DIVERGING PARALLELS

A COMPARISON OF AMERICAN AND EUROPEAN
THOUGHT AND ACTION

THE EUROPEAN ASSOCIATION FOR
AMERICAN STUDIES

DIVERGING PARALLELS

A COMPARISON OF AMERICAN AND EUROPEAN
THOUGHT AND ACTION

EDITED BY

A. N. J. DEN HOLLANDER

E. J. BRILL
LEIDEN
1971

CONTENTS

INTRODUCTION

The themes of the study conferences organized by the European Association for American Studies have always been chosen with an eye to the possibility of a specific European contribution to the understanding of American phenomena. American civilization, like any other culture, is an interdependent system of countless elements, based upon linked premises and categories whose importance is in no way the less because they are so seldom verbally expressed: they are taken for granted. It was the aim of the EAAS conferences in Rome (24-27 September 1967) and in Brussels (13-16 October 1970) to explore some of these tacit assumptions and to make them explicit. We have tried to do so by a method of comparison, by demonstrating that Americans and Europeans frequently do the same thing in very different ways, ways that are culturally determined.

Each different way of life—the American, the French, the British—is based on its own assumptions about the ends or purposes of human existence, about the ways and means by which social goals should be achieved, about what people have a right to expect from each other, about what constitutes fulfilment and failure.

In the course of history there has never perhaps been a civilization as self-conscious as our modern "Western" one. It has studied itself for centuries, it is still probing and sounding, investigating its furthest recesses and one might think that the number of assumptions that are strictly implicit, in the sense of never having been stated or discussed by anyone, must be negligible. Such a suggestion, however, will appeal more to those who belong to any national culture than to those who stand outside it.

It remains true for investigations of Western culture, no less so than for research on "primitive" civilizations, that the outsider enjoys specific advantages. These may not outweigh his handicaps, but this consideration is beside the point. The history of European comment on things American demonstrates clearly enough that comparison may lead to the constructive imagination that increases the effectiveness of our grasp of civilizations other than our own. American visitors to Europe, European travellers in the United States know quite well that forms and significances which seem obvious to an outsider, may be denied outright by those who created the pattern.

Meanwhile, insiders and outsiders share the interesting propensity of modern human beings, that they try to understand themselves and their own behaviour.

The tenet of America's Uniqueness, assertions of the non-comparability of "European" and "American" civilizations because of the supposed "exceptional" nature of American development have been heard. While granting that all comparison is limited in its possibilities, that some comparisons are impossible, we maintain that comparing the comparable remains both possible and rewarding. The Old World and the New have so much in common that the discernment of differences can no doubt be a promising approach to further insight as well as broader understanding.

An international body of scholars like the E.A.A.S., all "outsiders" as regards the United States as well as all other European countries but their own, may therefore be particularly well suited to investigate the diverse ways in which Americans and Europeans belonging to various national cultures, perform certain tasks, achieve certain ends, think about certain problems. In Rome and in Brussels, members of the Association came together to ask, perhaps to answer, the question of whether American and European societies present us with variations upon basic patterns and if so, what some of these variations are and how they have their roots in the larger fabric of a national society and a national culture.

The approach of the two latest E.A.A.S. study conferences thus smacked of anthropology in its interest for cultural similarities and differences, its attempts to "see ourselves as others see us", its discussions of the whys and wherefores of foreign ways, of the problems that beset a world that is full of foreigners. The central theme of the two meetings: The American Way—the European Way, has proved to be felicitous and not easily exhausted; it brought forth lively discussions, opened new perspectives, stimulated further thought. The Association herewith presents an anthology of the papers read at the meetings, in the conviction that they will interest a wider public.

A. N. J. DEN HOLLANDER

D. C. WATT

DIPLOMACY AND INTERNATIONAL RELATIONS

In the aftermath of the Second World War, and in the opening years of the cold war, the bulk of intellectual thinking on international relations in western Europe was based on the assumption that there was a recognisable group of states bound together by a common historical experience, common traditions and a common culture which could be loosely called "the West". Most of its members were joined together by the common experience of being attacked by Nazi Germany. The revivified Germany (and Italy) of the post war years which by a desperate effort, not always given its proper value by its former enemies, had sloughed off and brought under control its authoritarian and aggressively nationalist past, joined them in an equally common anxiety about the military predominance in central Europe of the Soviet Union. There was talk of "Atlantic Union",[1]—and indeed, with the exception of Austria and Switzerland, the only European states which lay outside the great advance of Russian power to lines of influence it had not enjoyed since the end of the Napoleonic era, were, in fact, riparian states of the Atlantic or of its Mediterranean extension.

Parallel with these developments, at least from the late nineteen forties onwards, one can trace the beginning of a common "European" consciousness. In its internal aspects it took various forms ranging from outright federalism through the administrative federalism of the Action Group for Europe to a reviving nationalism expressed within a European framework, "l'Europe des patries". But all its manifestations had one thing in common, an increasing awareness that they were not Americans, that in some, at first only ambiguously defined, way there were distinctive American and European ways of doing things. This realization was perhaps most clearly defined in France. But its elevation to the status of a doctrine within a generalised secular religion by that self-styled reincarnation of the humble Maid of Domrémy, should not prevent the recognition that this consciousness of difference between "European" and "American" moves, beliefs, ethos, and

---

[1] The "Atlantic Declaration" was in fact signed on 19 January 1962.

ways of doing things was very widespread throughout western Europe even by the end of the 1950s, even among those who were opposed both to the Gaullist and to the nuclear disarmers' attempts to exploit it. Even in Britain, where "Atlanticism" was only a thin veneer over a much more long established "pan Anglo-Saxonism", consciousness of the American failure to accept what "Atlanticists" and "Anglo-Saxonists" had assumed were the bases of their sense of community in quite the same way as their advocates on the eastern shores of the Atlantic, had begun to make itself apparent around the turn of the 1960s. So that even in Britain where old illusions die even harder than other kinds of lost causes, consciousness that Britain is, whatever this may mean, more "European" than "Atlanticist" is now fairly firmly rooted.

Since this consciousness of a "European" identity, expressed at the lowest as a feeling that the American identity was in some way not "European", grew out of a general experience of multilateral contacts with Americans at all levels of international activity, it is hardly surprising that the first fields in which these differences were perceived were in the style, the methods, the whole approach to international affairs of the Americans and their various European partners. What is surprising is that, on the whole, there has been remarkably little published work on these differences: and such as there is has stemmed more from the Nescafé school of instant sociologists and from the political advocates of national isolationism in the various European states than from academics.

It will be the main theme of this paper to argue that the main differences between the American and the European approaches to international relations, defined here not as an intellectual discipline, but as relations with the external non-American (or non-European) world stem basically from two sources; the differing theories of the state embodied in American and European constitutions, and the different perceptions of themselves and the external world embodied in the American and European traditions.

Before one proceeds with such a contrast one owes it to one's American, if not to one's European, readers and listeners to tighten a little more sharply one's definition of the Europe with which America is being contrasted. Since I am by discipline a historian, and this is a contrast which will be drawn over time, the kind of definition I will be using is ostensive, classificatory perhaps, rather than normative. My examples on the European side will be drawn from the European democratic rather than the European-authoritarian ends of the spectrum of European political experience. This is basically because events have shown that, in the long run, hereditary authoritarianism has not given way in Europe to plebiscitary populist authoritarianism but rather to what might be called a mixed meritocratic-plutocratic limited democracy. At the moment the only authoritarian states in Europe that can in some way be regarded as part of the European tradition are those of the Iberian peninsula. And there is good historical warranty for regarding them as having split away from the common path of European experience after 1830.[1] Neither post-Ottoman Greece nor post-Ottoman Turkey can be regarded as part of the west European tradition, the legacy of classical Greece and the modernism of Kemal Ataturk notwithstanding.

The basic contrasts in this paper are those to be drawn between the United States on one hand and Britain, France, Weimarian and Bonnisch Germany and non-Fascist Italy on the other. This is not to imply anything against the "European" quality of our host country, Belgium, or her Dutch and Luxembergian neighbours on the one hand or the Scandinavian countries on the other. It is just that studies of international relations of the kind this paper draws on have been greatly limited in Belgium and the Netherlands by the archival policy these countries have pursued; while I am debarred from all but the most superficial exploration of the Scandinavian literature by linguistic shortcomings.[2]

By far the greatest source of differences on the side of the administration of foreign policy lies in the unique nature of the American head of State. The Founding Fathers of the United States, unhampered by a hereditary monarchy with its attendant nobility, succeeded in solving the basic problem faced by all systems of government in Europe in the eighteenth century—how to legitimize the continuance of a system in which the head of state was the sole agent of government in a period when legitimisation by religious authority was no longer acceptable either to those who governed or to those who were governed. The President of the United States is an eighteenth century be-

---

[1] See for example, Raymond Carr, *Spain, 1808-1939*, Oxford 1966.

[2] See however Nils Ørvik, "From Collective Security to Neutrality. The Nordic Powers, the League of Nations, Britain and the Approach of War, 1935-1939", in K. Bourne and D. C. Watt, *Studies in International History*, London 1967; the same, *Sikkerhetspolitikken, 1920-39*, Oslo 1961: Folke Lindberg, *Scandinavia in Great Power Politics, 1905-08*, Stockholm 1958.

nevolent despot legitimised by popular election, checked by a popularly elected assembly and a written constitution with a Supreme Court to interpret it—and this has had the most far reaching effects on the conduct and management of America's external relations.

The first and most obvious effects that the nature of the American Presidency as a temporary elected eighteenth century enlightened (if limited) despot has upon the conduct of American external relations is in its dual effect upon the President's relations with the Department of State and with his chosen representativesa broad. The dual role stems from the dual nature of the Presidency—as being both despot and electee. As despot the departments of state are his servants. His Cabinet are his advisers, recognised by the constitution in that they must be "advised" and "consented" to by the Senate, but in all other respects closer to the Cabinet of a Frederick the Great than to the Cabinets of Britain, of the third and fourth Republics of France or those of the other European democracies. As electee, his Cabinet posts must go, as must his principal ambassadorships, as rewards to those who helped him to the nomination as his party's Presidential candidate or in the Presidential election itself.

It is thus in the nature of things that a President's relations with his Secretary of State, his other Cabinet ministers and his ambassadors abroad, should reflect the nature of the political coalition which has secured his nomination and election. Some posts will go to his most faithful supporters. Others to those whom he has had to placate or win over. His chances of re-election, his influence on the nomination of his successor will depend on these uncertain alliances and ambitions. For if one has to go back to the eighteenth century to find analogies to the constitutional despotism of the American president, one has no parallels, save that of the ill-fated crown of Poland, later than the seventeenth century elections to the head office of the Holy Roman Empire, for an elected despot. And in, for example, Franklin Roosevelt's relations with Joseph Kennedy, his ambassador to the Court of St. James,[1] or with Woodring, his Secretary of War,[2] one can see again the clouded relations of the Emperor Ferdinand with Maximilian of Bavaria or the Great Elector.[3]

[1] On Joseph Kennedy see William W. Kaufmann, "Two American Ambassadors: Bullitt and Kennedy", in Felix Gilbert and Gordon Craig, *The Diplomats, 1919-1939*, Princeton 1953; Richard Whalen, *The Founding Father*, New York 1965.

[2] On which see John W. Blum, *From the Morgenthau Diaries, Years of Urgency, 1938-41*, Boston 1965, p. 37.

[3] See C. V. Wedgewood, *The Thirty Years War*, London 1938.

Thus the most stable relationships between Presidents and Secretaries of State in this century have existed between those Presidents who had no anxieties as to their election and have therefore picked their Secretaries as trusted advisers rather than as allies rewarded for their part in the electoral victory. The relationships between Theodore Roosevelt and Elihu Root, between Harding and Charles Evans Hughes, between Coolidge and Kellogg, Hoover and Stimson, Truman and Acheson, Eisenhower and Dulles have all been of this kind. The cases of Theodore Roosevelt and Truman are proof that this relationship of confidence does not require, as is sometimes argued, that the President be a Louis XIII or a William I content to abide by the guidance of a Richelieu or a Bismarck.

There have on the other hand been Presidents who sought, so far as possible, to evade the problems of their "over-mighty" allies by excluding them from office and by conferring the most important offices of state, as the Tudor monarchs did in Britain, on men whose position and stature in political terms depended entirely on the favour of the President. Wilson's first Secretary of State, William Jennings Bryan, was an overmighty ally whose long leadership in disaster of the Democratic party Wilson felt obliged to reward. In all other respects he was as fitted for the position as the Emperor Caligula's horse for that of consul. His second Secretary of State, Lansing, belongs much more closely to the Tudor models, though he was more a Wolsey than a Thomas Cromwell. For the full illustration of this development one has to turn rather to President Kennedy's choice of Dean Rusk and Robert McNamara. Rusk, a Georgian lawyer, Rhodes Scholar, soldier and State Department employee was in no sense a political appointment—nor did he come from any of the milieux from which Presidents traditionally selected their Cabinet ministers or ambassadors. McNamara's case was only superficially different. Though he came from the Chairmanship of Ford Motors it was a post he had only just attained, and that by sheer merit. In no other respect can he be compared with industrial barons such as his predecessor as Secretary for Defence under Eisenhower, "Engine" Charlie Wilson of General Motors.

Bad relations between President and Secretary of State or ambassador can thus stem from either of the two aspects of his office in which the President is unique. They may arise because the President does not trust or cannot work with a political ally with whom for political reasons he would prefer not to break. This is the basic reason for the appalling relations which existed between Wilson and Bryan, between Franklin Roosevelt and Cordell Hull, and between Truman and Stettinius. But they may arise also because of the character of the President and from the fact that it lies within his power to employ the machinery of State in whatever way best suits his own personal style of governance. To decide why a Roosevelt or a Kennedy placed as much reliance on the employment of personal emissaries as they did requires a detailed analysis both of the domestic political and the politico-managerial factors in each case. With Roosevelt his use of a Norman Davis,[1] a Murray of Elibank[2] or a Harry Hopkins[3] stemmed basically from his secretiveness, his distrust of political allies, and his need to establish as close a personal relationship as he could with foreign statesmen whose co-operation was necessary to him. On the rare occasions where he used a political appointee, as he did with Ambassador Dodd in his soundings in Berlin on the possibility of a conference on economic disarmement in the fall of 1936[4], it was an appointment with whom he was in emotional sympathy and one which was, in any case, an appointment with very little weight in domestic American politics. To weigh it properly one should set by its side his instructions to Murray of Elibank that on no count should Ambassador Kennedy be informed of his clandestine contacts with Neville Chamberlain[5] in the last three months of 1938 and the assurances he conveyed to Chamberlain that America's economic resources would be made available to support Britain if she were engaged in war with Germany, whatever the state of America's neutrality legislation.

The case of John Kennedy is different. Technological means had made the employment of a personal emissary much easier in his day than it was in the time of Roosevelt. It took Norman Davies a week to reach Britain or Brussels in 1937. He could, it was true, converse with his President by transatlantic telephone, though this was not

---

[1] See on Norman H. Davis, Thomas C. Irwin, "Norman H. Davis and the Quest for Arms Control, 1931-1938", (Ohio State Univ. Ph. D., 1963); Dorothy Borg, *The United States and the Far Eastern Crisis*, Cambridge, Mass. 1964, pp. 403; D. C. Watt, *Personalities and Policies*, London 1965, pp. 83-99, "Britain, the United States and Japan in 1934".

[2] See Lord Murray of Elibank, "Franklin Roosevelt, the Friend of Britain", *Contemporary Review*, vol. C/XXXVIII, June 1955.

[3] Maurice Waters, *The Ad Hoc Diplomat*, The Hague 1963.

[4] See Francis L. Loewenheim, "An Ilusion that shaped History" in Daniel R. Beaver (Ed.), *Some Pathways in Twentieth Century*, Detroit 1969.

[5] Murray of Elibank Papers, National Library of Scotland, Folio 8809, Memorandum of 21 October 1938.

entirely satisfactory. By 1961 a George Ball or a McNamara could be in London in eight hours and fly back the next day, if needs be, to inform his President and confer with him on what had transpired. Kennedy tended therefore to use whoever seemed the most appropriate man to hand. To negotiate with Mr. Khrushchev on Berlin, a long slow process dependent on the establishment of personal respect between the two, he used his ambassador in Moscow.[1] To deal with crises such as *Skybolt*, the original multilateral force proposals or the negotiations on Britain's entry into Europe, he turned rather to the man whom he had chosen to act as his principal adviser, as it might be a McNamara for *Skybolt*,[2] a George Ball for Europe[3] or an Arthur Schlesinger Junior for Latin America,[4] irrespective of whether the individual concerned came from his appointments to the bureaucracy or from his own kitchen cabinet, the White House staff.

If one turns to the European states chosen as comparison, one has to recognize at once that with the European dependance on the parliamentary cabinet commanding a majority in the national parliament, whether that majority is achieved by the comparatively monolithic parties of Great Britain, or the shifting political coalitions of the Third Republic, the Cabinet is an alliance of political figures elected and representative, with no term other than electoral strength set on their office and commanding political power not in the once-and-for-all delivery of votes in an election but in the continuous delivery of support in parliament. The British Foreign Secretary, His (or Her) Majesty's Principal Secretary of State for Foreign Affairs, may share with the Secretary of State that curious eighteenth century nomenclature which placed as the first duty in the affairs of state on the Sovereign's servants, after that of managing his Treasury, that of conducting his relations with other monarchs. But he is much more than the monarch's first servant after the Premier. He is usually one of the two or three most powerful political figures in the Cabinet. The sole cases where this has not been so have been where the Prime Minister wished effectively to be his own Foreign Secretary without having to incur, as Macdonald did in 1924, the added burden of managing the day to day work of the Foreign Office. The most recent case of this sort was

---

[1] D. C. Watt, (Ed.), *Survey of International Affairs, 1961*, London, 1966, pp. 213, 217-18.

[2] Idem, *Survey of International Affairs, 1962*, London, 1970, pp. 162-63.

[3] George Ball, *The Discipline of Power*, London, 1968, pp. 81-82.

[4] Arthur Schlesinger Junior, *The Thousand Days*, London 1965, pp. 158-67.

the relationship between Sir Anthony Eden and Mr. Macmillan, his successor, with Mr. Selwyn Lloyd. This is a relationship still virtually unexplored by contemporary historians. That it was not a happy one and that it came to a disastrous end is however a matter of record. The relationship between Churchill and Eden during the years 1940-45 or between Chamberlain and Halifax in the years 1938-40 have also been put in the same category, but recent evidence has made it clear that their relations were less a matter of rider and horse than of a closer and rather different kind of symbiosis.[1]

Indeed for the closest parallels one has to go to the period of *Kanzler-demokratie* in post-war Western Germany or the Gaullist experiment in Presidential democracy in the French fifth republic. What is interesting in Bonn is that the years of Adenauer's dotage showed that the relationship between, for example, himself and Heinrich von Brentano were a deviation from the norms rather than, as was feared at the time, the reestablishment under the patina of parliamentary democracy of the *Bismarckischen Geist*.[2] He was forced by the collapse of his parliamentary majority to accept a Foreign Minister, Dr. Schroeder, whose methods and views he detested. Since that date the difficulties that have arisen, as between Brandt and Kiesinger at the time of the *Grosse Koalition* or between Brandt and Scheel since the 1968 elections, are those inseparable from any coalition, despite the fact that constitutionally the Bundeskanzler is a more powerful figure than a British or a French premier. One need look no further than the tensions existing between Chamberlain and Eden, or between Lloyd George and Curzon for a parallel. In brief the difficulties that have arisen in European practice between Heads of Government and their Foreign Ministers have stemmed either from conflicts of personality or from the strains of a coalition of equals rather than from the complicated system of one-way rewards and spoils inherent in the President's relations with his Secretary of State and his ambassadors.

The employment of political appointees in diplomatic positions and of personal emissaries by the West European parliamentary democracies has been quite different. It is true that in the past the number of British political appointees in diplomatic posts needs to be augmented

---

[1] D. C. Watt, *Personalities and Policies*, pp. 177-86, "Divided Control of British Foreign Policy—Danger or Necessity?". Max Beloff, *The Intellectual in Politics*, London 1970, pp. 19-34, "Prime Minister and President".

[2] Arnulf Baring, *Außenpolitik in Adenauer's Kanzlerdemokratie*, Munich 1969, esp. pp. 1-48.

by the Viceroys, Governors-General of Dominions, Governorships of Colonies and High Commissionerships, as well as holders of that curious British institution, developed during the second world war and applied occasionally thereafter, of the Minister of State stationed permanently abroad, for the comparison to be really valid. Even then while a Royal Duke could be sent to govern the Bermudas or to act as Governor-General of an antipodean Dominion for a time, these were to be the exception rather than the rule. Colonial Governors were usually career men. Governors-General of Dominions were not infrequently retired soldiers of considerable personal ability, still able to contribute something to the State and lacking in any overt party attachment. And the position they filled, while being more than merely honorific, did not make them direct instruments of British external policy subject to continued directives from London. Direct political appointments such as that of Lord Head, a Conservative War Minister, to Nigeria, or of Malcolm Macdonald, son of Ramsay Macdonald and a Cabinet Minister before 1939, as High Commissioner for South-East Asia, have in them an element both of respect for the judgement of the men concerned and of political exile.

Setting these cases aside, the bulk of British political appointments to ambassadorial posts abroad fall into two quite separate categories. Some stem from problems of coalition warfare, and are indeed carried over into the field of coalition peacemaking. Such appointments as those of Lord d'Abernon in Berlin, Sir Auckland Geddes in Washington and Lords Derby and Crewe in Paris have an element of this (though it is to be noticed that they date from the only period in British politics in which an individual was trying to build his own political party by methods which reportedly included the sale of honours and the employment of a personal spoils system). The appointment of Sir Stafford Cripps in Moscow (1940-42), of Lord Halifax in Washington (1942-46), of Duff Cooper, Lord Norwich, in Paris (1944-47), of Sir Samuel Hoare, Lord Templewood, in Madrid (1940-45) certainly come into this category. There have, of course, been deliberate attempts to politicise some posts, most notably by the Wilson government, with its appointment of Lord Caradon as head of the British delegation to the United Nations and John Freeman, first to New Delhi and then, in mistaken anticipation of a Democratic victory in the 1968 elections, to Washington. Such posts however have a natural tendency to depoliticise themselves either by the resistance of the professionals to the process (which has, for example, resulted in Lord Caradon's replacement by his professional deputy) or by the transformation of a political appointment into a career one after the change of government. Duff Cooper, a Conservative First Lord of the Admiralty (1937-38) continued to serve as ambassador in Paris under a Labour government—and the new Conservative government took its time in finding a replacement for John Freeman in Washington, despite his former editorship of the *New Statesman*.

It is when one turns to the employment of personal emissaries by the West European democracies that one can see how the exigencies of external relations exercise an effect far beyond that of problems of domestic political management. None of the West European bureaucracies like the personal emissary, who is by their definition nearly always an amateur, even where, as with Neville Chamberlain's employment of Sir Horace Wilson, the permanent under-secretary of the Treasury, he is, in his own field, a professional. Nevertheless one has to be pragmatic. Whereas Chamberlain's employment of Wilson and others is widely condemned as an inefficient deviation from the norm, where Britain is dealing with an authoritarian regime, where personal relations to the head of state or government are important, the British have shown themselves ready to use whatever means they have to hand. The leaders of the Secret Intelligence Service are not beyond a little personal diplomacy (most marked in the cases of Sir William Wiseman and Sir William Stephenson in Anglo-American relations in the two world wars).[1] In the case of Lord Harlech's embassy to the United States it was less his political eminence than his long standing friendship with President Kennedy which made him the obvious choice.

France has not been behind Britain in the use of personal emissaries, though the peculiar nature of French politics has produced very few political figures willing to accept the exile of a permanent embassy; they prefer to be *anciens ministres* in Paris rather than servants of the Quai d'Orsay abroad. The use of the personal emissary moreover came naturally to those accustomed to the personal *Cabinets* of the leading political figures and the great role played by intermediaries

---

[1] On Sir William Wiseman see Sir Arthur Willert, *The Road to Safety*, London 1952; W. B. Fowler, *British-American Relations 1917-1918. The role of Sir William Wiseman*, Princeton 1969; on Sir William Stephenson see H. Montgomery Hyde, *The Quiet Canadian*, London 1962; see also the memoirs of the Chief of Air Intelligence in the 1930s, Group Captain F. W. Winterbotham, *Secret and Personal*, London 1970.

in the construction, if not in the maintenance, of those everchanging coalitions. Especially in relations with the dictators, missions such as those of Lagardelle in 1935[1] and Baudouin in 1939[2] between the governments of the day and Mussolini, were a natural outgrowth of the problem of relations with personal dictators.

Behind the differing natures of the American system of elective limited absolutism and the various European parliamentary cabinet systems there are further implications that need exploration. These have to do with the nature of the foreign policy-making élites in America and Europe. In Europe these élites tend to be long serving, their members so continuously in service that whatever their individual social origins they tend to grow together as a group and their shared assumptions become backed by a network of social contacts and relationships such as to give the élite to which they belong a fairly permanent character. Theoretically this should be modified by changes in office among the political members of the élite—but in practice, even among the various political parties, there tend to develop long-term experts in external relations with its allied fields of defence, international economics and finance and overseas aid and investment. This tendency is noticeable even in Britain, where the development of specialist parliamentary committees is in its infancy. In the continental European powers where parliamentary committees on foreign affairs play an important part in the legislative process this tendency is greatly strengthened.[3] It is reinforced by the development of international parliaments and gatherings of parliamentarians on the one hand and institutes and associations for the study of international affairs on the other. The role this is playing in the emergence of élite groups common to the European states has so far not been examined by any political scientist, to the best of the author's knowledge.

This continuity in élite group membership is of particular importance where the balance between political and professional bureaucratic status and influence is disturbed. It is however to be mentioned that these élites also include political commentators and academics, both of whom play an important role in the ventilation and analysis of disagreements within the élite and in the maintenance of consent

[1] Hubert Lagardelle, *Mission à Rome*, Paris 1955.
[2] Paul Boudouin, "Un voyage à Rome", *La Revue des deux Mondes*, 1 May 1962, pp. 69-85.
[3] On the French parliamentary committee for Foreign Affairs under the third Republic see J. E. Howard, *Parliament and Foreign Policy in France*, London 1948.

to and acceptance of élite leadership in the field of foreign relations among the general mass of those politically involved in their particular societies. As with the political and professional bureaucratic members of the élite, its academic and journalistic membership tends to be long-serving, moving perhaps from one mode or organ of communication to another and from all of these into the field of foreign correspondent and back to their own countries. The same is true of a fifth element, those in positions of responsibility in private industry, in finance, trade and shipping etc., whose main work lies in the field of overseas economic and financial relations. Even with the addition of this last group their length of service, their concentration in, at most, two or three centres of activity, and their numbers make for a degree of collective agreement that is the more surprisingly strong for its habitual understatement.[1]

When one turns to the United States, the picture is changed very radically by three factors. The first is the sheer size of the country, the decentralisation of economic activity caused by its regional differences in industry, markets overseas, outlook on foreign affairs etc. The second is the number of those whose positions in industry, politics, journalism, academic life and in the administrative bureaucracy would make their European equivalents at least candidate members of the foreign policy-making élites in their own country. The third is the distorted balance between its political members, their permanent division into parliamentary and political administrators, and the disparity in power between this second group and the professional bureaucrats brought about by the system of elective limited absolutism already referred to.

The effect of this is to introduce a number of distortions. The first is to deprive the parliamentarians of any but the most public and indirect influence on the formation and conduct of external relations save in a critical and destructive sense. As a result only that handful of Senators and Representatives who enjoy the President's confidence (and they, of course, change somewhat as one elected absolutist succeeds another) are members of the American foreign policy-making élite in any sense comparable with their European equivalents. A second is to devalue the long-term professional members of the civilian side of the American bureaucracy and to make them hesitant and

---

[1] On the British foreign policy-making élite see D. C. Watt, *Personalities and Policies*, 1-15.

reserved vis-à-vis their political mentors. They are effectively denied
access to all but a handful of the top policy-making jobs within both
the State Department and the overseas embassies, save in so far as
they become identified with a particular party.

By a curious paradox however the long term military members of
the bureaucracy enjoy no such devaluation, save where the general
character of civilian attitudes to the military prescribes it. Traditionally
the advisory bodies of senior military and naval figures acted as military advisers not only to the absolutist and his administration but also
to the Congressional Committees charged with keeping the absolutist's
actions in the fields of defence and the armed services under constant
scrutiny. Thus, whereas British, French and other west European
military figures have occasionally campaigned individually and collec-
tively with considerable force to obtain the policy which seemed most
advisable to them, they have rarely if ever campaigned as an organised
body to attempt to persuade their parliaments to reject a treaty signed
by their own government as, for example, the General Board of the
U.S. Navy campaigned in Congress to secure the rejection of the
1930 London Naval Treaty.[1] This was elsewhere a phenomenon confined to those absolutist states where military and civilian authorities
existed as coequals in theory, the civilians being slightly subordinate
in fact, as in Czarist Russia or Bismarckian Imperial Germany. They
do not always campaign effectively; the General Board was defeated
in 1930 as was MacArthur in 1951. But apart from Foch's attack of
folie de grandeur at Versailles[2] and the Beresford-Fisher row in Edwardian Britain,[3] Europe has no recent parallels save in France in 1958-61,
where what was at issue was not the use of parliamentary methods
to defeat an administration's policy but a *coup d'état*.

So far as the politico-administrative élite in the United States is
concerned, one has to note one element, albeit a dwindling element, of
continuity among its number. This is provided by the East Coast Ivy
League wealthy patrician element, the product of a limited number
of private schools and universities. Again this is an element that needs
exploration. But the existence of figures such as Acheson, Harriman,
Christian Herter, David Bruce and others, whose service as foreign

---

[1] See Raymond O'Connor, *Perilous Equilibrium*, Kansas 1962.

[2] See Jere Clemens King, *Foch versus Clemenceau: France and German Dismember-
ment, 1918-1919*, Cambridge, Mass. 1960.

[3] See Arthur W. Marder, *Fear God and Dreadnought*, Vol. II, London 1916, pp.
39-45.

affairs experts for their chosen parties goes back their full working careers, and who move back into banking, the law, the universities or state politics, remaining available to serve either administration if their service is requested, has provided an element of continuity and authority in the conduct of American foreign policy which to some extent offsets the lack of power and influence of the professional bureaucrats of the State Department and the Foreign Service. Against these one has to set the gradual decline in power, influence and authority of this group in both parties, as the balance within the parties moves westwards and southwards.

So far, in this comparison between America and the European countries, attention has been focussed on the differences between the governmental aspects of the different foreign policy-making processes. It has been argued that these stem basically from the fact that, lacking the obstacle of a hereditary monarchy, the United States were able to solve the problems of legitimising authority, as these were seen in the eighteenth century, by basing that authority on an elective process, albeit an indirect one. In other respects however the principal bearer of authority remained as the eighteenth century had conceived him, an absolute monarch whose absolutism, whose exercise of power, was limited by the rule of law, embodied in a written constitution, safeguarded by an independent judiciary and watched over by an elected assembly which retained the power of the purse. It need hardly be said that an assembly, even one elected to be both federal and national, which has to operate within this general framework, is a very different kind of assembly from those which function in the various European countries. Whether these fall into the French republican tradition of an assembly which is itself the final repository of sovereignty, or whether they follow the British, Scandinavian, Dutch and Belgian models whereby sovereignty resides with the King's ministers in parliament, the role the elected assembly plays in the field of foreign policy is bound to be totally different. In eighteenth century terms the state was still very much the territorial extension of the monarch's personality. External relations were conducted between monarchs and their courts. They were pre-eminently a field reserved for the monarchical prerogative. This did not change, and was not changed by making the monarch elective. The only changes introduced were those which limited his powers to make war, his powers to make treaties and his powers to make appointments. Of these the first and the third at least stemmed much less from a distrust of the way in which the Presidential prerogative might be exercised, than from the process by which the founding states abandoned their thirteen separate sovereignties only piecemeal and with reluctance to the new federal power. The second was inherent in the separation of powers, since treaties became part of the domestic law of the countries which conclude them.

The effect of this is that, save where the conduct of foreign policy requires the voting of funds or the ratification of treaties, the President of the United States is absolved from the necessity of seeking parliamentary or popular support for his actions in a way for which there are few parallels in the European democracies. America offers few parallels to the reversal of the Hoare-Laval plan by the British and French governments of the day, or the Suez debâcle in 1956. The closest American parallel to the first is the abandonment of their Big Navy plans by Harding's administration and the Congress elected in 1920 in the face of organised pressure by American religious and civil organizations advocating naval arms limitation.[1] The Kennedy regime survived more or less unharmed the collapse of the Bay of Pigs assault on Cuba in 1961. And the general consensus of historians of Wilson's failure to obtain the necessary two-thirds majority in the Senate for the ratificationof the Treaty of Versailles centres on his lack of competence as a manager of Congress, not on the inherent impossibility of the task. It is interesting to note that attempts to extend Congressional control over the Presidential exercise of the prerogative have been defeated, as was the Ludlow amendment in 1938[2] and recent attempts made in the aftermath of the use made by President Johnson of the Congressional resolution passed in 1964 after the alleged attacks by North Vietnamese naval craft on ships of the American Navy.

Where the Senate exercises more power than its British, French or West German equivalents, is in its powers of investigation. The weakness of the British position rises from the general weakness of the British parliament as against the executive, though the effectiveness of the parliamentary question and the emergency debate are often underestimated, while those of the Senate Foreign Affairs committee, where legislation is *not* in question, are frequently exaggerated.

---

[1] See Adelphia Dane Bowen Jr., "The Disarmament Movement, 1918-1935", (Ph. D., Columbia, 1956), pp. 20-33.

[2] On the Ludlow Amendment see Robert W. Divine, *The Illusion of Neutrality*, Chicago 1962, pp. 219-21.

II

So far attention has been focused on those contrasts between the American and European approaches to external international affairs which arise from the differences between the foreign policy-making machines in America and Europe. It has been argued that the American system in practice leaves far more to the prerogative of the elective co-head of state and government, than the European does to the head of government. In practice the conduct of foreign policy in America is in many respects more absolutist, more authoritarian in the United States than in the democracies of Western Europe.

This may at first sight seem a very startling statement: but the degree to which it contravenes what is the view generally accepted, especially by American writers, about the conduct of and approach to foreign affairs of the United States, is the measure of the strength of the second main source of contrasts between the American and European democratic approaches to foreign affairs, diplomacy and international relations. This lies in the differing perceptions of the nature of their own system of government and of all other systems of government, with which they have to have contact if they are to be involved in international relations and diplomacy, held by the leading writers on and practitioners in the field on either side of the Atlantic.

The dominant school of thought in the United States, since the elections of 1912 and 1916 welded Populists and Progressives into a single coalition behind Wilson, has laid particular stress on the strength and importance of public opinion and of the influence of the public on the formation of foreign policy. For a brief period, roughly from the Republican victories in 1892 and 1896 to the debâcle of the Bull Moose party in 1912, it looked as if the United States might develop the same élitist attitude to international relations as prevailed in Europe. The possibility was never very high—but it existed. The election of Wilson (for all his admiration of the English political tradition in domestic politics,) and his appointment of Bryan as his Secretary of State, put paid to that prospect for ever.

This prevalence of a "populist" approach to international relations and diplomacy manifests itself in all kinds of ways. In the academic world it is revealed in the manner in which the study of the diplomacy, or still more the foreign policy, of a particular country or at best a region, seen as the external aspect of its domestic history, is institutionalised throughout the American academic world, whereas posts in the history of international relations such as those which predominate in France, Italy or Britain are found only as adjuncts to the theoretical study of contemporary international relations, if they are found at all. It shows equally in the extraordinary prevalence in the study of the contemporary international scene of abstract theories and models which rest on a polarised abstraction from purely American experiences. In 1964 I attended a two-day conference on the Marshall Plan as a field for historical research, the first day of which was devoted to the discussion of subjects to be investigated on the American side, the second to those worthy of investigation on the European side.[1] The American diplomatic historians attending the conference thought and spoke almost exclusively of the influences of sections of of American opinion, interest groups, minority groups and the like on the formulation of opinion, topics which the bulk of European historians would investigate only after all efforts to penetrate the processes of policy formulation at the Cabinet, ministerial and bureaucratic levels had been abandoned for lack of access to archival materials or participant's testimony.

These attitudes are the reflection of a dominant doctrinal approach to problems of America's external relations, which has distinct analogies to the ideologies of the eastern powers. When crossing to Europe in 1918 on the George Washington, President Wilson bade his entourage remember that the statesmen of Europe with whom they were about to negotiate were in no way representative of their peoples.[2] He is said to have remarked, on returning from the tour of Europe he embarked on before the Versailles Conference opened, that the dumb eyes of the people haunted him.[3] He came to believe that the hopes of the peoples of Europe, whom he separated entirely in his mind from their elected representatives, so recently elected and by margins much greater than his own, were pinned on him rather than on their own leaders. This concept of the people, dumb, inarticulate, managed by the self-promoted élites who govern them, at once innocent, positively good, primaevally naive, is not unknown in Europe. Indeed it is the stock in trade of the European radical tradition, although that tradition is usually voiced not by the people themselves but by

---

[1] For a record of the proceedings of this Conference see Robert W. Ferrell and Jerry N. Hess, (Eds.), *Conference of Scholars on the Marshall Plan, 1964*, Independence, Missouri, 1964.

[2] Notes of Dr. Isaiah Bowman, 10 December 1918, James T. Shotwell, *At the Paris Peace Conference*, London 1957, pp. 75-78.

[3] Harold Nicolson, *Peace making 1919*, London 1964, p. 50.

the déraciné, alienated intellectuals at the fringes of the ruling élites, as it was, for example, by the English radicals of the Union of Democratic Control from whom Wilson obtained so many of his ideas.[1] What is important to note is that, whereas in Europe this is a deviant tradition, in the United States, certainly since 1912, it has become the dominant tradition, not in the least invalidated by those who point out its inconsistencies with the evidence or its actual irrelevance. The whole bitter debate over Vietnam in the United States has turned frequently on allegations that one or the other side represent the Vietnamese people and that, *ipso facto*, their victory is morally ordained. The few European voices which have pointed out that this argument is essentially nonsensical, in that there is no such entity, in the political sense in which both sides employ the term, as the "Vietnamese people", remain largely unheard.[2]

By a curious paradox this doctrinal approach to international politics has infected even those who think of themselves as realists. A realistic foreign policy is judged as much by its accordance with the abstract canons of "realism" as any other of the alternative doctrines. It is a remarkable experience to find a discussion of American foreign policy of any era in this century, either contemporary or historical, which focuses on its degree of success in attaining its ends or its degree of accuracy in perceiving the actual outlines of the problems with which it had to deal. As a result those Presidents and Secretaries of State whose policy was actually successful and whose perceptiveness clear, acute and accurate, figures such as Theodore Roosevelt, Henry L. Stimson, Dean Acheson for example, figure as the villains and failures in a historiography whose heroes are Wilson, Charles Evans Hughes and Franklin Roosevelt. John F. Kennedy is still regarded with considerable ambivalence. But if he is, as current trends would indicate, in process of being sent to join the villains, it will be for his success in Cuba, South East Asia, the Congo, the test ban treaty and Berlin rather than his failures as over relations with Britain and western Europe. Dean Rusk has already been disowned, even by Kennedy's defenders.[3]

Together with this populist ideology there goes a considerable

---

[1] See Laurence W. Martin, *Peace without Victory*, New Haven, 1958; Arno J. Mayer, *The Political Origins of the New Diplomacy, 1917-18*, New Haven 1959.

[2] See, for example, Dennis Duncanson, *Government and Revolution in Vietnam*, London 1968.

[3] See, for example, Arthur J. Schlesinger Jr., *The Thousand Days*, pp. 384-87.

ambivalence over the limits of national interest. Isolationists, who set very narrow limits on the national interest, do it in essentially populist terms, limiting the "people" to the American people whose sons must not, for example, be sent to die in "foreign wars". Their opponents however, echoing Wilson, would deny that the "People", Freedom and Democracy have to have been born under the American flag or to have taken out naturalisation papers. A century of mass immigration has made such arguments "nativist", an ugly word for what in other countries could well have been once called patriotic. The problem is complicated by the difficulty of defining an American except in ideological terms by relation to his activities. No doubt the Protestant ethic of salvation through good works rather than grace enters into this too. But in practice this attempt to define citizenship by relation to abstract qualities, an attempt whose darker side is the obsession with symbols such as "the flag" or the loyalty oath is without parallel in the history of western Europe after the end of the seventeenth century, when attempts to define citizen loyalty in terms of religious faith withered with the onset of the Age of Reason.

What this means in practice is that Americans have the utmost difficulty in distinguishing their concepts. Supporters of the main line of American policy since 1947 move easily in their discussion of world affairs between concepts such as "America", "the West", the "Free World" as groups holding policies, sharing the same interests, involved in the same decision making processes, as though the terms were virtually interchangeable.[1] While by contrast Americans who oppose this see nothing inconsistent in the deification of Che Guevara or Ho Chi Minh, whom they see as representative leaders of the Peoples International, the *Weltvolk* as it might be, whom the American ruling élites, the barons of the "military-industrial complex" are oppressing. They see nothing wrong, any more than Wilson did in 1914 in Mexico, in imposing a leader on a foreign country, providing his credentials are recognisably "democratic"; if his actions are rejected by his own people, this is merely a temporary aberration. The degree of persistent anti-Germanism in America, like the deeprooted antipathy to President de Gaulle, stems from the logical dilemma that Hitler's popular support in Germany or de Gaulle's refusal to accept France's role as an outlying part of a *Weltvolk* centred on Washington imposes on them. If Hitler was popular in Germany this must argue something

---

[1] For a recent example see Walter C. Clemens Jr., "The Soviet World Faces West", *International Affairs*, Vol. 46, No. 3, July 1970.

basically evil, *unmenschlich* or *unweltvölkisch*, in the German people. If de Gaulle denies the universal applicability of the American scale of values, then he too must be evil.

At a rather different level this universalist approach leads to a considerable impatience with the sovereignty and interests of America's smaller allies. One can see this manifested in the callousness with which the Papuans of Dutch New Guinea were sacrificed to the cause of good relations with Indonesia by the Kennedy regime in 1962;[1] in the inability of the Kennedy regime to understand the implications for the sovereignty of America's allies, of Mr. McNamara's remarks at Athens and at Ann Arbor in 1962 on the military irrelevance of small deterrent forces,[2] a speech which, together with the cancellation of the *Skybolt* missile programme, did more to defeat President Kennedy's Grand Design than any of President de Gaulle's evocations of Germany's past in his execrable German; in the use of American financial pressure to bring about a dismantlement of the sterling area in 1946-47 and to attempt to force the pace of development in Europe in 1949-50.[3] In each case the American action has been justified and defended in terms which only carry conviction, if it is accepted that the U.S. government in some sense is super-sovereign, super-representative of the interests of the peoples of its allies.

The belief that foreign policy has to be conducted in accordance with a universalist "doctrine" and that the decisions and actions out of which a foreign policy is constructed are justifiable only in relation to their degree of accordance with the principles of that doctrine has further implications. By contrast with the limited pragmatism with which European theorists and practitioners in the field of international politics have approached their subject, their American opposites have been interested, often to the point of obsession, with the nature of political power, or at least that part of political power which relates to international politics. Where European writers on international politics, from Grotius onwards, have concerned themselves mainly with the legitimisation of power, leaving discussion of its nature and employment basically to the school of military theorists of which Henry Humphrey Evans Lloyd, Jomini, Clausewitz and Douhet

---

[1] See *Survey of International Affairs 1962*, pp. 376-403, and the sources there cited.

[2] Ibid., pp. 82-84. For the text of the Ann Arbor speech see *Documents on International Affairs, 1962*, pp. 369-76. See also William W. Kaufman, *The McNamara Strategy*, New York 1964.

[3] See D. C. Watt, *Personalities and Policies*, pp. 53-80, "American Aid to Britain and the Problem of Socialism".

are the most distinguished,[1] Americans face no such problems. Legitimacy in the use of power is supplied by the moral basis of the general universalist doctrine which inspires their approach to international politics. Instead, from Admiral Mahon to the Rand Corporation's theorists, their interest has been directed to the nature and best means of employing power in international politics. In this field and in this alone, the much vaunted pragmatism of the American approach to life for a moment asserts itself. But the arguments which follow are again far from pragmatic, being at best abstractions from experience, where they are not theoretical inferences from a set of principles adopted *a priori*.

Four separate approaches to political power can be easily distinguished. There are the theoreticians of military and sea power from Admiral Mahon to the theorists of warfare in the nuclear age from Bernard Brodie to McNamara and Kissinger.[2] There are the believers in moral power from Wilson to John Foster Dulles, whose techniques, rhetorical and legalistic, lead to the final section of this paper, a comparison of European and American methods of diplomacy. There are those who attempted to refine these by developing other non-violent forms of power, of whom Franklin Roosevelt's ideas on quarantining aggressors,[3] George Kennan's containment and Dean Acheson's role in the conception of the Marshall Plan[4] are perhaps the most interesting examples. And there is the new school of sociological engineers who lack a major figure, save perhaps in Walt Rostow's theories of economic development,[5] but whose doctrines have been put into action in development aid projects from Point Four to the Alliance for Progress,[6] in the whole body of C.I.A. practice from the subsidising of existing non-Communist international fronts such as the I.F.C.T.U., the Congress for Cultural Freedom and the International Union of Students, to the whole, much more un-American, range of "dirty tricks"

---

[1] See Michael Howard, *Studies in War and Peace*, London 1970, pp. 21-36, "Jomini and the Classical Tradition in Military Thought".

[2] Howard, pp. 154-83, "The Classical Strategists".

[3] See John McVickar Haight Jr., "Roosevelt as Friend of France", *Foreign Affairs*, April 1966, and Laurence W. Pratt, "The Far East and the Anglo-American Naval Conversations of January 1938", *International Affairs*, 1971.

[4] See Joseph Jones, *The Fifteen Weeks*, New York 1955; Dean Acheson, *Present at the Creation*, New York 1970.

[5] Walt W. Rostow, *The Stages of Economic Growth: a non-Communist Manifesto*, Cambridge 1960.

[6] David M. Baldwin, *Economic Development and American Foreign Policy 1945-1962*, Chicago 1966.

of the militant anti-Communist organizations involved in Teheran in
1953, in Guatemala in 1954 and in the Bay of Pigs debâcle. To this
one must add such projects as the Peace Corps,[1] and the various crash
programmes designed to produce as rapidly as possible American-
trained, American-oriented and pro-American élites in the newly
emergent states of Africa and South East Asia,[2] and the illfated project
for the academic study of the promotion of revolution in Chile exposed in the mid-1960s.[3]

It is however from the early believers in moral power through the
appeal to the people that the greatest difference has opened between
American and European diplomatic methods. This lies eventually in
the development of "open diplomacy" to a point where public oratory
and the open press conference become themselves major methods of
international communication. To this one must add the development
of parliamentary diplomacy in which the methods by which majorities
are sought and obtained in the United States Congress are applied to
the organization of majorities for resolutions introduced into the
General Assembly of the United Nations.

These are not of course methods which have remained private to
the Americans, and their definition needs to be refined. Diplomacy
by oratory falls into two basic categories, that designed as a form of
communication with other governments and that designed as a form
of propaganda aimed at the domestic support enjoyed by other
governments. The distinction is basically one of motivation. Wilson's
speech of January 1918, embodying his famous Fourteen Points, was
intended essentially to fall into the second category. It was the action
of the German government in October 1918 which made it into the
first. It was thus an extension by accident rather than intention of the
technique Wilson had developed with the Peace Notes of 1916,
documents couched in the form of traditional diplomacy but transformed in practice into instruments of the New Diplomacy by their
simultaneous publication. The technique puts Wilson slightly ahead
of his Soviet rivals. (President Cleveland's Venezuelan message of
1895 and William II's famous telegram to President Kruger of the

---

[1] David Hopgood and Meridan Bennett, *Agents of Change. A new look at the
Peace Corps.* Boston 1964.

[2] Robert Ellsworth Elder, *The Foreign leaders Programme, Operations in United
States*, Washington, Brookings Institute, 1961.

[3] Irving Louis Horowitz, *The Rise and Fall of Project Camelot: Studies in the
relationship between Social Science and practical politics*, Cambridge Mass. 1967.

Transvaal are much earlier examples. The Monroe doctrine itself is perhaps the earliest.) But Trotsky's famous comment, on assuming control of the Soviet commissariat for foreign affairs, that all he intended to do was to issue a few manifestos and then shut up shop, is perhaps the most extreme statement of the techniques of open diplomacy these two super-powers of the future were developing. There are of course earlier examples of the speech intended as warning rather than communication. Lloyd George's Mansion House speech of 1912, made at the height of the Agadir crisis, and the Kaiser's famous Tangier speech of 1905 which opened the first Morocan crisis are examples of this technique. It was however one which has been sparingly employed, and then only as a means of overt diplomatic pressure coordinated and orchestrated with more traditional forms of diplomatic communication as well as the traditional military methods of manoeuvre, partial mobilisation, naval concentrations etc. What was new with Wilson and Lenin was this preference for the manifesto over all others forms of diplomatic communication, an example which was to be eagerly adopted by the European plebiscitary autocrats of Nazism and Fascism, by the Vatican (some whose earlier encyclicals, especially that of 1871 on Papal infallibility and Leo XIII's *De Rerum Novarum* could perhaps be regarded as prototypes of this form of communication), and by the representatives of the lesser powers seeking on the podium of the League of Nations a means of universal communication which their otherwise exiguous diplomatic resources denied to them.

When one turns to the use of the press conference as an instrument of open diplomacy, problems of definition loom rather larger. The use of individual organs of the press as semi-official channels of communication is a nineteenth century device, and the use of an official press is at least as old as Napoleon. Bismarck's famous instigation of the *Krieg in Sicht* articles in the *Kölnische Anzeiger* and the Berlin *Post* in April 1875 show that the technique was already well-established in the 1870s, though in this case the exercise rebounded on the head of its initiator. The Kaiser's *Daily Telegraph* interview of 1908 represents a widening of the technique, since it involved an element absent in the earlier examples, that of relying on the news value of the action itself rather than control of the journal involved as the principal means of obtaining publicity for the action.

The press conference itself is however a newer and more recent development. It became a necessity as a result of the development of an international press that was commercially viable and therefore in itself beyond the control of particular governments. Again there is a gap in the historical study of this instrument of communication. Regular conferences were given, on and off the record, by statesmen in the 1920s and 1930s though they were rarely used as instruments of international communication even by Franklin Roosevelt. Roosevelt was not unskilled in the use of the press interview or the selective leak as witness, to give two examples, his use of *the Times'* Washington correspondent in October 1934 to warn the British government against a rapprochement with Japan,[1] and his use of Arthur Krock of the *New York Times* in August 1936 to float the idea of an international conference on peace through world trade.[2] But for the full development of the press conference as an instrument of diplomatic communication one has to wait until John Foster Dulles, an example developed by President Kennedy but encountered in its fullest and most stylised forms in the press conferences given by Europe's most distinguished admirer and imitator of the American model of elective absolutism, President de Gaulle. It is however fair to point out that President de Gaulle's model has been followed by no other European head of government, not even by Mr. Harold Wilson, who experimented very widely with various forms of public communication during his six years as prime minister of Britain, without however hitting on any very new variant of the original techniques of open diplomacy. With Mr. Dulles and President de Gaulle the press conference became a means of evading as well as augmenting normal methods of diplomacy.

The last form of populist diplomacy to which reference has already been made is that of lobby diplomacy as practised today at the General Assembly of the United Nations. There has been disgracefully little study as yet of the methods by which majorities were sought in the League of Nations. Such evidence as is available suggests that Britain and France concentrated basically on voting their client states in the Dominions on one hand and through the mechanisms of the French alliance system in Eastern Europe on the other. In the case of Germany the one case which is most extensively documented is the pressures brought to bear on what would now be called the "non-aligned" members of the League Council at the time of the Rhineland crisis

---

[1] See D. C. Watt, *Personalities and Policies*, p. 95.
[2] See Arthur C. Krock, *In the Nation, 1932-1966*, New York 1966, p. 63.

of March 1936.[1] Here all the pressures were applied not in London when the Council was meeting but in the respective capitals of the states concerned using normal diplomatic channels. The only real novelty lay in the number of states against whom pressure was simultaneously orchestrated.

The techniques used first by the United States in the General Assembly of the United Nations seem to have been developed at the Pan-American conferences, especially those of 1936 and 1938, as a substitute for the cruder forms of pressure abandoned in the Good Neighbour policy.[2] Again they require far more precise study and documentation than is at present available. What is significantly American in this is the effort put into and the importance attached to the securing of a regular majority behind American sponsored resolutions as a means of pressure to be employed against the Soviet Union.[3] This too is a post-Rooseveltian phenomenon, embodied in its ultimate form in the Uniting for Peace Resolution of 1950. The United States was to find the Soviet Union an apt pupil—and has come, correspondingly, to attach less importance to resolutions of the General Assembly. But the fact that the U.S. delegation to the United Nations is regularly headed by a political figure of at least cabinet status, if not rank, and that its size and organization has led to its being called the "other State Department" show the importance it still holds in American eyes.[4]

To sum up then—the principal differences between the American and the Euro-democratic approaches to diplomacy and international relations lie in this: America combines a system of government which, even if its head is elected and limited by a written constitution and an elected assembly, is basically akin to the systems of monarchical rule obtaining in eighteenth century Europe, with an ideological attitude to the problems of foreign relations which judges actions by their accordance with the values of the ideology and which seeks to influence the widest possible range of opinion in the countries with whose actions it is concerned. Its methods of diplomacy accord with

---

[1] See *Documents on German Foreign Policy*, London and New York, 1966, Series C. Vol. V, passim.

[2] See for example Julius Pratt, *Cordell Hull*, New York 1964, Vol. I, pp. 168-76, on Hull's role at the Lima Conference in December 1938.

[3] For a characteristically unsympathetic note on this see Conor Cruise O'Brien, *To Katanga and Back*, London 1962, pp. 18-25.

[4] See Arnold Beichman, *The "Other" State Department. The United States Mission to the United Nations—Its role in the making of foreign policy*. New York 1968.

the populist and universalist nature of its ideology. Common to the Euro-democracies is a system of government which basically has at its head a career political oligocracy which is allied with an élite which is sufficiently socially cohesive and sufficiently continuous in its membership over time to be only intermittently open to American populist methods and is progressively if slowly regaining its consciousness of its difference from the United States and its own common European identity. The kind of populist universalist approach which the United States embodies is in Europe basically a heresy, a deviation from the European norm, as it has been ever since a misreading of Montesquieu and the revolutionary ardour of a Tom Paine finally divided what was essentially a culture founded by refugees from Europe from its European roots.

URS SCHWARZ

THE CONDUCT OF WAR

American and European Practice

I. War and Civilization

We do not like to think of war as of an element of culture and civilization. The word itself, the visions it evokes, personified by the four horsemen of the Apocalypse, is revolting to the human mind. The very concept of war as the application of force and violence, sometimes carried to its extremes, to the relationship of nations or social groups is in contradiction to the values we conceive as belonging to human culture and civilization. Yet, conflict between societies and between organized nations as such has always existed since social structures have emerged from the mist of pre-history, and conflicts will naturally continue to be with humanity until the end of its days.

Such conflicts may in a future yet to be built cease to assume the forms and proportions of war. It is one of the high hopes of humanity to succeed in eliminating war from the realm of international relations. In spite of appearances, in spite of the threatening and chaotic aspects of the world to-day and a bloody war going on, there are reasons for hope. Significant steps have already been made towards the banning of war as an accepted institution of international intercourse, after the end of World War II, when the Atomic Age dawned, when the United Nations were founded, when the strategic balance between world powers was discovered. And steps have been made towards limiting war when it occurs.

It is significant that after the end of World War II not one single conflict has been started by a declaration of war in the legal sense. In a recent study of conflict in the twentieth century[1] eighty wars and smaller armed conflicts are listed in the short period alone between the first Vietnam war of 1945 and the Nigerian civil war which broke out on July 7, 1967.

The Secretary of Defense of the United States, Robert McNamara,

---

[1] David Wood, *Conflict in the Twentieth Century*, Adelphi Paper No. 48, London, Institute for Strategic Studies, 1968.

in a speech in 1966 referred to 164 internationally significant out-
breaks of violence between 1958 and 1966, of which fifteen were
military conflicts between two or more states. In only two of these
cases was a state of war recognized to exist within the meaning of
international law, namely in the conflict of the Arab states with Israel,
and in the war of 1965 between India and Pakistan. Since 1948, when
after the establishment of the State of Israel hostilities broke out between the new state and its Arab neighbors, the Arab governments
insisted that a state of war existed between the opposing nations. In
1965 Pakistan asserted for legal purposes that it was in a state of war
with India, despite the fact that no declaration of war had been issued.[1]

So much for the present and for the future. When we look back
to the past and even to the most recent past, we see how much of
the times has been filled with wars and how much energy, courage,
thought and talent has been devoted to the unproductive and rather
destructive art of warfare.[2] The word "unproductive" refers, in this
context, of course to culture and civilization as such and as a whole,
and not to some specific fields of science and technology where war,
to the embarrassment of a humanity devoted to peace, has proved
to be almost too productive. It is, therefore, not possible to objectively
interpret events past and present, including the development and
growth of ideas, not possible to really fathom the psychology of a
people without looking into its relationship to conflict, into its attitudes towards warfare. By comparing the positions of various peoples
and nations we may gain, in addition to deeper understanding of the
reasons for differences between them, a surplus of insight in the nature
and way of thinking of each individual nation under observation.

Whoever reads the treatises on ancient Oriental warfare, sees,
emerging before his eyes, divested of the disguises of myths and
artistic embellishments, the real body of Indian cunning and dedication to violence and Chinese strategy and statecraft. We are thinking
of the *Arthashastra*, the Indian teachings in government by the South
Indian scholar Kautilya in the 4th century before Christ, and in the
famous writings of the Chinese philosopher and civil servant Sun Dzu,
who wrote a little later in the same century. Whoever reads Thucydi-
des' *Peloponnesian War* (400 b.C.) recognizes the real face of ancient

---

[1] Dietrich Schindler, "Aspects contemporains de la neutralité", *Académie de
droit international*, Recueil des cours, II, 1967, Leyden, 1967, p. 283.
[2] Robert W. Tucker, *The Just War*, Baltimore, 1960, p. 12.

Greece, and how much it is the father and mother of modern state-craft, in its best and in its worst aspects. Whoever accompanies Niccolo Machiavelli to Cosimo de Medici's park in Florence and listens to the discussions between Cosimo's noble friends and Fabrizio Colonna on *l'Arte della Guerra* (1521) discovers so many fresh aspects of Renaissance Italy.

A comparison between European and American views on and practice of war equally will bring out characteristic patterns of behaviour and may perhaps shed light on the obscurer reasons for differences dividing an Atlantic world which otherwise has so much in common. Such comparisons may best be conducted by dividing the field of investigation in two sections. The first will deal with the underlying philosophies concerned with the conduct of war and with specific problems such as views of the relationship of policy and power, military sociology, relationship of the civilian, the soldier, the scientist and the technician, the philosophy of leadership (II).

The second section will be concerned with the application of the principles we have discovered in actual military operations, in the strategies and tactics applied in American and European warfare, and show how they are reflected and illustrated by them (III). Finally, we shall point to the innovations and fundamental changes brought about by the present era of limited war (IV).

II. The Philosophies of War

Views on Peace and War

European thinking on the relationship of peace and war is best reflected by the famous phrase of the German thinker and strategist Carl von Clausewitz (1780-1831) "War is the continuation of politics with the admixture of other means". This sentence has, as we know, been quoted and misunderstood and wrongly interpreted millions of times in the light of equally misquoted and misunderstood passages of Clausewitz' writings. Yet, in essence, it assimilates war to the foreign policy of a state: It is as legitimate an activity of a government as its conduct of diplomacy. But as diplomacy is directed towards the achievement of political goals, so should war address itself to well defined political results. It should be subordinated to its political aims and consequently limited in its extent, scope and violence precisely by these objects.

After the Napoleonic wars (1798-1815) with their disastrous results for Europe, which had gradually transgressed their political goals and become wars in the abstract, Europe returned to the classical view that wars were to be waged for limited political objects, that arms should be the *ultima ratio regis*. Under this law the Crimean war (1854-1856), the Italian wars (1859-1870), the Austrian—Prussian War (1866), the Franco—Prussian war (1870-1871) were waged. This traditional European concept was replaced only in the 20th century by the new and catastrophic invention of total war, which actually developed during the second Thirty Years War (1914-1945) and came to a climax with the explosion of two atomic bombs over Japan.

The Clausewitzean thinking corresponded very much to the traditional attitudes of European governments, which were generally timid and inefficient (and still are), relatively powerless, most of the time in conflict with their own public opinion and political parties, and therefore careful to avoid foreign conflicts. The result was that wars generally only started by inadvertence, accidentally and negligently, and grew to larger proportions because of the weakness rather than the strength of the contestants. The exceptions were France under the rule of Napoleon Bonaparte, Prussia under Bismarck and the German Empire under Wilhelm II.

International public law, following Hugo Grotius' *De iure belli ac pacis* (1625) and Emmerich von Vattel's *Droit des gens* (1758), especially the Third Book, On War, developed the law of peace and war, which invested war, once it was declared in proper and due form, with the majesty and legitimacy of a rightful action of a prince or government. The Hague Peace Conferences of 1899 and 1907 actually did not address themselves, for this reason, to the sources of war, they did not outlaw war but rather tried to prevent conflict by the introduction into international relations of subtle judicial instruments and procedures borrowed from the domestic law of civilized nations. In addition, they tried to limit war, once it had broken out, by juridical laws of warfare. The Geneva Conventions on the protection of non-combatants introduced the element of humanitarian international law, which also, in a limited yet significant way, builds a dam against violence.

The juridical doctrine of lawful war had generated a moral doctrine of just war. Just war could be reconciled with the commandments of Christ and with Christian love of mankind, as long as the war was fought in self-defence and only against armed forces, sparing, as far as possible, the non-combatants. Consequently, in Europe the pessimistic philosophers who accepted war as a necessary evil or explained or justified it by the laws of nature and evolution and by the inherent characteristics of the human being, by far outnumber the optimists who predicted that the causes of war will be overcome and therefore war itself. Among the pessimists of course figure Darwin, Hegel, Marx, Nietzsche, Burckhardt, Lenin; among the optimists Comte and Spencer.

American thinking on peace and war, on the other hand, starts from the psychological trauma of a generation who had left Europe behind in order to evade oppression. It started from the experience of nation-building in a virgin land and from the thoughts which particularly appealed to the inhabitants and builders of such a land. The historically erroneous mythical concept that the golden age, an *etas aurea*, had preceded the sinful and warlike past and present, may have been another component of the American dream. In a new land which was not affected by the sinful past it would be possible to live near Nature and to revert to the golden times. The Republic was founded on the basis of the Enlightenment. Separated by the Oceans from Old Europe, where tyrants and princes fought their permanent and meaningless wars, America was to be the "earthly paradise" where reason and justice made war unnecessary and impossible. This thinking was re-inforced by the—mistaken—view that the Oceans constituted a barrier protecting the New World from the Old. It did not occur to most Americans that the Oceans were the easiest lane of access and that their protection lay in the hands of the British Navy and not of winds and waves.[1]

Additional strong impulses for this thinking on peace and war were derived from the evolutionary theory initiated by Auguste Comte and Herbert Spencer, who assumed that war belonged to primitive and feudal societies and would be eliminated by the development of an industrial society, and of democracy. The United States, according to the Jeffersonian conception, had begun their march as an agricultural society, yet, at an early date, and definitely after the Civil War, had sought progress under the sign of industrialization. They were fast progressing in that direction and, therefore, there could be no doubt in their mind that war for them was going to disappear.

When war nevertheless occurred, as was the case from 1775 to 1783, when the United Colonies fought for their independence from England, again from 1812 to 1814 and again from 1861 to 1865 and in

---

[1] Louis J. Halle, *Dream and Reality*, New York, 1958, p. 32.

1898, and throughout the century against the Indians and the Mexicans, this was considered as an unfortunate aberration from normal, which was peace. Wars were not for America. In his message to the Congress on December 8, 1914, President Woodrow Wilson referred to the European war then going on as "a war with which we have nothing to do, whose causes cannot touch us."

This leads directly to the basic attitude of Americans in war. Since war is opposed to the true order of things, and since war has to disappear by the progress of humanity towards its true destination, war has to be conducted in the spirit of ending it as soon as possible. This has deeply influenced the American views on the relationship of power and policy as well as strategy and tactics in every conflict, in which the USA were involved.

Americans are unconcerned by the causes of war and concentrate only on the question who initiated the use of force. The one who started the war departed from the norm; his war is therefore unjust. He who defends himself against the aggression tries to re-establish normalcy; he is waging a just war. He is, therefore, entitled by the justice of his cause to use any extent of violence.

The Relationship of Policy and War

For the European nations, which for centuries have lived in an almost permanent state of war or at least in close neighborhood to some war going on, foreign policy and armed conflict were no real alternatives. The diplomat and the soldier were used to working hand in hand. Their task to guard a country's integrity, its prestige, to expand its power, were, although the instruments differed, intimately linked. Their respective activities were interrelated and the artisans themselves, belonging to the same class of society, with the same allegiance to the ruler, had most things in common.

The American view, on the other hand, that war is alien to the nature of American society and to the very nature of the American nation and its destiny, created an altogether different attitude towards the relationship of policy and war, of diplomacy and power.

The traditional outlook, which prevailed from the beginnings of the Republic until the end of World War II, generated an absolute distinction between the government's activity in peace and in war. The line dividing policy and war formed a real watershed.

As soon as war broke out the military were asked to assume the direction of events. The only object of war would be and could only be to end the war. No other war aims really counted. When President Wilson on March 5, 1917 asked the Congress to authorize a declaration of war on Germany, he said: "We...shall, if necessary, spend the whole force of the nation to check and nullify its (the enemy's) pretensions and its power... We are glad...to fight thus for the ultimate peace of the world and for the liberation of its peoples... The world must be made safe for democracy."[1]

These were the war aims of the United States at the outset of World War I. They actually can be reduced to one object: Bring "ultimate peace" to the world. Democracy corresponding to the American pattern, spread all over the world, was not the object in itself. It was the guarantee, since war was alien to American democracy, that wars would never again break out and disturb the peaceful existence of the United States. In the course of the war, however, it became mandatory to state some sort of political aim for the enormous effort undertaken by the whole nation. Political war aims appeared at the outset merely as restatements of general principles of morality and law, freedom of the seas, self-determination of small nations. Only towards the end of the struggle the war aims became more articulate and were finally formulated in Wilson's address to the Congress of January 8, 1918, in what was soon to be called the "Fourteen Points". They did not represent, however, a well planned strategy for war and peace, and even less a concerted strategy of the Allied powers, but rather a projection of what Wilson personally believed to be the wish of the American people and, therefore, of all the peoples of the world able to express their will.

The unhappy experiences of the two wars of the American revolution and the Civil War, where domestic politics of the low order had interfered with the war effort every time when it became necessary to mobilize more of the nation's forces or to appoint higher military commanders, added to the firm conviction that war and policy should be and remain separate domains. President Franklin D. Roosevelt adhered in principle to this doctrine. This did not prevent him, however, from introducing once in a while considerations of electoral expediency in his conduct of the war. After December 7, 1941, when the United States were drawn, by the Japanese attack on Pearl Harbor,

---

[1] Edgar E. Robinson and Victor J. West, *The Foreign Policy of Woodrow Wilson, 1913-1917*, New York, 1918, p. 382.

into World War II, the President insisted that he should be considered and referred to as Commander-in-Chief rather than as President. He excluded the Secretary of State from his War Council. Throughout the war the member of the Cabinet responsible for the conduct of the foreign policy of the government was never admitted to any of the international conferences related to the conduct of the war, which the President and the military chiefs attended.

This fact is not only to be explained by personal incompatibilities between the President and the Secretary of State, but by the firm conviction held by the President and most of his fellow Americans that diplomacy ends where war begins. This idea was shared by many. Even the Secretary of State himself, Cordell Hull, gave testimony to this view by a significant remark of his. When late in 1940 a document on the strategic options open to the US in the world conflict then in its opening stage was to be submitted to the President, it was signed by the Secretary of War and the Secretary of the Navy. The Secretary of State refused to sign, although he was, in general, in agreement with the policy set out in the document. He pointed out that as head of a civilian department he was doubtful whether he could join in submitting to the President a military statement of the situation.

The result of this voluntary abdication of diplomacy and the will to renounce any political direction of the war had far reaching results. One of these results was, as we shall see later, that the military commanders in the field whose only mission was to "end the war" were invested with the supreme power to take military decisions which later would prove to have momentous political implications and results.

This thinking finds characteristic expression in connection with the Civil War, when General Schofield sharply criticized Sherman's March to the Sea as not at all consistent with the "dictates of established principles in the conduct of a military campaign." The whole disdain for politico-military concepts was expressed in his words: "It was, perhaps, not *war* but rather *statesmanship* upon which Sherman was about to enter."[1]

Or in remarks by General Omar N. Bradley in his memoirs on World War II where he explains why he chose not to take Berlin. He writes: "I could see no political advantages accruing from the capture of Berlin that would offset the need for quick destruction of

---

[1] John M. Schofield, *Forty-Six Years in the Army*, New York, 1897, p. 311.

the German army on our front. As soldiers we looked naively on this British inclination to complicate the war with political foresight and non-military objectives."[1]

The gulf between policy and power was only bridged after the end of World War II, which in itself was still conducted according to the traditional concepts. The armed forces of the US had been demobilized, in traditional fashion, and billons worth of equipment destroyed, after the war was ended—since wars in the future would not recur. The United States soon were to discover that the deep involvement in world affairs, created by the gigantic war effort, was irreversible. The occupation of Germany, Japan, Italy, Austria and Korea involved the deployment of some military power. When in 1947 the US had to assume in the place of Great Britain the protection of Greece and Turkey against its domestic and foreign enemies, the die was cast. Political and military planning henceforth went hand in hand. When the aggression against South Korea in 1950 called forth a new and unprecedented military effort, at the same time a new form or war developed from this conflict—new for America: Limited War. The very essence of limited war is that political decisions accompany, step by step, and direct from day to day the military effort, and every military step is taken with the political aim in mind.

The new doctrine found its consecration in a special message on the Defense Budget of President John F. Kennedy of March 28, 1961 to Congress where the President stated that "Diplomacy and defense are no longer distinct alternatives, one to be used when the other side fails—but must complement each other."[2]

Military Sociology

The relationship between a people and its armed forces is always the outgrowth of the social history of a nation and generally reaches far into the past. For this very reason it is not possible to discover one single European pattern of the sociopolitical relationship between the soldier and the citizen. It varies from country to country and has undergone everywhere deep changes in the course of the centuries which did not follow at all parallel lines.

---

[1] Omar N. Bradley, *A Soldier's Story*, New York, 1951, p. 544.

[2] Congressional Quarterly Almanach, 87th Congress, 1st session, XVII, Washington, 1961, p. 895.

The European countries had a professional military class which was to a large proportion identical with the nobility, and possessed by proud traditions. When the system of government was the monarchy, which applied until 1917 to all European nations with the only exceptions of France, Portugal and Switzerland, the military were closely linked to the throne and represented the uppermost layer of society, more respected than wealth, learning, art. The military system, which in earlier centuries had been based on professional soldiers—volunteers and not so volunteers—was shattered by the French revolution. It was replaced by the new concept of national mass armies raised by conscription. The French and Napoleonic solution was, however, not universally accepted, and after 1815 the period of the Restoration brought practically the return to the professional army in most of the countries. It was Prussia which developed the compromise solution which combined the advantages—and, as was later discovered, the drawbacks—of both systems. It was the cadre-conscript army, which combined the professionalism of officers and non-commissioned officers with the weight of masses of enlisted men and which permitted the creation of sizable reserve forces. After Prussia's victories over Austria and France this solution was almost universally adopted in the last decennia of the 19th century in Europe.

The system was designed for providing the mass armies which were later to fight the "total wars". The new mass armies required masses of armaments and equipment, which in turn engendered an industry capable of mass production closely linked to the military needs. Such was Europe involved in a cobweb of military power, for which the weak civilian authorities were no match—except the ones in the democratic Scandinavian states, in Great Britain and Switzerland with their age-old and stable institutions.

The protest against this involvement in warlike postures generated the pacifist movement, which towards the turn of the century seized a small part of the intellectuals and a large section of the worker's movements. This movement, however, as 1914 was going to prove, was pathetically powerless because of its total lack of real understanding of the underlying sociological facts and the real nature of the dangers for peace. It could not prevent nations from being dragged by the sheer weight of their military institutions, to which no civilian leadership corresponded, into the abyss of war.

The sociological pattern of the military institutions in the United States of America is, of course, deeply influenced by the British experience, but not by the continental experiences. The permanent conflict between Parliament and Crown which culminated in the 17th Century in the Bill of Rights, had shaped the outlook of the early settlers. Since the Bill of Rights declared that a standing army, unless raised with the consent of Parliament, was illegal, for the American a standing army was contrary to the freedom which he had found and which he cherished. Alexander Hamilton[1] had to use all his power of persuasion in order to prevent a clause from being inserted in the Federal Constitution, copied from the Declaration of Rights of 1774 that "standing armies are dangerous to Liberty". George Washington, from 1775 to 1783 when he disbanded his army, was constantly engaged in a fight against a military system under which militia and volunteers were mobilized by the legislatures for a limited period and then disbanded. A persistent lack of discipline found expression in frequent mutinies.

The Civil War bore testimony time and again to this specific American thinking on war, to its reaction to the professional soldier, its belief in *ad hoc* forces and amateurs. In 1861 Abraham Lincoln had to conduct the operations against the Confederacy with forces which were disbanded after a few months and replaced by new even less trained soldiers and with a large proportion of newly promoted officers. The initial success of the Confederates was due to the excellence of their initial higher command echelon, built around professionals.

The Navy's position was different. Similarly to the situation in England it was much less afflicted by these views. It seemed unlikely to the American mind that the Navy could become a political threat to freedom, since it has to stay off shore. Its very nature called for professional skill and long-serving personnel. The Navy was considered from the outset, in union with the Oceans on which it sailed, as the permanent element for the protection of the nation and its ideals from outside interference.

One of the foremost American military writers, Lieutenant General John M. Schofield, wrote in 1897 that the Navy would protect the "vast national interests and honor", whereas a small standing army, as the "model and instructor" would permit the USA to rely on mobilization of its citizens in case of an emergency. This would, in the General's words, correspond to the "perfect ideal of a peace-loving yet military republic".[2]

---

[1] *The Federalist*, No. 24.
[2] John M. Schofield, op. cit., p. 366.

The stubborn belief in amateurism, the conviction that political leaders would in case of war also be good military leaders, trusted by their subordinates, runs through the whole fabric of American military history. In the early months of the American participation in World War I President Wilson expressed his doubts about the ability of the professional soldier to cope with the new situation, when he wrote that this war, being completely unprecedented, was, in a sense, a war for amateurs.[1]

It was an American tradition and characteristic to have government run by amateurs as well. Few Secretaries of State have been professional diplomats.

A deep change occurred after the end of World War II. The interpenetration of the military element and the scientific community, of defence procurement and the national economy, had grown to an unprecedented degree. After the victory won over the Axis powers military leaders, the war heroes, similarly to events after the Civil War, were drafted for electoral or otherwise political office. Generals like Eisenhower, Marshall, Bedell Smith, Bradley, Le May, Goldwater were eagerly accepted by the nation or at least sectors of the nation as the new leaders in the fields of politics, learning, diplomacy, industry. The condition of this transition of the military into the political domain was, however, that he completely became a civilian.

Civilian, soldier, scientist, technician

As we have seen, in Europe the ascendancy of civilian power over military power was not always recognized as an essential of a well organized society, and is of a relatively recent date. Even where constitutionally the precedence of the civilian before the military was granted, the facts often pointed in the opposite direction. The reasons were the dominating social position of the military in so many countries, the weakness of the civilian leaders and the at least nominal position of the monarch as commander-in-chief of the armed forces. In really well organized and smoothly functioning societies such as in Scandinavia, Great Britain and Switzerland, the pre-eminence of the civilian authority over the military power was never questioned in the past hundred years.

---

[1] Elting E. Morison, *Admiral Sims and the Modern American Navy*, Boston, 1942, p. 359.

The totalitarian governments, on the other hand, true to their origin and their nature, concentrated military and civilian authority in one hand. In this special case it would be impossible to say whether the political authority gives directions to the military arm of the state or vice versa. Among them the Union of Socialist Soviet Republics represent a curious mixture reflecting the traditional interpenetration of military and civilian power which was characteristic for the Russia of the Tsars. The front positions are occupied by civilians—which may carry high military titles—but their dictatorial position is based on the armed power of the Army and the Police, which exercise, subject to the changes of their relative position resulting from a complicated power play, the corresponding influence on the civilian authorities.

In the United States, the nation with the oldest written constitution still in force and an extraordinary stability of its institutions, which have withstood war, civil war and many staggering changes, the primacy of the civilian authority has never really been questioned. This relationship of authority finds its most vivid and visible expression in the constitutional provision that the President of the United States is commander-in-chief of the armed forces.

Yet, much stronger than this formal rule are the political and sociological facts and traditions. In times of peace the military withdraws to his assigned position, which is to develop the efficiency of his service and to wrest the highest possible amount of money in the form of military credits from the Congress for the acquisition of arms, munitions, airplanes, ships, the training of men, and to use that money by feeding it to the corresponding industries. Far from him the desire or even the thought to make political decisions.

Even the Department of Defense with its own political planning staff, with the wealth of information it collects, with its worldwide network of bases and forces, with the overwhelming power it wields is a very tame giant. It is directed by a civilian appointed by the President and confirmed by the Senate. He is the executive force behind the strategic decisions of the administration. We must remember that the criticism of the war in South East Asia—and this seems typical— in spite of one or the other loud demonstration in front of the Pentagon, is not directed against the military as such. It is addressed to the President's office. Criticism of the military- industrial relationship, of the system of conscription, of the reserve officers training system in the Universities is levelled against the civilian authorities much more than against the military establishment.

However, when war breaks out—and we are here referring to classical, declared wars of the past and not to the limited wars or semi-wars of the present—then the civilian authority steps down and calls upon the military. Their task: Win the war for ending the war. The civilian arm does it without fear, since it knows that the military man will find it natural and proper to be subordinated again to the civilian authority once his task is completed.

A profound difference exists between the European approach to military technology and the American approach. Again it is to be explained by differences in the fundamental traditions. The European armies found it difficult, even in an industrial age in full development, to cut loose from their origins. The origin was the feudal past, where the land and agriculture had been the main source of wealth of a nation and the basis of its armed forces. When for years the horse had ceased to be a source of energy and a necessary instrument of transportation, European armies would go to war, as late as 1939, with endless columns of horse-drawn cannons and vehicles of every kind. Technological innovation was slow and concentrated on the navies, which by definition and by tradition used other sources of energy than the muscles of men and horses—the wind, steam—long before these innovations were widely applied in industry, agriculture and in armies. In analogy to the navies the navies of the air, the air forces, started from technology and were consequently closely related with the scientist and the technician.

American armies were made, throughout history, when they were needed. They had to carry with them the ideological ballast of the prevailing views on power and policy, on peace and war, on the social position of soldiers and sailors in the nation. But they never were burdened with obsolete material. They were made by a nation wich had needed and used technology for the building of a new land: railroads, steamships, the electric telegraph, harvesting machines. Consequently, technological achievements immediately found entrance in the armed forces and were put to the service of warfare. This development was favoured by the influential position of the Navy, which, similarly to Europe, was leading on the path of harnassing science and technology to the defence effort.

In Europe it was Great Britain, the classical naval power, which was foremost in using, when World War II approached, and in the context of the war, sophisticated technology, such as radar, and scientific methods, such as quantitative analysis, for solving complicated strategic problems and preparing far-reaching military operations. Problems of air defence, of sea transportation, convoys, submarine warfare, aerial warfare against Germany and Italy could not be solved by rule of thumb and with the help only of common sense and experience. The United States of America had to turn to the same methods when confronted with the appalling problems of a war to be waged on two fronts, across the Atlantic and the Pacific Oceans. The scientific approach became an absolute condition of success when the decision was taken to apply nuclear power to the war effort and to make the atomic bomb.

From the war effort, where the scientific and quantitative approach had proved so successful and where advanced technology had triumphed, the new methods and the new men were carried into the post-war era. They shaped military technology, strategic planning, the evolution of weapons systems, the fast developing strategic research and speculation. From the position thus gained these methods spilled over into the realms of civilian technology and space research, in the methods of business administration and industrial production, and were brought back to Europe, where they actually had originated.

Philosophy of Leadership

One deep difference between European and American practice will easily be discovered when one looks at the methods of leadership in war and its underlying philosophy.

The application of the rule by American leaders that "war excludes policy" will often leave, as we shall see, a political vacuum. The political authorities refrain from taking decisions which actually would belong to them, until the war is ended and until they again assume their role. The military High Command, in turn, which directs and conducts the war, is not directly interested in the political outcome and even feels not authorized in any way to consider this outcome. This would mean mingling politics and the military effort, which is considered inadmissible. The military command does, therefore, not issue instructions or orders referring to political matters. This will leave to the military commander in the field full discretion to act, if act he must, and to assume the responsibility for the political outcome. He is, of course, supposed not to think of the political implications of his military decisions, which according to military orthodoxy have to aim exclusively at the destruction of the enemy's army or fleet.

This almost absolute discretion with respect to a decision's political outcome stands in sharp contrast to the detailed orders and instructions as to their execution given the commander by his superiors on military matters. The American High Command, from George Washington down to George Marshall, had to deal with a high proportion of non-professionals, of civilian leaders who had been transformed in an emergency into military leaders. They did not have the same background—sociologically and professionally—as their superiors who probably were professional soldiers and products of the Service Academies. From this relationship—professionals who are used to work together with "amateurs"—stems the American practice of giving detailed orders for the fulfillment of a given task. Similar considerations apply, *mutatis mutandis*, to business and industry. Minor details there used to be settled by the head office, which simply cannot imagine that a subordinate can make the right decision, especially when he is a foreigner or in a foreign land.

Another reason for this American view on leadership may be technological. The Americans fought their great wars—with the exception of the revolutionary wars—in an epoch when methods of transmission were already fairly developed and when, therefore, the High Command was physically able to instantly intervene. For the Europeans wars were conducted throughout centuries where it took two hours to inform Athens of the victory of Marathon, and for a messenger from Rome two weeks to reach Caesar in Gallia, and several weeks for a dispatch to reach the Duke of Medina Sidonia in the Great Armada. European tradition, therefore, is one of great independence especially of the Naval commander during a campaign.

An example of the American philosophy of leadership is provided by the invasion of the Philippines in 1944. General Douglas MacArthur was to land, according to plan, on the southernmost island, Mindanao, and later on the smaller island of Leyte. When MacArthur reported the weakness of the Japanese air arm on the Philippines and suggested an abbreviated procedure, he was not entitled to make the decision himself. He had to be expressly authorized by the Joint Chiefs of Staff in Washington to bypass Mindanao and to land directly on Leyte.

A minor incident may further illustrate the American philosophy to lead from the top. During the Cuba missile crisis of 1962 the Secretary of Defense, Robert McNamara, in the heat of action, tried to tell over the radio telephone a destroyer captain in the Caribbean

Sea what he was to say to a Russian captain of a merchant vessel which he had summoned and stopped. Admiral Anderson found this procedure not proper and pointed out to McNamara that such direct interference in details could not be admitted. The incident, of course, belongs to the context of a confrontation and not of war and is therefore not entirely typical.

The European philosophy on the chain of command is different. European practice is to designate to the commander directing operations in the field the object he is to achieve, perhaps with indications as to priorities and timing. Then he is free to decide how best to execute his orders and to settle all the details. This is partly a result of the already mentioned lack of adequate means of communication in earlier periods, partly a result of the Prussian experience. The Prussian Army had highly trained and experienced commanders assisted by officers of the General Staff, who formed by reason of their training and their tradition a closely knit community of doctrine and thought. It is also a leftover from the Napoleonic wars which were fought by professionals, and especially of the experience with naval power, where full freedom of action had to be given to the commanding officer of the fleet.

III. STRATEGY, OPERATIONS, TACTICS

When Policy Ends

All the preceding comparisons of European and American views on military policy and on the conduct of war provide the basis for an investigation on how European and American practice of warfare differ and how far they coincide. And we have to discover how the differences find expression in the realm of strategy, operations and tactics.

From the view that war is opposed to the ordained and normal order of things, to the idea of leaving its conduct entirely to the soldier or to the civilians who have transformed themselves into military leaders, there is only a short step. This leads to the undivided responsibility of the military commander in the field for the most vital decisions which may have perhaps endless political consequences.

A few examples may illustrate this point. After Pearl Harbor, President Franklin D. Roosevelt held, on December 16, 1941, one of his War Councils. At that date the Philippines had been attacked by the Japanese after destruction of large proportions of the American aircraft stationed there, and it seemed most unlikely that this advanced position could be held. The President, therefore, decided that "the Commander of the Asiatic Fleet would have discretionary authority as to how long he could remain based on the Philippines and to his direction of withdrawal—to the East or to Singapore". For the President—as for President Wilson 24 years earlier—war had begun and policy had ended. The decision how long he could remain in Manila Bay certainly belonged to the Commander of the fleet, since it immediately related to his assessment of the situation and his conduct of operations. The decision, however, whether the American fleet stationed in the Far East should join the British in Singapore would be of the utmost political significance. Would henceforth the American fleet participate in the defense of the British, Dutch and French possessions? Would it join the US fleet in the Eastern Pacific? Would it perhaps steam to the Panama Canal and take up positions there? These decisions of the highest strategic importance were casually left to the Admiral commanding the ships.

The question whether Berlin was to be taken by the American armies in 1945—which was to decide perhaps on the future relationship between the Soviet Union and the West and did shape 25 years of diplomatic struggles—was never even discussed in Washington. It was left to the military commander in the theatre. General Eisenhower, in turn, did not seem to be interested in this question of detail, since it seemed exclusively of political instead of strategic relevance, and his mission was not a political but a military one. So he left it to the local commander, General Bradley, who decided not to listen to the British suggestion to take Berlin ahead of the Russians, because his only mission was to destroy the enemy's army.

On January 22, 1944, in the middle of the battle for Italy, an American force was landed at Anzio, near Rome. After discussions the British and the American Staff had decided upon the operation— a compromise between two conflicting views—which was designed to break the stalemate then existing at the Italian front. The landing was unopposed but was not exploited by the over-cautious commander. Using the total surprise achieved he easily could have captured Rome. However, he had not received any order to this effect. True to the tradition not to engage in "politics", but to defeat the enemy, the decision what to do after the landing, which was of highest political significance, was not taken by the High Command. It was left to the military commander on the spot. This offcer, not finding any enemies there to be defeated, did nothing. He did not move out of the beachhead initially secured until the Germans had gathered their forces around it and almost succeeded in defeating the invador.

The bombing of Japan started, after a few preliminary raids, in November 1944 after airfields on the islands of Guam, Saipan and Tinian had been secured. The operations began, true to the American principle, on the assumption that only military targets should be hit by precision bombing by daylight. This method proved ineffective against the widely dispersed Japanese war industry. General LeMay therefore decided to change the bombing procedure. He engaged his bombers in night raids with incendiary bombs instead of high explosives. With this decision obliteration bombing of Japanese cities had begun. One raid on Tokyo in the night of March 9 to 10, 1945 destroyed 250.000 houses and killed 85.000 people. The concept of just war, the principle that only military objectives should be attacked, which was widely proclaimed at the beginning of the war as the essence of American strategy, in opposition to the strategy of dictators, had gone overboard. It had gone by a decision of the local military commander, who acted absolutely within his authority as long as he did everything to win the war.

When the first experimental atomic bomb had been exploded on July 26, 1945 in Nevada, the commander of the US Army Strategic Air Force was instructed, on the same day, to deliver the first "special bomb" as soon as weather would permit visual bombing, after August 3, 1945, on one of four specifically mentioned Japanese cities. August 3 was assumed to be the date by which the Japanese could have offered surrender under the terms of the Potsdam declaration issued on July 26. Long studies, discussions and soul-searching had preceded this order given to the air force. Yet, after it had been given, the responsibility for selecting the date and the target among the four cities mentioned was left to a local commander. No further order was given, not even the one to deliver the second bomb. It was dropped on a day selected by the commander of the air wing and on the target selected by the commander of the airplane which carried the bomb—who was authorized if necessary to change from Kokura to Nagasaki. Again, decisions which shook the world were taken by the commanding officers on the spot, who acted within the discretion granted to them under the principle that it was the military's business to know how to win the war with the weapons they had been issued.

All this does not exclude that within the military ladder of command the authority of the commander may be narrowly limited. We have dealt with this problem in the context of the philosophy of leadership. He will be told by his superiors, who perhaps sit in Washington, exactly what to do, and when to do it and how—in the realm of his military responsibilities. Yet, the political implications may not be considered by the same superiors, since they are not concerned with policy but only with winning the war. Therefore, the subordinate commander may be free to make military decisions which actually are of the highest political significance.

From the idea that war has to be won by utterly defeating the enemy's forces and not by policy-oriented manoeuver,—war excludes policy— the deep strategic division between the British and the Americans in the course of World War II developed. These controversies illustrate like nothing else the difference between American and European practice. They became visible in practically every decision which had to be taken in the course of the war by the Combined Chiefs of Staff, and it is impossible to enumerate them all. A few examples may suffice.

The American war plans centered around the idea that Germany should be defeated first and later Japan. Throughout the war the Americans defended this basic strategic concept—the defeat by one massive onslaught by land forces of the armies of the principal foe— against the British and their policy-oriented proposals and plans.

For the Americans the obvious and the only possible course of action was to build up an invasion force on the British Isles and then to launch an attack against Western Europe. The British, hard pressed in the Near East, advocated a landing in North Africa which would open possibilities for operations of highest politico-military importance against "the soft underbelly" of the enemy powers. The decision to undertake late in 1942 the landing in Morocco and Algeria was made jointly by President Roosevelt and Prime Minister Churchill, against the strong opposition of the American Chiefs of Staff. It was one of the instances where the President overruled his military advisers, and one of the few occasions where political considerations decided on military operations.

Once the Southern coast of the Mediterranean secured, there was no plausible reason for the Americans not to follow the British and to exploit the success by an operation against Italy. In August 1943 the capture of Sicily forced the capitulation of the Italian government, and in September the Italian mainland was invaded. This was the last concession the Americans were to make to British "statesmanship". They were now firmly determined to return to "war". No additional diversion from the final attack "Overlord", to be undertaken in the summer of 1944 against the French coasts, was to be admitted. The British proposals for other operations—the capture of Rhodes, the opening of the Dardanelles which should bring Turkey into the war on the side of the Allies, landings in Yougoslavia, a thrust into Eastern Europe ahead of the Russians, were firmly resisted. The landing in Southern France, "Anvil", which took place in August 1944, had been decided upon as part of the massive effort of "Overlord". After the success of the landing on June 6, 1944 in Normandy, the British proposed to cancel this operation, which now seemed unnecessary to them, and to use the available forces for a landing in the Adriatic. This was emphatically declined by the American Chiefs of Staff.

When what remained of the Japanese navy was destroyed in October 1944 in the South of the Philippines, in the engagement of Leyte Gulf, and when in April 1945 Iwo Shima was occupied by the Americans and Okinawa invaded, there could be no doubt that Japan was defeated. In spite of this evidence, plans were laid for a massive invasion of Japan by the Allied Armies, beginning on the southern Island of Kyushu and working its way up towards the north. One million casualties was the estimated cost of the operation.

On June 18, 1945 at a meeting of the War Council President Truman approved this plan, to which the military had not offered an alternative. John J. McCloy then brought up the idea of using the atomic bomb as a warning for Japan. He then records that someone suggested almost casually, when the meeting was already breaking up, that serious attention should be given to an attempt to end the war by political means. McCloy then remarks in his memoirs: "Now this incident indicates that at the time everyone was so intent on winning the war by military means that the introduction of political considerations was almost accidental."[1]

As a forceful expression of such attitudes a remark by Senator Hickenlooper may be quoted. When in the Senate hearings on the Military Situation in the Far East in 1951 (MacArthur Hearings), the Senator criticized the British, he said: "...our military tactics and strategy in this country have always been of an aggressive nature; we believe

---

[1] John J. McCloy, *The Challenge to American Foreign Policy*, Cambridge, Mass., 1953, p. 42.

in getting the thing over with; we believe in an aggressiveness rather than muddling through."[1]

We see, therefore, on the one hand the British viewpoint derived from the traditions of a sea power which had practiced war through centuries against ever changing groups of foes, supported by an equally changing group of allies. Operations were conducted as well on the European Continent as in India, in Egypt, in America, on the Krim, in Mesopotamia, and they all were part of one national strategy, the aim of which was to prevent the rise of a hegemonial power in Western Europe, by the deployment of British sea power and—if feasible—without an overseas engagement in war on land, which should be left to allied powers. On the other hand was the American trend to end the war by destroying the enemy's power to make war.

Concentrated Power

Opposed to the British strategy is the American view to the effect that war is to be avoided and should never be initiated as a means of achieving national goals—the idea of "just war"—and, when it breaks out, should be terminated by the utter destruction of the enemy's power to make war. The thrust will be directed against the enemy's heartland and the seat of his military might—the navy and the army— and no portion of one's forces must be diverted from this one and single purpose by politico-military considerations of any kind. In support of this image of American practice in war one often mentions the term "unconditional surrender", as used by President F. D. Roosevelt on January 23, 1943, after the conference of Casablanca. At that conference the overall strategy to be employed against the Axis powers had been discussed and partly determined. We now know that no decision of the conference was at the bottom of Roosevelt's remark made before the press on that day. He was referring, of course, to General Ulysses S. Grant's famous note to the commandant of Fort Donelson on February 16, 1862 "No terms except an unconditional and immediate surrender can be accepted". This phrase, part of American folklore, the perfect expression of a national ideal of

---

[1] *Military Situation in the Far East.* Hearings before the Committee on Armed Services and the Committee on Foreign Relations, U.S. Senate, 82d Congress. 1st session (Washington, 1951), p. 493.

"toughness" and the longing of the American mind for "all or nothing", had come, almost inadvertently, to the president's mind when
he wanted to convey to the journalists the impression of the conferees'
determination to defeat Germany and to stand unwaveringly on the
side of the Soviet ally.

We have now seen how American strategy is distinguished from
European—especially British—practice. The American wish to achieve
"all or nothing", to use massively the available physical power, to
use machines instead of men, to "get the thing over with", finds a
full expression in the strategic decisions as well in the Civil War
(1861-1865) as in the wars in Europe in 1917/1918 and in World War
II from 1941 to 1945. Yet, it also shapes the pattern of military operations and even of tactics.

From Civil War days we might remember Picket's charge at Gettys-
burg on July 3, 1863, the siege of Petersburg from June 1864 to April
1865. In 1917 the belief in the massive offensive, in the concentration
of forces presided over the American war effort in France. The American generals Pershing and Bliss finally convinced the Allied powers
to adopt a unified command. In World War II the examples of American operations and tactical procedures which point to the absolute
concentration of forces are to be counted by the thousands.

When the landing in North Africa was planned in 1942, the British,
well versed in the tactics of peripheral warfare, suggested a thrust
into the Mediterranean with troop landings in Algeria and Tunisia
and Admiral Cunningham's ships right in Bizerta. The Americans,
however, could not visualize any other approach than to begin at
the far end, in Morocco, securing ports and staging areas, railroads
and roads, and then to work their way east. Finally, a compromise
solution was offered by General Eisenhower, to the effect that several
months were lost.

After the landing on the Italian mainland in September 1943 all
the British suggestions of diversions, amphibious operations, of a
politico-military approach—the Italian government had capitulated—
were defeated. The American High Command established a continuous front across the peninsula and pushed it, in frontal attacks, preceded by massive artillery fire and aerial bombardment, across mountains
and valleys northwards until the attack bogged down. The already mentioned amphibious operation at Anzio was undertaken half-heartedly
and remained unsuccessful, because it did not occur to anybody to
think of the politico-military potentialities.

In the attack against Japan General MacArthur could not visualize
any other approach than that of taking one island after the other, from
which the foot soldiers could step to the next island, with all the heav-
iest gear imaginable, and thence to the Chinese mainland and from
there to Japan. The Navy and the Air Force, which by then—1943—
seemed to be impressed and partly won over by British and Churchille-
an practice, advocated a more imaginative and daring course—"leap
frogging" the Japanese strongholds. The controversy ended with a
compromise.

The conflict between General Eisenhower and Field Marshal Montgomery towards the end of World War II has been widely reported
and commented upon. When the Allied armies had broken out of
their beachheads in Normandy and Provence and were pursuing the
battered German armies across France, Montgomery suggested a
swift thrust across the Rhine into the Ruhrgebiet, in order to deal
a deadly blow to the German war effort. Eisenhower, on the contrary,
insisted that the allied armies be brought up to the so-called Siegfried
Line (which partly existed in German propaganda only), their logistic
support secured, and that only then the massive onslaught should
be made with the object of "destroying the enemy's forces". This
was the course of action adopted, with the result that the Germans
won breathing space, held out throughout the winter, and that the
Soviet armies could penetrate deeply into the heart of Western Europe.

One incident of this very winter is also characteristic: the reborn
French army, fighting under General Eisenhower's orders, had pene-
trated, in the last days of 1944, into Alsace and had taken Strasbourg.
The symbolic value of this feat of arms for France and for the rest
of Europe was perceived by everybody. When the Germans started,
at Christmas, their surprise counter—offensive in the Ardennes,
Eisenhower decided to concentrate all available forces against this
area and therefore to withdraw from Alsace and from Strasbourg.
General de Gaulle refused to execute the corresponding orders, fearing
the political implications of the withdrawal. It is interesting to note
that Eisenhower and the American staff did not even think of the
political consequences of the move and simply could not understand
the French arguments.

Similarly in naval operations the American urge for massive, concentrated action finds frequent and full expression. The classical writer,
who reflects this basic thinking, and who transmitted it to a world-

wide audience—way beyond the American military—was of course Admiral Alfred Thayer Mahan (1840-1914). He influenced American strategic thinking, around the turn of the century, in an almost un-believable way. He became by an extremely wide—and loose—inter-pretation of his writings, which were mostly a historian's work, the classic of European and American imperialism. His views were em-pirical and conservative, and this explains probably why he appealed so much to the military mind, both in America and in Europe. The effect was that his teachings, which were on the strategic level, were carried over unthinkingly into the realm of military operations and tactics.

Mahan was a believer in the decisive role of the battleship and of concentrated action of the undivided fleet against the seat of the enemy's sea power—his battlefleet. From this the rule was derived "never divide the fleet". It found its pathetic expression in a letter written by President Theodore Roosevelt on March 3, 1909 to President-elect Taft. He wrote: "Dear Will: one closing legacy. Under no circumstances divide the battleship fleet between the Atlantic and the Pacific Oceans prior to the finishing of the Panama Canal."[1]

This was world strategy. Yet, the rule "never divide the fleet" which so admirably corresponded to the principle that only a massive, concentrated effort could destroy the enemy's forces—which was the only object of war—was carried as a shibboleth into tactics. As a consequence, as late as in World War II, tactical commanders in many instances did not dare to detach sections of their respective fleet in order to deal with weak enemy forces.

In the battle of Leyte Gulf of October 1944, which we have already mentioned, Admiral Halsey, attracted by a Japanese decoy force, left his assigned task of protecting the troop landings on Leyte Island because he thought it more important "to destroy the enemy's fleet". Catastrophe was avoided thanks to the weakness of the Japanese in this late stage of the war.

The urge to attach much importance to well defined doctrines, to a specific formula, which finds expression in the use made of Mahan's legacy, reflects another facet of American politico-strategic thinking. It is a consequence of the dominant pragmatism. The American mind easily refuses to think in the abstract. It takes its

---

[1] Elting E. Morison, ed., *The Letters of Theodore Roosevelt*, Cambridge, Mass., 1952, vol. VI, p. 1543.

inspiration from preceding events, preferably when "all the facts are in", and likes to react to facts. In analogy to the legal system, which is based on judicial decisions and the doctrines derived therefrom, foreign policy likes to deduce "doctrines" from decisions which have been taken under specific circumstances. We know that the "Truman Doctrine" made Vietnam possible, we know the "Eisenhower Doctrine" for intervention in the Middle East, the "Johnson Doctrine" for economic and social intervention in Latin America and the "Nixon Doctrine" which still awaits application. Equally, doctrines as the ones extracted by Mahan from naval history, by Jomini and Clausewitz from the Napoleonic wars, or Ferdinand Foch's tactical theories derived from the 19th centuries wars, were destined to deeply influence the American practice of war. They were applied, as soon as they appealed to American preconceived ideas—concentration, application of massive force, offensive, destruction of the enemy's forces—in a different setting and on levels for which the "doctrines" had not been designed.

IV. The Period of Limited War

Assimilation of American and European Thought

Many of the basic differences which used to distinguish European from American practice of warfare, have faded away after the beginning of the era of limited war.

The strategic speculation and research, which developed from the process of making and using the atomic bomb and from the entirely new aspects of the balance of power derived from the existence of all-destructive weapons, re-introduced the old concept of limited war. How alien this concept of limiting the use of violence in war is to the American mind can easily be gathered from what has been said until now. The more remarkable is the achievement of the American mind in having reverted to the old truths of Europe that war can be and must be limited. The new-old concept crystallized in America around the experience of the Korean war (1950-1953), where neither overwhelming air and sea power nor nuclear weapons had usefully and effectively been deployed.

Limited war, of course, is opposed to the traditional conceptual framework of American strategy: no destruction of the enemy's forces by massive concentrated power, no unconditional surrender, no clean-cut division between power and policy, no exclusion of the politician from decision-making, no clear cut distinction between peace and war. Therefore, there can be no doubt that limited war, whether waged by Europeans or Americans, will have to follow similar rules derived from its very object—to permit readjustment without going to extremes. Laws developed mostly by civilian American strategic research and analysis, and practiced mostly by American or Soviet forces, will in the future govern limited warfare. The character of this type of warfare, which is strictly linked to well defined political objects and has to remain, in the employment of force, within the limits set by the political environment, requires a strong and continuous direction and supervision by the highest military and political authority.

During the Korean war, this requirement, which was not understood or accepted by General Douglas MacArthur, was cause for one of the most spectacular conflicts between civilian and military power and ended in the recall of the General and the victory of the President. We know that ever after the conduct of limited war has been centered in Washington. The conduct of the Seventh Fleet during the Gulf of Tonkin incident in 1964 was directed from Washington. We know that the targets of the bombings in North Vietnam in 1965 and 1966 were every day decided upon in the White House. We know that the British-French landings at the Suez Canal in 1956—the first limited war operation conducted independently by European powers— were directed in detail, with the corresponding results, from London.

One of the interesting facts of the era of limited war, which also includes modifications of the general strategic doctrines, like the introduction of the principle of "flexible response", was, that the roles of Americans and Europeans have, to a certain extent, been inverted. Europeans used to be critical of the American tendency of "all or nothing", of their dislike for political manoeuvre, of their belief in massive employment of force. "Massive retaliation", when formulated and announced by Secretary of State John Foster Dulles in 1954, was greeted with sharp criticism and with dismay in Europe. When gradually the Americans developed their thinking on limited war, on flexible response, some Europeans again criticized this turn of events. The French had adopted their own doctrine of massive retaliation. The Germans felt secure only under the most massive threat by American power. Only gradually the new American conceptions were accepted.

Conclusions

To conclude, we find that the most recent strategic developments, the need of limiting force in the modern world, has an unifying effect. The strategic environment is practically the same for the whole world. It seems therefore likely that governments and military establishments are bound to overcome differences which have been created by their traditions and by their own mental processes. The facts of life will prove stronger. More and more unified views will prevail. In the implementation of any kind of policy and strategy, however, when human beings have to act under stress, the national character, national traditions, deep seated preferences and revulsions, may emerge again. It is therefore useful and necessary to study the behaviour of nations and their soldiers and airmen and sailors in the past, if we want to understand their positions in the present and to predict their postures in the future.

A SHORT BIBLIOGRAPHY

Aron, Raymond, *Paix et Guerre entre les nations*, Paris, 1962.

Buchan, Alastair, *War in Modern Society, an Introduction*, London, 1966.

Foot, M. R. D., *Men in Uniform*, London, 1961.

Greenfield, Kent Roberts, *American Strategy in World War II: A reconsideration*, Baltimore, 1963.

Hermann, Carl Hans, *Deutsche Militärgeschichte, Eine Einführung*, Frankfurt a.M., 1966.

Howard, Michael, ed., *The Theory and Practice of War*, London, 1965.

Kissinger, Henry A., ed., *Problems of National Strategy, A book of Readings*, New York, 1965.

Mahan, A. T., *The Influence of Sea Power Upon History 1660-1783*, Boston, 1890.

Mosen, Wido, *Eine Militärsoziologie*, Neuwied, 1967. (With an extensive Bibliography).

Osgood, Robert E. and Robert W. Tucker, *Force, Order and Justice*, Baltimore, 1967.

Ropp, Theodore, *War in the Modern World*, New York, 1962.

Schwarz, Urs, *American Strategy: A New Perspective*, Garden City, New York, 1966.

Smith, Dale O., *U.S. Military Doctrine*, New York, 1955.

Sokolowsky, Marshal V. D., ed., *Military Strategy*, London, 1963.

Tucker, Robert W., *The Just War*, Baltimore, 1960.

HANS R. GUGGISBERG

THE USES OF THE EUROPEAN PAST IN
AMERICAN HISTORIOGRAPHY*

I

American historiography has always been preoccupied with American history. This is still the case in our present time. It is a natural phenomenon which applies in the same sense to other nations. Like other nations, too, America has always had historians who devoted themselves partly or exclusively to the study of the history of foreign lands. Within their guild they always were and still are a minority. Their position *vis-à-vis* the reading public and also *vis-à-vis* the subjects of their interest is more problematic than that of the historians who concentrate on the national past. For the American historian of foreign lands the question of a specific historical sense is not only inescapable but also more difficult to answer than for his colleague who writes on American history. As Leonard Krieger has pointed out a few years ago, this historical sense may be defined as the capacity to understand the temporally distant in its own terms together with the consciousness of its relations with the familiar. When the American historian of extra-American (i.e. in our case European) history finds the temporal distance extended by the geographical and cultural distance, he is quite naturally tempted to start out by asking of his subject: "What is it to me or I to it that I should aspire to study and understand it?" This basic question can lead to interesting historiographical results, but it can also lead into the sterility of mere antiquarianism.[1]

It is quite evident that these same perils also threaten the European historian who studies a problem in a European field outside the history of his own country. There is, however, an important difference: although the temporal distance is the same, the geographical and cul-

* First published in the Journal of American Studies, vol. 4 no. 1 (July 1970). Reprinted by permission of the Editors of the Journal and of the Cambridge University Press.

[1] Leonard Krieger, "European History in America", in John Higham, Leonard Krieger, Felix Gilbert, *History,* Humanistic Scholarship in America, The Princeton Studies, Englewood Cliffs, N.J.: Prentice-Hall, 1965, p. 235.

tural distance is always shorter. Even in our time of microfilms, photostats, travel grants and visiting professorships, it still remains something else for an American to become a specialist of, say, the Italian Renaissance than for a German or an Englishman. The American still has to overcome more technical obstacles on the way toward the subject of his interest. But first of all he needs a strong and un-wavering conviction of the basic unity of Western history. If, in the course of his studies, he has gained this conviction and then sets out to write European history, he has gone through a longer and less self-evident development than the European whose ancestors never turned their backs to the Old World. The greater distance of the American's point of observation does not have to be a disadvan-tage, however. A wider horizon can be surveyed at one glance, and details which seem to justify controversy when examined at close range may lose their significance in favour of the general contours of the wide plains and hills which link the great peaks to each other. If the distant observer strives to explore a certain summit or a particular valley and takes upon himself the toils of a long and difficult journey, he always carries in his mind this picture of the whole horizon, and while on his way he has a great deal of time to meditate upon it.

Old and new American works on European history are not interest-ing merely because in some instances they contain original interpreta-tions of certain facts or developments. They also show us what kind of European topics were of particular importance to educated Ameri-cans in particular periods of time. In addition to reflecting various historiographical influences from Europe they help us recognize the changing pattern of the Old World's image in the New. And this is the reason why a considerable number of them are of general signifi-cance to the student of American intellectual history. It goes without saying that in this context their scholarly qualities are often less impor-tant than their weaknesses.

It cannot be doubted that a discussion of the uses of the European past in American historiography is incomplete as long as it is concern-ed exclusively with works on European topics. It ought also to take into account the great achievements in the field of American history and examine their treatments of the European background. We will indeed have to point to some of these works, but for the sake of clarity I should like to base the following remarks mainly on the American contribution to European history proper.

If we look over the whole development of interest in European history within the general development of American historiography, we can distinguish two basically different ways of linking the history of the Old World to the historical experience of America. The first is characterized by a chronological conception: European history is considered mainly as a pre-history of America, as a kind of introductory phase in which the ideas and traditions that were to make the American nation what it is, began to emerge but did not find their true and lasting fulfilment. The second approach is based on the consciousness of a historical community in which America and Europe play equal roles as parts of the same Western World. The first approach naturally led American scholars to the study of the earlier periods of European history, while the second furthered their interest in the more recent developments. In addition to this it can be generally observed that American historians who adopted the first way of looking at the European past tended to be primarily interested in the history of political institutions, religion and culture, while the adherents of the second method showed a distinctive preference for problems of international relations, diplomatic and economic history. But we must be careful not to oversimplify our case. It is not possible to define every American book as belonging to one or the other of these categories. In the minds of many authors both ways of looking at the Europeans past seem to have melted into each other. There are, on the other hand, historians of great fame whose stand can be rather easily recognized. The conviction of the basic unity of European and American history is always there; the question is, however, how this unity is defined. The historians who see the European past mainly in terms of a pre-history or pre-formation of American fulfilments tend to stress the unity of cultural heritage. Those who see European history as a part of an Atlantic context are more inclined to define it as a unity of fate.

Down to the end of the nineteenth century, American scholars of European history were mainly interested in the unity of heritage. It is only natural that the idea of an historical unity of fate should have impressed them more and more at the time when the United States attained the stature of a world power and became involved in the global conflicts and problems which characterize the twentieth century. This apparent shift of emphasis in the American outlook on the European past is a phenomenon of crucial importance. In dealing with it here, we have to discuss two specific problems: its origins and its historiographical consequences.

It is generally agreed that the great turning point in the development of historical writing in America falls into the last quarter of the nineteenth century. Prior to this period, American historiography was—in Leonard Krieger's words—"amateur in authorship, romantic in tone, literary in style, nationalist in mission, and multivolumed in scope". During the 1870s and 1880s it became increasingly professional, scientific (as the phrase was), expository, and "if not exclusively monographic at least limited in its canvas".[1] In a general survey one may thus speak of an "amateur" and a "professional" era, if one keeps in mind that the amateur contribution did not suddenly disappear after about 1880. If we examine the "amateur" era of American historiography for its interest in European history, we find ourselves confronted with a striking, almost paradoxical situation. In the seventeenth and eighteenth centuries when North America was still tied to Europe politically, Americans wrote practically no European history. In the first three quarters of the nineteenth century, when the American republic consolidated its political and national identity, American men of letters wrote a number of very important works on the history of the Old World. It is, of course, true that in the Colonial period many educated Americans were aware of the European context of the American experience. Puritan historians wrote Providential history that included the traditional Christian concept of the Four Empires, the conflict of God and Satan for the souls of Christians, and the dramatic story of the Reformation and religious persecution as background for the narrative of New England.[2] The historians of the Revolutionary generation had a more secular point of view, but many of them were convinced that the American Revolution was part of the history of mankind and had to be written as such. How well the leading men of this period were acquainted with the then available literature on British history has been shown in an informative study by H. Trevor Colbourn.[3] But the fact remains that in the whole Colonial and Revolutionary period no historical work on a European subject was written in America.[4]

---

[1] *Ibid.* p. 238.

[2] *Ibid.* p. 239.

[3] H. Trevor Colbourn, *The Lamp of Experience: Whig History and the Intellectual Origins of the American Revolution*, Chapel Hill: University of North Carolina Press, 1965, pp. 21 ff.

[4] If we peruse the leading histories of the Colonial past and of the Revolution, we can see that the reference to the European background is in most cases very scant. It is noteworthy only in Cotton Mather's *Magnalia Christi Americana* (1702)

II

Not the Colonial but what is usually called the "National" period of American historiography saw the beginning of serious and comprehensive study also in the European field. Famous names come to one's mind at once: Washington Irving, William Hickling Prescott, John Lothrop Motley. All of them wrote multivolume works and won immediate recognition as historians both in America and in Europe. Their aims were literary. They produced romantic works of art, full of pageantry and local colour. They loved the great scenes, the heroic "tableaux" of famous events and episodes. They wrote for a general public of educated readers whom they wanted to teach moral lessons and to edify. Formal composition and effect were almost as important to them as contents and documentation.[1] Yet the choice of their subjects was not based upon historical picturesqueness alone. In most of their works they treated problems of European history which could either be seen as background to the early history of the American nation or be compared with certain phases of its early development. Thus Irving wrote his *Columbus* (1828), Prescott rose to fame with his *History of the Reign of Ferdinand and Isabella, the Catholic* (1838) and Motley produced his six volumes on the Netherlands' struggle for freedom and national independence (1856 ff). All these subjects were apt to fascinate the contemporary American reader and indirectly to confirm his conviction of the distinctiveness and uniqueness of the American experience. In one form or another all these works dealt with the evolution of political, religious and individual freedom out of political and religious tyranny. Seen from this angle, Irving, Prescott and Motley fulfilled a cultural function very similar to that of Bancroft, Palfrey and their successors who treated the national theme. Irving and Prescott started out from the same point of juncture between European and American history. But the Boston gentleman of letters went much further than the enthusiastic amateur from New

---

and in Thomas Prince's *Chronological History of New England* (1736). But even here we do not perceive more than a fragmentary image of the Old World. Mather points to Europe as the site of the incomplete Reformation which was to be gloriously perfected in America. Prince presents the reader with a summary of the history of mankind as an introduction to the history of New England because he wants to show "the age of the world when this part came to be known to the other". Krieger, *loc. cit.* p. 240.

[1] David Levin, *History as Romantic Art: Bancroft, Prescott, Motley, and Parkman*, Stanford, California, Stanford University Press, 1959, pp. 3-23.

York whose real interests and abilities lay outside the field of disciplined historical research. In long years of labour and constant struggle
to overcome his physical handicaps, Prescott built up a monumental
survey of Spanish history which led from the unification of the
Iberian kingdom in the fifteenth century to the height of colonial
expansion and European preponderance under Philip II. The connexion of this great theme with the early history of America was not
Prescott's only motive, however. There were other impulses, perhaps
more objective ones: the general interest in Spanish history and culture
which prevailed in the United States in the first half of the nineteenth
century, the personal influence of George Ticknor, the attractiveness
of an exciting subject that had not been treated before and the awareness of newly accessible sources which could be brought to the reader's
attention. But that was not all. There was still another aspect which,
in Prescott's view, placed the history of the Spanish nation into the
general context of the course of Western civilization: the development
of liberal Teutonic traditions and institutions into fruitful national
vitality. The promotion of this development was, to the American
historian, the great achievement of Ferdinand and Isabella. They had
unleashed the forces of cultural energy that founded the New World,
but at the same time they had created the pattern of authoritarianism
which ultimately led to the extinction of individual liberties and to
the decline of the Spanish empire. This tragedy was not brought about
by the absolutist principle of royal power alone. Even more important
was the fact that the Spanish monarchy submitted itself to the religious
bigotry of the Church. Here we have the theme of Prescott's last work,
the unifinished *History of the Reign of Philip the Second* (1855 ff.).[1]

It cannot be doubted that Motley was a much less able historian
than Prescott. His interests were simpler, his ideas about the historian's
task more naive. Yet an obvious similarity of the historiographical
aims places him close to his older New England colleague. In his
representation of the contemporary American motives in writing
European history Motley is much more transparent. The great theme
which he discussed in his weighty volumes was "the dangers which
come from superstition and despotism and the blessings which flow

---

[1] Hans R. Guggisberg, "William Hickling Prescott und das Geschichtsbewusst-
sein der amerikanischen Romantik", *Jahrbuch für Amerikastudien* 11 (1966), 176-93:
Krieger, *loc. cit.* pp. 241 ff.

from the maintenance of religious and political freedom".[1] This theme was, to him, the expression of a universal law which governs "all bodies political as inexorably as Kepler's law controls the motion of planets. The law is Progress; the result Democracy".[2] If Prescott had written the history of Spain to show his American readers the example of a national development contrary to that of their own country, Motley described a parallel case, and he did not hesitate to point out the parallelism whenever possible. In the introduction to the first volume of *The Rise of the Dutch Republic* we find the following characteristic sentence: "The maintenance of the right of the little provinces of Holland and Zeeland in the sixteenth, by Holland and England united in the seventeenth, and by the United States of America in the eighteenth centuries, forms but a single chapter in the great volume of human fate; for the so-called revolutions of Holland, England, and America, are all links of one chain."[3] Much more than Prescott, Motley pressed the thesis of the Teutonic origins of Democratic institutions. This brought him close to Bancroft, who also saw the early history of the United States mainly in terms of a renaissance of Teutonic, i.e. Anglo-Saxon, traditions of freedom—traditions which had for centuries been buried under the weight of European feudalism. Motley went further than that. His admiration for the continuity of Germanic traditions both in the Old and in the New World made him overlook all the contemporary differences between German and Anglo-American culture, so that he could exclaim: "Ever since the great rising for freedom against the Roman empire, down to this hour, Germany has been the main source of European and American culture. The common mother of nations and empires—alma mater felix prole—she still rules the thought of her vast brood of children; Franks, Goths, Saxons, Lombards, Normans, Netherlanders, Americans—Germans all."[4] With his teutonism Motley obviously stands in a historiographi-

---

[1] John L. Motley, *History of the United Netherlands from the Death of William the Silent to the Twelve Years' Truce*, vol. 1, London, 1901, p. iv.

[2] John L. Motley, *Democracy, the Climax of Political Progress and the Destiny of Advanced Races: An Historical Essay*, London, 1869, p. 6.

[3] John L. Motley, *The Rise of the Dutch Republic*, vol. 1, London, 1896, pp. liii-lv. Cf. Krieger, *loc. cit.* p. 243.

[4] John L. Motley, "Historic Progress and American Democracy", in *Representative Selections, with Introduction, Bibliography, and Notes*, ed. by Chester P. Higby and B. T. Schantz, New York, 1939, pp. 105 ff.; Levin, *History as Romantic Art*, pp. 86 ff.; Hans R. Guggisberg, *Das europäische Mittelalter im amerikanischen Geschichtsdenken des 19. und des frühen 20. Jahrhunderts*, Basel & Stuttgart: Helbing & Lichtenhahn, 1964, p. 33.

cal tradition that can be traced back to eighteenth century England and to Montesquieu.[1] As an American historian of the romantic generation he seems to anticipate some of the ideas of the later "scientific school" and of such national historians as John Fiske, James Kendall Hosmer, and John William Burgess.[2]

For the romantic historians of America the study of European history had two main functions. Primarily, European history was "prenatal" American history in the period when the destinies of the two continents were still tied to each other, or in the earlier period when American history in the proper sense had not yet begun. The secondary function was the indication of continuing political and religious conflict in the Old World at a time when these problems came to be solved in the New. The emphasis throughout lay on the common heritage of ideas. By illustrating the fruition or stagnation of these ideas in various European countries, the American historians were able indirectly to demonstrate to their readers the difference as well as the uniqueness of the American development toward democracy.

III

In the second half of the nineteenth century, and particularly after the close of the Civil War, a number of new tendencies started to dominate the general development of historical study in the United States. Together with an increasingly critical attitude toward the sources went a general acceptance of evolutionary thought. Behind this stood the influence of the German historical school on the one hand and that of Darwinism on the other. One of the most important results of the new movement was the reform of the teaching of history in American universities, the adoption of the seminar method and the establishment of what was called "the school of scientific history". The influence of the German historical school was mainly an influence on methodology. German historicism was never really integrated into American historical thought. It was only in the present century that the philosophical framework of nineteenth century German historiography began to be studied and appreciated in the United States.

---

[1] Colbourn, *The Lamp of Experience*, pp. 25 ff.; Guggisberg, *Das europäische Mittelalter*, p. 31.

[2] Guggisberg, *op. cit.* pp. 61-5.

Again, this happened under a foreign influence, namely under that of the German refugee historians, many of whom had come from the school of Friedrich Meinecke. By the disciples of the American "scientific school" of the late nineteenth century Ranke was very highly praised, but his works were not widely read.[1]

To the study of European history in America, the rise of the "scientific school" did not bring immediate changes in outlook. The emphasis on the continuity of cultural heritage persisted, and the approach remained mainly chronological. To most students of the famous seminar at Johns Hopkins which, under the leadership of Herbert Baxter Adams, became the most important centre of the "scientific school", European history was of real interest only as long as it could be seen as a development preceding the Colonial period of North America. The interest of the "scientific historians" was thus limited to the field of medieval institutions, mainly of Anglo-Saxon England. Teutonism, now as a "scientific" thesis of historical continuity, was in full bloom. It flourished not only at Johns Hopkins, but also at Harvard, where the somewhat more critical Henry Adams had introduced the new methods of teaching and research, and at Columbia, where John William Burgess became one of its most outspoken advocates.[2] It cannot be overlooked that the "scientific school" also produced a number of historians who, in their later lives, became specialists in European history. We shall see, however, that the development of their European interests was mostly due to other and stronger influences than those they had met in their graduate school days.

Outside the history seminars, European history continued to be written in the traditional fashion. Large works on great themes were produced, some of which have kept their scholarly validity for a long time. The emphasis on European-American continuity was still in many cases based on the religious motif. But no more than in the earlier period can this continuing focus upon religion be explained as a pure and general concern for religious history as such. Religion functioned—if we may quote Leonard Krieger once more—"...as a constant principle of identity in terms of which the changing modes

---

[1] Jurgen Herbst, *The German Historical School in American Scholarship*, Ithaca, New York, Cornell University Press, 1965, pp. 99-128. Cf. George G. Iggers, "The Image of Ranke in American and German Historical Thought", *History and Theory* 2 (1962), pp. 17-40.

[2] *Ibid.* pp. 112 ff.; Herbst, *op. cit.* pp. 112 ff.; Guggisberg, *op. cit.* p. 63.

of Western culture acquired meaning and coherence for Americans. In a century of political isolation the traditional religious motif remained the main substantive theme locating America in world history".[1] A general tendency toward specialization can be observed in these new works. In some of them the scientific concepts of the time are clearly discernible as the starting points from which the investigation of the past was undertaken. Both John William Draper and Andrew Dickson White projected an intellectual conflict of their own time into the Ancient and Medieval past of the Old World: the struggle between science and religion. Draper was a trained physiologist who became an amateur historian because he believed in the possibility of investigating the past of mankind with the methods and tools of science. He was an evolutionist and a firm adherent of Comtean positivism. As the author of a *History of the Intellectual Development of Europe* (1863) and a concise *History of the Conflict between Religion and Science* (1874) he appears to the modern reader in the somewhat anachronistic role of a belated eighteenth century encyclopedist. His aim was to show the contrast between the dark "age of faith", which lasted to the end of the fifteenth century, and the enlightened "age of reason" which began with the Renaissance and found its fulfilment in modern America. White was less onesided in his historical views, but their general pattern was the same. This becomes obvious already in the title of his most significant historiographical achievement, the *History of the Warfare of Science with Theology in Christendom* (1896). White was a professional historian who later became a leading university reformer and eventually a diplomat. He wrote on European history out of his sense of what was needed in America. As he says in his *Autobiography* (1905), he desired to confront his readers with the European past to help them "understand our own time and its problems in the light of history".[2] In his treatment of the sources he was more critical than Draper, but like his older contemporary he sought to demonstrate the fundamental necessity of a liberal attitude in religious matters in order to secure cultural progress. Behind this pragmatic aspiration stood the conflicts which accompanied the foundation of Cornell University as a non-sectarian institution. Here, White was directly involved: he was the first president of this new American university.

---

[1] Krieger, *loc. cit.* p. 245.
[2] *Autobiography of Andrew Dickson White*, New York, 1905, vol. 1, p. 83.

The conjunction of growing historical criticism with the preservation of the thematic tradition found its most impressive demonstration in the works of Henry Charles Lea. This wealthy Philadelphia publisher again wrote as an amateur, but he turned out to be a more significant historian than many of his professional contemporaries. His contribution was twofold: like his "scientific" colleagues he developed institutional history as the most reliable basis for the study of any period. In addition to this he refrained from making particular moral judgements, because he believed that the historian should insist on the priority of the facts and let the facts alone "teach their appropriate lesson". Yet he remained within the historiographical tradition of his century. As a historian of institutions and more particularly of legal institutions he became a specialist on the history of ecclesiastical law. His greatest works were the *History of the Inquisition in the Middle Ages* (1888) and the *History of the Inquistition in Spain* (1906-7). In a number of auxiliary studies which appeared before, between, or after the two *magna opera*, Lea investigated such themes of ecclesiastical law as auricular confession, indulgences, sacerdotal celibacy, and the persecution of witchcraft. Unlike most of his professional contemporaries of the "scientific school", Lea had never studied in Germany nor been a member of one of the new history seminars in the United States. Nevertheless, he became one of the great masters of historical criticism and rose to international renown as well as to the presidency of the American Historical Association (1903). Together with Prescott he may be counted among the greatest American pioneers in establishing the European background of American history. Still, his image of the European past, and particularly of the Middle Ages, remained onesided and pragmatic. It was dominated by dark colours. It cannot be said that Lea did not see the bright ones, but he was obviously not interested in reproducing them. Basically, Lea was not concerned with the cultural unity and uniqueness of the Middle Ages but with the spirit that stood behind the institutions of the Church and caused these institutions to become obstacles to the development of "human progress". "Human progress", to him, was liberty of conscience, tolerance and democracy. Like most of his educated fellow-Americans, Lea believed that the preservation of these ideals was the sacred task of his nation. To the historically minded readers of this nation he demonstrated a great example of what had happened in the (pre-American) European past when men had not yet realized how important it was to preserve these ideals. Although he was technically far more advanced, Lea's historiographical achievement, when viewed from this angle, may certainly be compared to that of Prescott.[1]

Among Lea's contemporaries there were several historians who also addressed themselves to the study of European Church History. Most of them wrote on the Reformation and on the history of particular Protestant movements. Although their writings were generally less comprehensive in scope and more specialized in the treatment of their subjects, they too emphasized the chronological connexion between the European and the American past. The conception of the unity of heritage was easier to defend in such books than it had been for Lea in his histories of the Inquisition. Moreover, a new motive of historio-graphical endeavour became visible: the author's self-identification with a specific denominational tradition that had started in the Euro-pean Reformation and then taken roots also in the New World. This self-identification could, of course, engender a kind of popular litera-ture without any historiographical value. But it could also lead to the production of informative works of high scholarly quality. That this happened is convincingly shown in Henry Baird's volumes on the history of French Protestantism, in Samuel Macauley Jackson's bio-graphy of Zwingli and in Williston Walker's book on Calvin.[2] De-nominational identification has furthered American investigations of European Church History down to our day. It must be recognized as one of the reasons why relatively many American scholars have become leading authorities particularly in the fields of Anabaptism and evangel-ical radicalism, i.e. in fields which have for a long time been left unploughed by European scholars.[3]

IV

The nineteenth century American perspective on European history was not, as we have seen, fundamentally changed by the ideas and

---

[1] Guggisberg, *op. cit.* pp. 85 ff. Cf. Krieger, *loc. cit.* pp. 248 ff.

[2] Henry M. Baird, *History of the Rise of the Huguenots of France* (1879), *Huguenots and Henry of Navarre* (1886), *Huguenots and the Revocation of the Edict of Nantes* (1895); Samuel M. Jackson, *Huldreich Zwingli* (1900); Williston Walker, *John Calvin, The Organizer of Reformed Protestantism, 1509-1564* (1906).

[3] Cf. the works of Roland H. Bainton, Earl Morse Wilbur, Harold Bender, George H. Williams and many others. The significance of the present American contribution to Reformation research is easily recognized in such periodicals as *Church History, The Mennonite Quarterly Review*, and the German-American *Archiv für Reformationsgeschichte*.

methods of the "scientific school". The thematic tradition and the preponderance of the ideas of continuity and unity of the cultural heritage persisted for an amazingly long time. It was only in the last decade of the century that the first intimation of a fundamental re-orientation came into the light. Here again, our attention is drawn toward the work of an outsider. In several respects, Alfred T. Mahan's famous trilogy on the influence of sea power upon history appears to the modern reader as a traditional nineteenth century product.[1] It covers a general theme in great detail; its emphasis is upon narrative synthesis and upon the reinterpretation of published materials; its style is formal and ponderous at times. The purpose of the work is pragmatic; the author admits that "the practical object...is to draw from the lessons of history inferences applicable to one's own country and service".[2]

The new element was first of all the subject. For the first time in the nineteenth century, an American author dealt with the European past outside the traditional fields of legal, institutional, moral or ecclesiastical history. And he even went as far as to devaluate these preoccupations of his predecessors in favour of secular interests and power as the prime moving forces of history. Although this position had long before become a familiar one in domestic history, it was new in the American perspective on Europe. Like the earlier authors, Mahan was concerned with the connexions between European and American history; this is obvious already in the first two volumes and particularly in the third, which deals with the War of 1812. But behind his narrative lay an expanded concept of the American—European community. It was no longer only a community of continuing traditions but a community of simultaneous destinies on both sides of the Atlantic Ocean. Mahan was the first American scholar of European history who saw the Old World and his own nation as equal partners in a specific development of political involvement. With this he became the harbinger of a new American outlook on the European past—of an outlook which was eventually to be dominated by the idea of the unity of fate. This re-orientation produced general results only after the turn of the century when political events were making the *rapprochement* of the American and European orbits more explicit.

---

[1] *The Influence of Sea Power upon History, 1660-1783* (1890); *The Influence of Sea Power upon the French Revolution and Empire, 1793-1812* (1893); *Sea Power in Its Relation to the War of 1812* (1905).

[2] *The Influence of Sea Power upon History, 1660-1783*, London, 1965, repr., p. 83.

Although the "scientific school" had not directly furthered the study of European history, it had drawn the attention of many American scholars toward the European background of their own national history. In spite of the fact that many former pupils of the founders of the "scientific school" eventually became severe critics of their teachers' ideas, a number of important general impulses had come out of the seminars of Herbert B. Adams and his contemporaries. The monograph, the doctoral dissertation and the textbook became the typical means of scholarly communication and increasingly superseded the multivolume treatments of general themes. This did not apply only to domestic history, but in the course of time it also changed the external appearance of the study of the European past. Some "scientific historians", while specializing in the American Colonial period, became increasingly interested in the immediate background of British history and established the so-called "imperial tradition". We think of Charles M. Andrews and Herbert Levi Osgood, but quite particularly of George Louis Beer, who became the greatest American authority on the *British Colonial System* (1908-12).

More influential than the impulses of the "scientific school", however, were those of the group of younger scholars who gathered around James Harvey Robinson at Columbia and adhered to the ideas he had laid down in his book on *The New History* (1912). These ideas do not require detailed enumeration here. What we must not overlook, however, is the fact that in the minds of Robinson and his followers the European dimension had always been prominent. Among these scholars there were several experts in European history. Robinson himself was one. During the formative phase of the movement before World War I Charles A. Beard not only collaborated on several textbooks on European history but also produced a monograph on *The Office of the Justice of the Peace in England* (1904). Carl Becker had not yet published the works that were to make him well known as an authority on American as well as on European history, but his dual interests reflected themselves already in his early teaching career. Among Robinson's first disciples, James T. Shotwell, Carlton Hayes and Lynn Thorndike were to become prominent in different areas of European history.[1] When looking upon the Old World, the New Historians emphasized the following principles with particular insistence: history is a continuous process; its chief goal is to learn from the past in order to

---

[1] Krieger, *loc. cit.* pp. 260 ff.

contribute not only to the understanding but to the improvement of the present. The historian must encompass all the varied interests and activities of man; he must try to understand conditions and institutions and not simply reproduce the facts. He must take into account the insights gained by the social sciences. Many of these ideas were rather a modernization of than an antithesis to the established tradition. But as far as European history was concerned, the impulses of the New History undoubtedly caused a general intensification of interest. This interest was firmly based on the consciousness of common contemporary connexions and common destinies. It was therefore only natural that the New Historians desired to expand the thematic horizon: they called for more intensive study also of modern European history.

The experience of World War I did much to fulfil this wish. It exhibited the community of American and European political interests and the unity of fate within Western Civilization in so fundamental a way as to make it predominant in the approach to European history for more than one generation of historians. From 1917 to the crisis of the 1930s the emphasis was primarily on the history of external relations. Thereafter one can observe a growing interest also in domestic problems of European countries. During the war, many leading historians had become acquainted with the complexity of diplomatic relations and foreign policy through their collaboration in organizations such as the Board for Historical Service. Prominent specialists of European history were called to serve as experts in the American delegation at the Paris Peace Conference. To them and to their later colleagues the war evinced the political community between America and Europe. It confirmed their conviction that the study of diplomatic history was of particular importance also for the determination of America's role in the history of the world.[1]

During the period of isolationism the American interest in modern European history did not abate but kept on growing persistently. This fact can certainly be understood as an expression of the "antithetical magnetism" of Europe for American intellectuals which Daniel Boorstin has pointed out as a general characteristic of the 1920s.[2] Diplomatic history was indeed the field in which a great number of outstanding works were produced. Most of them dealt with the events that had led to the joint Allied war- and peace-making enterprises,

---

[1] *Ibid.* pp. 263, 269 ff.
[2] Daniel Boorstin, *America and the Image of Europe*, New York, 1960, pp. 23 ff.

while some reached further back into the international developments of the three last decades of the nineteenth century. It was in this field also that a great national controversy erupted: the conflict between the revisionist and anti-revisionist interpretations of the origins of the war and of American intervention. This conflict was observed with particular interest in Germany, and the most prominent exponent of revisionism, Harry Elmer Barnes, could for a time enjoy the admiring appreciation of a considerable German audience. Barnes was to take part again in the controversy about Franklin Roosevelt's foreign policy which was fought out among American historians after 1945.[1]

Diplomatic history was the most prominent but not the only field of modern European history to which American historians addressed themselves between the two world wars. Many turned to economic and social history or to the theme of nationalism and imperialism. These subjects were studied particularly at Columbia, where Shotwell and Hayes continued to represent the traditions of the New History.

Besides this great expansion of American interest in modern European history, the study of the Middle Ages and of the early modern period had by no means died out. On the contrary: American medievalism reached the high level of its quality which has remained traditional down to our day, in the same 1920s when the intensification of interest in modern Europe took place.[2] Many of the leading scholars had received their training in the seminars of the "scientific school" and had consequently started out on their professional career as specialists of institutional history. Like their colleagues in the modern field, they also began to expand the range of their interests under the influence of the New History. After World War I they came to the European archives in increasing numbers, started to explore them systematically, and soon they felt fully capable of competing with their European fellow-medievalists on an equal level of scholar-

---

[1] Warren J. Cohen, *The American Revisionists: The Lessons of Intervention in World War I*, Chicago, 1967. Günter Moltmann, "Revisionist Historiography in the United States and its Importance for German-American Relations in the Weimar Period", *Deutschland und die USA 1918-1933* (Schriftenreihe des internationalen Schulbuchinstituts, Bd. 13, Braunschweig, 1968).

[2] The visible symbol of this impressive development was the foundation, in 1925, of the "Mediaeval Academy of America". Since 1926 this organization of scholars published the journal *Speculum*. It was to be the counterpart of the *Journal of Modern History* which was founded three years later as the professional periodical for European history since the Middle Ages. Although the number of trained medievalists was still comparatively small in the 1920s and 1930s, their interests covered a wide horizon. Cf. Guggisberg, *op. cit.* pp. 173 ff.

ship. By 1930 several successful attempts had already been undertaken to present the history of medieval culture as a whole or in some of its most important aspects. A number of these works have become classics in their field on both sides of the Atlantic Ocean, e.g. Henry Osborn Taylor's *Medieval Mind* (1911) or Charles Homer Haskins's *Renaissance of the Twelfth Century* (1927), not to speak of that unique and truly "unclassifiable" masterpiece of the old Henry Adams, *Mont-Saint-Michel and Chartres* (1913). Alongside these extraordinary achievements went many reliable textbooks and source-collections for the benefit of students and a great number of monographs or extensive works on special topics. Of particular importance was the American contribution to the history of medieval science, notably in the weighty volumes of George Sarton and Lynn Thorndike. Out of these works came a remarkably severe attack upon the Burckhardtian concept of the Renaissance. In their emphasis on the continuous and unbroken expansion of man's knowledge of nature, these American historians saw the Renaissance not as a new revival of intellectual forces but rather as a period of rest between the Middle Ages and the Enlightenment, or even as a period of regression.[1] This "revolt of the medievalists" against the established pattern of historical periodization was parallelled by similar attempts at re-orientation in Europe, but nowhere was it so exclusively based upon the idea of the continuity of scientific progress as in the United States.[2] American medievalists of the 1920s and early 1930s excelled in other fields, too, notably in economic history, paleography and in history of art, but here their interpretive achievements were, on the whole, less original.[3]

In general, the American scholar's outlook on the Middle Ages was naturally free from national prejudice. This was, as Haskins himself pointed out, his great advantage, because it enabled him to see common elements of medieval civilization more clearly than his European confrère.[4] Indeed, we observe American medievalists again and again

---

[1] George Sarton, *Introduction to the History of Science*, 3 vols. in 5 parts, Baltimore, 1927-1948; Lynn Thorndike, *A History of Magic and Experimental Science*, 8 vols. New York, 1923-1958. See especially Sarton's essay on "Science in the Renaissance", in J. W. Thompson, G. Rowley, F. Schevill, G. Sarton, *The Civilization of the Renaissance*, Chicago, 1929, p. 79. Hans R. Guggisberg, "Jacob Burckhardt und Amerika", *Jahrbuch für Amerikastudien* 13 (1968),pp. 53-68.

[2] Wallace K. Ferguson, *The Renaissance in Historical Thought: Five Centuries of Interpretation*, Boston & New York, 1948, pp. 329 ff.

[3] Guggisberg, *Das Mittelalter*, pp. 137-50.

[4] Charles Homer Haskins, "European History and American Scholarship", *American Historical Review* 28, January 1923, p. 226.

emphasizing the cultural unity of the Middle Ages in contrast to the diversity of the modern world. And in addition to this we find that the American medievalists of the 1920s and early 1930s were proudly conscious of the fact that the intellectual heritage of the Middle Ages belonged to them just as much as it belonged to the Europeans who seemed culturally closer to it.

If the American historian who, in the years between the two world wars, devoted himself to the study of modern Europe, emphasized the American-European unity of fate, his colleague in the medieval field quite naturally tended to stress the conception of the unity of heritage. This has not changed to the present day. The American contribution to European history has continued to receive fruitful impulses, first of all from the refugee scholars who came to the United States as victims of National Socialist persecution, and then again from the experience of the Second World War. As a consequence of all this, the American awareness of the community of destinies within the Western or Atlantic world has become more and more distinct.[1] It stands behind the works of such scholars of "Atlantic history", as Preserved Smith, Carl Becker, Louis Gottschalk and Crane Brinton. It provided the intellectual basis on which the *Journal of the History of Ideas* was founded in 1940. In more recent years it has again become evident in Robert R. Palmer's panoramic study on *The Age of the Democratic Revolution* (1959-64).

The extent of the refugee scholars' influence upon the development of the study of European history in the United States is still very difficult to characterize and to evaluate. We cannot and shall not venture to do it here. In order to attain a reasonably reliable basis for a general judgment we would have to consider not only the works of the refugee scholars themselves but also of their many pupils. It cannot be doubted that through their writing and teaching the European emigrants have greatly intensified and deepened the American understanding of the European past in a great number of more or less specialized fields. In some of them, e.g. in medieval studies or in contemporary history, the definition of a specifically American outlook must henceforth be undertaken with very careful differentiation. One can also observe that the guild of American historians, pupils as well as colleagues, has not failed to recognize the merits of the refugee scholars. This becomes evident in innumerable prefaces of books, in

---

[1] Krieger, *loc. cit.* pp. 288 ff.

many memorial articles and also in some "Festschriften". It became impressively manifest when, in December 1966, Hajo Holborn, the great German-born teacher of the history of Germany at Yale, was elected president of the American Historical Association.[1]

World War II expanded the horizon of American historians also beyond the geographical border lines of Europe. It has opened to them new vistas in the Asian and African world. As for Europe, the interest is certainly not diminishing. The production of learned books has become so vast, that the European observer can do no more than try to keep track of what happens in the field of his own specialization.[2]

It seems that in spite of this enormous expansion of scholarly interest and activity in European history, the general American perspectives upon the Old World's past have not undergone any fundamental changes since the time after World War I. We may safely assume that the great majority of American scholars in the field of European history could still agree with what Charles H. Haskins has already said in 1923: "Whether we look at Europe genetically as the source of our civilization, or pragmatically as a large part of the world

---

[1] On the influence exerted by refugee scholars, notably from Germany and Austria cf. Gerald Stourzh, "Die deutschsprachige Emigration in den Vereinigten Staaten: Geschichtswissenschaft und politische Wissenschaft", *Jahrbuch für Amerikastudien* 10 (1965), pp. 59-77, 232-66; 11 (1966), pp. 260-317. Cf. also Leonard Krieger and Fritz Stern, "Editors' Introduction", *The Responsibility of Power, Historical Essays in Honor of Hajo Holborn*, Garden City, N. Y., 1967; Franz L. Neumann, "The Social Sciences", in Neumann *et al.*, *The Cultural Migration: The European Scholar in America*, Philadelphia, 1953, pp. 4-26; Donald Fleming & Bernard Baylin (eds.), *The Intellectual Migration, Europe and America, 1930-1960* Cambridge, Mass., 1969. This volume, interesting and many-sided as it is, contains surprisingly scant information on refugee historians.

[2] Another problem, which we cannot discuss here, is the question as to the reception and influence of the theories and methods of the "Ecole des Annales" upon contemporary American historiography. That there is such an influence cannot be doubted, but it would not be an easy one to describe. It is astonishing to note how long it took for the works of Marc Bloch to be translated and published in the U.S.A. The writings of Lucien Febvre do not seem to have aroused much general interest among American historians. F. Braudel's *La méditerranée et le monde méditerranéen à l'époque de Philippe II* (1949, 1966) has been very severely criticized by Bernard Baylin, *Journal of Economic History* 11 (1951), pp. 277-82. One can perhaps say that the "Ecole" is not very influential as a block but some of its works, ideas and methods have been taken up with sympathy and interest. Cf. Joseph R. Strayer's "Introduction" to Bloch's *The Historian's Craft*, Manchester and New York, 1954. For information on this point I am indebted to Professor R. S. Lopez of Yale University.

in which we live, we cannot ignore the vital connections between Europe and America, their histories ultimately but one."[1]

---

[1] Charles Homer Haskins, "European History and American Scholarship", p. 215. Cf. Chester P. Higby, "The Present Status of Modern European History in the United States", *Journal of Modern History* 1 (March 1929), pp. 3-8.

W. H. G. ARMYTAGE

THE EDUCATIONAL IDEAL

I

"A great many young people in America are now convinced that the American system is a failure" editorialized the London *Times* on 29 September, 1970. Instancing the "squalid lost war" in Vietnam; "the disaffection" of the black population, the squalor of the cities and the rejection of the young by a conservative political establishment, the *Times* opined that these young "feel that America is no longer the country they were taught to believe in. The mythology has become irrelevant, the ideals tarnished".

This has not always been so. Nearly a hundred years ago an English peer, an old Etonian too, who later as prime minister won the Derby twice, reduced, in his words "the whole subject of contention into a single issue". He remarked "lay before the world the exact advantages offered by every state to its inhabitants and where would they go? We know already, for all uncared for humanity flows there now and does not return—to the United States. By that single test it seems to me that the merits of the United States as a community are sufficiently tested, and overwhelmingly established."[1]

One of the most impressive events of Rosebery's ten week tour (from 30 September to 17 December 1873) was a visit to a school of 1000 boys to listen to what were called "declamations", i.e. speaking in public. After doing so he confessed himself "much struck by the coolness with which these boys faced their schoolfellows and spoke out. An English boy "of their age" he reflected "would have blushed and giggled". As he walked around the school he discovered why "the method used here" he continued "appeared to be almost discussion".[2]

Rosebery's eye for self confidence in the young was sharp. He was an old Etonian, so devoted in fact that when old he commanded his servant to play the Eton Boating Song to him if he should begin to

---

[1] A. R. C. Grant and Caroline Combe, *Lord Rosebery's North American Journal —1873*, London, Sedgwick & Jackson, 1967, p. 138.

[2] *Ibid.*, p. 119.

die.[1] But before he died Rosebery spoke up for what he called "efficiency" in Britain. Indeed at the turn of the century he talked about it so much that someone wrote, rather unkindly

> "Rosebery continues to prance upon the moonbeam of efficiency and makes speeches at every street corner; but he might just as well call it the Absolute at once for all the meaning it has to him or anyone else..."[2]

These are three sides of the picture: youth not afraid to speak out, teaching by discussion and efficiency. I must now add a fourth: social mobility. Rosebery really appreciated this. "It is easy to taunt and deride...to denounce the whole state as one sinking mass of corruption"[3] he reflected, then asked "Is it a dream that I have been in a country where all are born equal before the law?...where each son of the soil carries in his wallet not the staff of a field-marshal, for field-marshals are abhorrent to the spirit of the country, but a possible passport to the White House, to the Bench of the Supreme Court, to every eminent position without exception that the state can afford. Where none as in heaven is before or after another, where none can afford to shut himself up in the shallow exclusiveness of wealth, lest he be left fixed though not a star, where every citizen is a conductor of the electric spark of political power."

So one of our past great aristocrats anticipated one of our most distinguished contemporary sociologists, Professor Glass, who argues that "even if there is little actual opportunity to rise in social status, the belief in a myth of opportunity may provide similar results; and perhaps part of the pride which Americans feel in their "open" society derives more from the image of nineteenth century U.S.A. than from any exceptional present reality".[4] I think such a concept is consistently reinforced by the general "efficiency" movement in the United States: since high ability jobs are held by high ability people, who can adapt more quickly to internal and external change, and are less likely to be squares. True, it breeds ulcers, neuroses and coronaries, but so does any form of urban life.

---

[1] Winston Churchill, *Great Contemporaries*, 1933.

[2] Raymond Asquith to John Buchan in 1901 quoted John Raymond "Rosebery" in *The Doge of Dover*, MacGibbon & Kee, 1960, p. 41.

[3] Grant and Combe, *op. cit.*, p. 138.

[4] D. V. Glass (ed.) *Social Mobility in Britain*, London, Routledge & Kegan Paul, 1954, p. 25.

II

One can summon up, from the dusty archives of travel books, government reports, productivity missions and the like, clouds of witnesses to fill out this external view of the American ideal. Professor Stewart Fraser has listed nearly a thousand such references to American education since 1900 and has a three volumed Ph. D. thesis on others before.[1] May I therefore cite one twentieth century writer whom Professor Fraser does not mention, whose "love affair" with America began in 1929 when he made the first of his three pre-war visits. Being a sensitive man, he realised that, "the psychological disposition of masses of people depends, far more than we are usually inclined to think, upon the myths they believe about themselves".[2] "Such myths" he went on "are not pure fantasy but they are crude and they correspond only very roughly to the true facts of a people's life". To him the spell-binding nature of the American myth was that "of a social equality and of equal opportunity for 'the pursuit of happiness' "—where "every man has the opportunity to better himself". But he sadly confessed he shook himself free of it after six visits, realizing that what America lacked was what he called a psychic or affective element of a visible past. To satisfy that hunger, armadas of American tourists were invading Europe to explore and record what they did not have at home. This sensitive soul was Sir Richard Rees, born in 1900 and educated at Eton and Oxford.

He was not the only one to say this (as he acknowledges): Simone Weil and T. S. Eliot were, in different ways, pointing out that such a loss (or unawareness) of a past was equivalent to the loss of the supernatural. But to Rees the American influence on Europe was destroying the European past as well, so much so that Europeans saw their own country "as a foreign country or an extinguished state, lime-lit by theologians or mapped by historians". He compared us to "somnambulistic motorists driving from nowhere to nowhere in pursuit of happiness along an ever broader concrete highway; and America is in the lead".[3]

---

[1] Stewart E. Fraser (ed.) *American Education Through Foreign Perspectives, Twentieth Century Essays*, New York, John Wiley & Sons, 1969, pp. 469-525.

[2] Richard Rees, *A Theory of My Time, An Essay in Deductive Reminiscence*, Secker & Warburg, 1963, p. 222.

[3] *Ibid.*

III

Sir Richard Rees' point of view, to which many people overtly subscribe, is that though America is "still enchanting thanks to the buoyancy of her myth and to the success with which she pursues it",[1] "... the enchantment only begins to fail when we remember that this pursuit is a heading rush to nowhere".

In other words Sir Richard wishes a destination.

Here his criticism really illumines the American educational ideal: that in its educational process the destinations emerge by the audit of past experience and its reconstruction in present practice—the emphasis is on practice. Or as its great guru John Dewey wrote in *Experience and Education*, education is "the intelligently directed development of the possibilities inherent in ordinary experience".[2] If this were a sermon, that would be my text. Moonshine you may say, perhaps wrongly, problem solving education with the aim emerging from the process has not only shown there is no shine on the moon but can freely question whether or no America should be reduced to a lunar landscape.

Dewey stressed the importance of the transaction between the individual and *what at the time* (my italics) constitutes his environment, the environment being "whatever conditions interact with personal needs, desires, purposes and capacities to create the experience which is had". "Even when a person builds a castle in the air" Dewey argued "he is interacting with the objects he constructs in fancy".

Continuity and interaction therefore intercept and unite with each other as long as life and learning continue; so a sane person constructs a world of related objects. That is why Dewey agreed that "we often see persons who have had little schooling in whose case the absence of set schooling proves to be a positive asset" since they have at least "retained their common sense and power of judgement; and its exercise in the actual conditions of living has given them the precious gift of ability to learn from the experiences they have."[3]

To show how education was "a continuous reconstruction of experience" Dewey founded his University Elementary School in 1896. Here means and end were identified. For to him education was the

---

[1] *Ibid.*

[2] John Dewey, *Experience and Education*, Collier Books, p. 89.

[3] *Ibid.*, see chapter 3.

way in which society improved and renewed itself. Hence his school, by activity methods, enabled children to rehearse problems of adult life in laboratory, workshop and outside, by offering tools to construct, create and inquire. It was not so much a drawing out process as a harnessing and orchestration of impulses. There was, as he said, no mystery, no wonderful discovery about it. "It is simply a question of doing systematically, and in a large intelligent and competent way what for various reasons can be done in most households"—the ideal home as it were, enlarged.[1] Indeed just as at the same time Frank Gilbreth was giving us the ideal American kitchen, Dewey was giving us the ideal American school.

IV

Dewey's intellectual forebears were a physicist and a biologist. The physicist insisted that everything must be verified against the experience of other people, that meaning should be judged by its consequences. The biologist agreed: ideas, to him were made true by events, i.e. were subject to the process of verification. Between them they provided not only Dewey but subsequent generations of Americans with a philosophy. They were of course C. S. Peirce and William James. Before they died in the second decade of this century their ideas were part of the American atmosphere.

Dewey's successors can be identified today among American cognitive psychologists, perhaps best represented by the Harvard Centre for Cognitive Studies whose director, Jerome S. Bruner, holds that "we are only now on the threshold of knowing the range of educability of man—the perfectibility of man. We have never addressed ourselves to this problem before".[2] Bruner's apostolate of the growth sciences has already won him an honorary degree from my own University of Sheffield.

Bruner's optimism that we have "never tapped the potential of human beings" is shared by Professor J. McV. Hunt of the Psychological Development Laboratory of the University of Illinois. He has recognized that "one of the major problems of our time" is the need "to

---

[1] John Dewey (ed.) *Selected Educational Writings* with an introduction and commentary by F. W. Garforth, London, Heinemann, 1966, p. 104.

[2] Maya Pines, *Revolution in Learning*, Allan Lane, The Penguin Press, London, 1969, pp. 37-8. Jerome S. Bruner, *The Process of Education*, Cambridge, Mass., Harvard University Press, 1960.

find ways of raising the level of intellectual capacity in the majority of the population".[1] This he hopes will be accomplished through bettering the early environmental encounters of children whereby future generations might gain, on an average, some 30 points in the I.Q. scale.

The third example of the lively persistence of American pragmatism can be seen in the establishment of the Office of Economic Opportunity which has commissioned a study of the ways in which children between the age of two and five, learn in a responsive environment. This study really began eleven years ago when its present director, Professor Omar Khayyam Moore, launched his Responsive Environments Laboratory at a Country Day School in conjunction with Yale University. Today with improved apparatus known as ERE (the Edison Responsive Environment, a typewriter which is programmed to talk, play games, read and show pictures), to this learning laboratory (which owes much to the engineering efforts of Richard Kobler) children can come for half an hour a day from a poor area in Chicago where illiteracy is high. Also financed by the Office of Economic Opportunity the laboratory is also used to teach reading to dropouts and illiterate adults.[2]

V

John Dewey was no febrile permissivist. For he pointed out in *School and Society* that "under present conditions, all activity, to be successful, has to be directed somewhere and somehow by the scientific expert—it is a case of applied science".[3] Here Dewey was in a tradition going back to Francis Bacon when he argued that the teacher should be an enabler, a situation controller, setting up problems for children which evoke interest, enable them to test hypotheses, and reconstruct their experience accordingly. For him every small town school was a potential Solomon's House where the junior New Atlantis might take a twentieth century shape.

By enfolding science firmly and bravely as a democratic activity he was also in a line that goes back to Henry Adams with whom William James described an encounter as like "meeting the augurs behind the

---

[1] J. McV. Hunt, *Intelligence and Experience*, New York, Ronald Press, 1961.

[2] R. D. Hess and Roberta M. Bear, *Early Education: Current Theory, Research and Practice*, Chicago, Aldine, 1967.

[3] Garforth, *op. cit.*, p. 94.

altar—and *none* of them were smiling". James added "powerful race these Adamses to remain plebians after so many generations of culture".[1]

For Adams' autobiography *The Education of Henry Adams* is a chromophotograph, reflecting various shades of grey in the American social scene up to the second world war. It is a sensitive, objective autobiography of the type Sir Francis Galton would have enjoyed, written at a level which makes it one of the essential transcripts of American experience.

William James' reference to the non smiling augurs identifies another component of the American ideal: a realistic concern with the future. The anticipatory stance in social thought in the United States, its concern with the future, is perhaps its most salient point of contrast with our own Alexandrine preoccupation with the past.

And Henry Adams was an anticipator. "I tell you" he wrote to his brother in 1862 with whimsical irony "these are great times. Man has mounted science and is now run away with. I firmly believe that before many centuries more, science will be the master of man. The engines he will have invented will be beyond his strength to control. Some day science may have the existence of mankind in its power, and the human race commit suicide by blowing up the world. Not only shall we be able to cruize in space, but I see no reason why some future generation shouldn't walk off like a beetle, with the world on its back, or give it another rotary motion so that every zone should receive in turn its due portion of heat and light".[2] As the son of the then American ambassador to England, the grandson of the sixth and the great-grandson of the second president of the United States, Adams was to haunt the corridors of Washington and Harvard for the next fifty years, listening, noting, recording and reflecting on the way in which science was becoming the master activity of the republic: a religion even.[3]

The basis of this religion is the infinite improvability of man. That is why science was applied to education at times with a persistence that has evoked amusement, incredulity and disbelief in Western Europe. Nevertheless this belief has certainly paid rich dividends in

[1] M. de Wolfe Howe (ed.) *Holmes-Laski Letters*, Oxford, 1953, ii, p. 103.

[2] Worthington C. Ford, *A Cycle of Adams' Letters 1861-1865*, Boston, 1920, p. 135.

[3] Ralph E. Lapp, *The New Priesthood, The Scientific Elite and the User of Power*, New York, Harper & Row, 1965.

material advance, social progress and social mobility, for today over 40% of the age group in the United States are at college, a total of some 7 million young men and women. And even if the colleges are at the moment attracting world wide attention by their vigorous protests against not only the Vietnam War, but the ruin of the environment by juggernaut technocratic advance, it should be a matter of admiration that so many of the future responsible citizens of the United States should feel so strongly and protest so bravely, for the United States was born out of protest.

VI

The cradles of this religion of science were the universities of the United States, 69 of which were stemmed from the Land Grant Act passed in 1862. These Land Grant colleges which developed into the great state universities with their conjoined experimental stations gave to the world such discoveries as hybrid corn (which gave America the equivalent of one year's extra crop during the second world war) and streptomycin (discovered during that war). They became the cathedrals of learning. Professorial seminars "almost constituted a series of cults".[1] The phrase is Laurence Veysey's and it is significant that his three examples were Stanley Hall, Frederick Jackson Turner, William Graham Sumner: a psychologist, a historian and a sociologist: all social scientists.

League tables of precedence in such matters are perhaps relevant, so it is worth noting that the ten largest producers of American scientists, asterisked in *American Men of Science* over the years 1903-1943 were, as might be expected Adams' own University of Harvard (401), Johns Hopkins (242), Chicago (215), Columbia (201), Yale (172), Cornell (155), Michigan (108), California (104), Princeton (85) and Pennsylvania (77)[2] (where Mr. Wilson's son Giles went for his Ph. D.) are but the leading institutions of a whole network that today are centres not only of pilgrimage but of sectarian ferment.

To obtain a profile of the group that hoped to graduate in the class of 1970 the American Council on Education began four years ago a

---

[1] The phrase is from Laurence P. Veysey *The Emergence of The American University*, Chicago: University of Chicago Press, 1965, p. 157.

[2] For this and similar evaluative tables see George W. Pierson, *The Education of American Leaders. Comparative Contributions of U.S. Colleges and Universities*, New York, Frederick A. Praeger, 1969.

survey of more than 200,000 freshmen in 251 colleges, universities and institutes of technology. These 200,000 were about a fifth of the total age cohort of freshmen which in 1966 numbered over a million. From this survey several interesting facts emerged: most expected to complete more years of schooling than their parents, 89% expected to receive bachelors degrees, 40% planned to go on for masters degrees and 10% planned to go on for the doctorate.

Professionally, 22% planned to become elementary or high school teachers, 21% to spend some time in the Peace Corps or VISTA before settling down, 12% to become businessmen, 9% to become engineers, 7% artists or entertainers, 4% lawyers, less than 2% college professors and 1% clergymen.

Note that the idealistic quotient was high—it is doubtful whether 40% of them graduated with their classmates in 1970, or that 60% will ever get their bachelors degree. Paul Wooding pointed out that "their responses gave no reason for despair about the younger generation" and that, if anything "the class of 1970 seems to be made up of fairly normal people who are apparently more socially conscious and less governed by economic motives than their parents".[1]

VII

I started by quoting from one great English newspaper: *The Times*. Can I continue by quoting from two others: the *Daily Telegraph* and the *Manchester Guardian*. A hundred and six years ago, a reporter for the *Daily Telegraph*, George Augustus Sala, pointed to an ideal beyond the warring armies by identifying an America which was neither "north" nor "south" which he called the Republic of Jones. "It may be that its President is a ... modern St. Simon, a Latter day Père Enfantin; and that here are the aspirations that were dreamt of in the New Atlantis, and Sir Thomas More's "Utopia" and M. Cabet's "Icaria" and M. Fourier's "Phalanstère" are realised". "Some of these days", he concluded, "this shadow may surprise us all, by proving to belong to a substance of some magnitude".[2]

By identifying America as the Republic of Jones i.e. of the common man, and discerning as its ideological (as opposed to founding)

---

[1] Paul Woodring, *The Higher Learning in America: A Reassessment*, London, McGraw-Hill Book Co., 1968, p. 67.
[2] Sala, G. A., *My Diary in America in the Midst of War*, 1865, vol. ii, p. 396.

fathers Bacon, Cabet and Fourier, this journalist showed considerable percipience, and confirms really what one has said about Adams and Dewey.

The other is of course Alastair Cooke of the *Manchester Guardian* who has described the ideal United States as shrinking to a microcosm in California. This state, he goes on is "a bubbling test-tube of the most characteristic problems of the United States" since "it faced a decade ago the kind of social ordeal that is now causing anguish all over". For from here comes the most serious threat to the authority of the university, the most exciting crash programmes for new schools— and the most flambuoyant criminal youth. "It used to be said" he continued "that you had to know what was happening in America because it gave us a glimpse of our future. Today, the rest of America, and after that Europe, had better heed what happens in California, for it already reveals the type of civilization that is in store for all of us".[1]

VIII

Certainly California was singled out by the Prime Minister's Committee on Higher Education in England as "particularly interesting".[2] For here is a "master plan for education" aiming at raising the total number of full time students to 660,000 by 1975, a figure now realised to be too low. The reasons for it are threefold and stem from the booming economy and innovation which motivates a greater proportion of high school graduates to go forward to higher education than elsewhere in the United States, and the fact that these colleges will have to be state-provided since the proportion of those students who can go or will be able to go to private colleges is much lower than elsewhere (about 1:5 in 1962 and 1:9 in 1975). A third reason for the "plan" was that in addition to the universities establishing "branch" campuses, so many junior and state colleges were founded and mooted that they looked like overlapping and duplicating facilities.

So the "Master Plan" sets targets for each sector, outlines the functions of each type of institution: university state college or junior college, and enables them to consort and consult on their common needs before presenting the bill to the state. The top 33$\frac{1}{3}$ per cent of

---

[1] Alastair Cooke, *Talk About America*. The Bodley Head, 1968, p. 234.

[2] *Committee on Higher Education. Appendix Five to the Report of the Committee appointed by the Prime Minister under the Chairmanship of Lord Robbins 1961-63: Higher Education in Other Countries*, London, H.M.S.O., Cmnd. 2154, V, pp. 283-285.

high school graduates were to go to the state colleges, the top 12½ to the universities thus limiting the expansion to these to 180,000 and 120,000 respectively in 1975.

The most significant role was cast for the junior colleges which were expected to triple their enrolment in 1975 to 290,000. These junior colleges provide the first two years of higher education, what is called the freshman and sophomore years, which when completed enables them to take their junior and senior years at the university. Cheap, local, with a high staff student ratio, these colleges have a specific "cooling out" function to prevent the creation of an academic proletariat. And like the colleges and the universities they are to work a four term year to ensure utilization of what they call "the plant" for 48 weeks in the year.

This has not been the first time that the "junior college" has excited comment in Britain for four years earlier the Central Advisory Council for Education, when examining the education of the 15 to 18 age group, asked: Is there a case for a junior college which would be essentially a full-time institution without part time students, and replied that though they were not sure they had the impression that there might well be an experiment especially since they envisaged a fourfold interest in that particular age cohort by 1980.[1] For it has been predicted that the junior college will assume a larger place than ever in American education during the next half century.[2] For as the educational highway becomes ever broader and congested it is essential to guide, mollify and accommodate those who cannot move quite so fast and who otherwise would become congestants. Such congestants are often frustrated and recalcitrant. Their recalcitrance has been described by a distinguished sociologist as "a symptom of dissociation between culturally prescribed aspirations and socially structured avenues for realizing those aspirations."[3]

---

[1] Ministry of Education: *15 to 18: A Report of the Central Advisory Council for Education* (England) *(The Crowther Report)*, H.M.S.O., 1959, vol. 1, par. 622, 624.

[2] Burton R. Clarke, *The Open Door College: A Case Study*, London, McGraw Hill, 1960, p. 7.

[3] Robert K. Merton, "Social Structure and Anomie" in *Social Theory and Social Structure*, new ed. Glencoe, Ill. Free Press, 1957, p. 134. Or as Lady Venables said: "students whose ambitions outrun their abilities certainly need to be helped to lower their sights, but on these courses there are probably a larger number with abilities...whose sights could possibly be raised from the shop floor with suitable encouragement". Ethel Venables, *The Young Worker at College: A Study of a Local Tech.*, London, Faber & Faber, 1967.

The two year college will offer an opportunity of enabling students
to "go out prepared for activities that satisfy them instead of being
branded as failures. They cross the finishing line before growing
weary of the race".[1] For Americans see choice as going through three
phases, (i) phantasy choice, (ii) tentative choice, (iii) realistic choice,
the latter being subdivided into exploration, crystallization and specifi-
cation. At this stage, adequate counselling and information is needed[2]
and this is what the junior college gives.

IX

That the junior college can develop in this direction is due to two
longstanding attributes of the American scene: firstly the electives
system whereby a student can choose modules of subjects right up to
first degree level before crystallizing on a specialism (even if he does
crystallize then); secondly the characteristic American stance towards
tomorrow. On the first, or electives system, much has been written
and said. I would merely like to say that it is a brick-building method
of education obliging on the student to look for his own cement to
link the various bricks together. On the second I would like to dwell
rather longer since I think it is the ultimate philosophical base of
American education.

"It can hardly be believed", said de Tocqueville, "how many facts
naturally flow from the philosophical theory of the indefinite perfectibility of man or how strong an influence it exercises even on men who,
living entirely for the purposes of action and not of thought, seem
to conform their actions to it, without knowing anything about it".[3]
His words, though written in 1835, characterise the flow of American
speculation about tomorrow. They were concerned not only with the
question "what's wanted?" as "what's in store?", with the implication
that a lot was. Certainly Jules Verne recognized, contributed to, and
at times borrowed from this store of technological fantasy. His idea
of a multivaned helicopter, The Albatros (in *Robur the Conqueror or
The Clipper of the Clouds* (1886)), was taken from the young American

---

[1] Burton R. Clarke quoted in "The 'Cooling-Out' Function in Higher Education", *American Journal of Sociology*, LXV (1960), pp. 569-576.

[2] E. Ginsberg et al. *Occupational Choice: An Approach to a General Theory*, New
York, 1951.

[3] A. De Tocqueville, *Democracy in America*, 1835, Part 1, Chapter 2 (trans. Henry
Reeve) 1835-40 (Saunders and Othey).

writer, Luis Senarens, who had been selling, since the age of fourteen, science wonder stories for boys.[1] Nor should we forget America of the year 2000 projected by Edward Bellamy in *Looking Backwards* (1888): the best and most influential of over a hundred and forty such fantasies written from that decade up to the first world war. After that war, as the masters of the craft began to operate, English social moralists like Huxley, Orwell and C. S. Lewis unashamedly used their protective techniques[2] not to hymn a mechanical millennium but to excoriate it.

Some of the mantic energies of these myriad rivulets of speculation about the technologies of tomorrow, disorderly and shallow as some of them were, were channelled by operational research and systems analysis; both built during the war.

Systems analysis was, after 1948, the special concern of the Research and Development (RAND) Corporation. Working for the U.S. Air Force under contract it developed cost-effectiveness techniques and, working for the Department of Defense, the Planning Program Budgeting System. It rediscovered the educational role of games. In doing all this it inevitably, and deliberately, became involved in technological forecasting, for which it developed a system of iterative opinion sampling known as Delphi.[3]

Other attempts to improve intuition are represented by brainstorms, buzz groups, and so forth. It is even claimed that a harvest of ideas can be gleaned by gazing at the human boss—or navel—a technique known as Omphaloskepsis, or by simply allowing researchers a long rein, so that they can emulate the three princes of Serendip and discover something whilst looking for something else.[4]

But omphaloskepsis and serendipity are not enough in a world of cost effectiveness, so the Ford Foundation established Resources for the Future Inc. in 1953 to consider social problems like land use, water, energy, minerals, pollution, and regional development. Such application has prompted further internal techniques of forecasting up to the year 2000.[5]

---

[1] S. Moskowitz, *Explorers of the infinite: shapers of science fiction*, Cleveland and New York, The World Publishing Co., 1963, p. 240.

[2] S. Moskowitz, *Seekers of tomorrow: masters of modern science fiction*, Cleveland and New York, The World Publishing Co., 1965.

[3] O. Helmer, *Social Technology*, London, Basic Books, 1966.

[4] E. I. Green, "Creative thinking in scientific work", in *Research, development and technological innovation*, Homewood, Illinois, Richard D. Irwin, 1964, p. 118.

[5] H. H. Lansberg, L. L. Fishman and J. L. Fisher, *Resources in American future-*

RAND has fathered several other forecasting institutes. In 1956 it hived off the System Development Corporation which specializes in technological forecasting in a management information system. System Development Corporation is building up an electronic data bank from which manipulative and manipulated information can be obtained, and indeed, models played against each other in such banks. This, according to Hasan Ozbekhan, enables possible futures to be conceived, created, compared and cased. As he says, such futures-creative planning "uses the future as an operational means to effect changes in the present, and through such changes brings the conceived future into being".[1]

Ozbekhan was merely laterally extending the philosophic revolution effected by the physicists and sociologists a generation earlier: a revolution whose most elegant exponent was Alfred North Whitehead, the English mathematician who, after teaching at Harvard for ten years described as "vicious" the assumption "that each generation would substantially live amid the conditions governing the lives of its fathers and will transmit those conditions to mould with equal force the life of its children". Whitehead considered as far back as 1933 that "we are living in the first period of human history for which this assumption is false". How right he was and how difficult it is for us to realize this nearly forty years later, and how authoritatively he could speak for he possessed the distinction, virtually unique amongst Englishmen, of being a fellow both of the Royal Society and of the British Academy and having held chairs at both the leading English and American universities. He insisted on the need for foresight. "We require" he wrote "such an understanding of the present conditions as may give us some grasp of the novelty which is about to produce a measurable influence on the immediate future". Stressing the fluidity and shifting nature of the immediate future he went on: "Rigid maxims, rule-of-thumb routine, and cast iron doctrines will spell ruin".[2]

patterns of requirements and availabilities 1960-2000. Baltimore, The Johns Hopkins Press, for Resources for the Future Inc.

[1] H. Ozbekhan, The idea of a "look out" institution, Santa Monica, California, System Development Corporation, 1965.

[2] A. N. Whitehead, Adventures of Ideas, London, Harmondsworth, Penguin Books, 1942, p. 114.

Whitehead might also have written

"The endless controversies whether language, philosophy, mathematics, or science supplies the best mental training, whether general education should be chiefly literary or chiefly scientific, have no practical lesson for us today. This University recognizes no real antagonism between literature and science, and consents to no such narrow alternatives as mathematics *or* classics, science *or* metaphysics. We would have them all, and at their best".[1]

In fact he did not, for this was taken from a declaration of intent three quarters of a century earlier made by a thirty-five year old chemist on assuming the presidency of the university where Whitehead was teaching: Harvard. The intent was to establish an electives system whereby each student would be held responsible for choosing whatever he wanted to study and had to accept responsibility of that choice. Such freedom was encouraged by the slow establishment of a unit or modular system whereby the student could sample in his freshman or sophomore years, units drawn from the whole range of arts and sciences. The chemist, none other than C. W. Eliot, found it a life long experiment. And that he succeeded was due merely to his capacity to outlive rather than outwit his opponents.

X

Like most other names I have mentioned in this lecture (C. S. Peirce, and William James) C. W. Eliot was trained in the methods of science and wished to organise the environment in the enrichment of human experience. Such an organization, with the huge technological sprawl that it involves, has put paid to the old American myth of the little red schoolhouse. Forty years ago Miss Evelyn Dewey assured an English Professor of Education that there were 200,000 single teacher schools in the United States. Today we hear stories that in New York they do already use the "terminal" of a course where the computer is in California.[2]

It looks as if a Laureate of *The Los Angeles Times* of forty years ago might have been right when he said:

---

[1] Charles W. Eliot, *Educational Reform*, New York, Century Co., 1898, p. 1.
[2] Sir John Adams, *The Teacher's Many Parts*, University of London Press, 1930, p. 33.

> "The red little school as the birthplace of brains
>   Is a legend the nation still cherishes:
> And if any fond hope of the future remains,
>   That hope will be lost when it perishes."[1]

Certainly the feeling of being lost in a vast impersonal machine pervades a number of recent criticisms of American education. One of the most fluent and persuasive of these critics, Jacques Barzun, has recently lamented a too rapid accretion of new functions over the past decade and a half not only by schools but by American universities; whose once single-minded, easily-defined entity has been thereby torn apart. As he says "a big corporation has replaced a once self-centred company of scholars and has thereby put itself at the mercy of many publics, unknown to one another and contradictory to their times."[2] But it is part of the regenerative strength of the American ideal that it generates such elegant and eloquent native critics who thereby further adaptations of growth. It has been the critics who prompted Operation Head-start in the gettos: a programme which has influenced the establishment of educational priority areas in Britain. Indeed so many of their adaptations of growth are visible that two years ago two Frenchmen asked "When are we going to decide to do something in Europe other than devise mocked up versions of organizations and methods imported from America, while the Americans themselves go on inventing new ones and are increasing their lead over the rest of the world?"[3] These two Frenchmen, Louis Armand and Michel Drancourt, are well known for their studies of American industrial domination in Europe.[4] They argued that the association of Europe should be accompanied by the association of educational institutions on American lines: a mutation so comprehensive because it is "quite impossible to make a success of it on the scale of any single nation" and must, therefore, be on "a European scale".

It is only when seen as an implication of the Treaty of Rome that the sheer magnitude of the operation appears. The so called European

---

[1] Louis Armand and Michel Drancourt, *The European Challenge*, London, Weidenfield and Nicolson, 1970, p. 25.

[2] Jacques Barzun, *The American University: How It Runs, Where Is It Going*, London, Oxford University Press, 1969, p. 3.

[3] Armand and Drancourt, op. cit., p. 190.

[4] Louis Armand and Michel Drancourt, *Plaidoyer pour l'avenir*, Coll. "Questions d'actualité", Paris, Culmann-Levy, 1960; and Michel Drancourt, *Les clés du pouvoir avec une conclusion de Louis Armand*, Paris, Fayand, 1964.

Institute at university level provided for by Euratom has not even taken shape, much less a kind of Eured programme.

For just as the American open door, supermarket type educational system was devised to homogenize people of different tongues, faiths, economic backgrounds and ethnic loyalities, so, if Europe is to become a viable entity, a Eured system will have to be established on the same lines. Transfer between two universities in the E.E.G. should be as easy as between any two universities in the U.S.A.[1]

---

[1] op. cit., p. 25.

R. H. PEAR

STUDENTS AND THE ESTABLISHMENT IN EUROPE AND THE U.S.A.

It is the student revolt in Europe and the U.S.A. which must concern us, for although it is not the only manifestation of anti-establishment attitudes, it is the clearest. We turn to this topic with some reluctance perhaps for it is now (in 1971) no longer novel, no longer does it inevitably make the front page; nor are its ideas particularly attractive, intriguing, or even, to many observers, relevant. Students moreover are not the only section of the community which feels alienated, frustrated, unable to experience that development of personality which both Marxists and Liberals declare to be the true end of man. Workers, cultural, geographical or historical minorities (like Ulster Catholics) also experience frustrations, but students have resources for continuous organisation and activity, for publicity, agitation, sit-ins, teach-ins, and the physical resilience of youth which, when properly employed, can almost bring the mighty to their knees. Cultural or political minorities, (e.g. Welsh, Scots) may have brief successes within the larger national political framework, and youths (other than students) can trouble the authorities on Saturday nights. Their leisure, college buildings and facilities and comradeship, can make students (in the absence of a revolutionary working class) the most insistent and formidable mouthpiece for modern discontents.

What we have to consider here is not a problem (to which there may be a solution) but a condition which may persist until it is no longer thought important. The condition is that of the considerable body of western youth who feel no deep sympathy for their countries' established values, and who have money, time and a permissive environment (and who are the targets of powerful advertisers) in which to emphasize their differences from their parents. "The generation gap"[1] is a useful shorthand description of an aspect of their condition, but as we may see later, strictly applied, it does not explain very much.

---

[1] K. Allerbeck, "Alternative Explanations of participation in student movements: generational conflict": paper presented to VIII World Congress International Political Science Association Sept. 1970.

However cautious we may feel about pinpointing the causes of this condition, a word must be said about where and when its beginnings were first perceived. Here we must note two different but connected facts. Firstly where and when did it first become fashionable, amusing, acceptable in the post war world to ridicule established values; secondly, when did student youth, taking advantage of this relaxation, take off into its own world of habits, words, values and criticisms? In England we might begin the era of sophisticated ridicule with the assumption by Mr. Malcolm Muggeridge of the editorship of "Punch". During his term of office Punch's values were revolutionized. It became contemporary, slick, and politically critical. It is entirely appropriate that Mr. Muggeridge (today England's foremost puritan lay saint and one of her best journalists) should be alive and well to deplore the results of the revolution he started.[1] In the America which so humourlessly suffered the outrages of Senator Joe McCarthy there was one publication which jeered continuously, "Mad" magazine written ostensibly by and for high school kids. It is worth a Ph.D thesis, for it must have been for many of the generation which took to student activism in the 1960's their first introduction to "Un-American" ideas. They read it, jeered at Conrad Hilton and the A.M.A. and were not struck dead, or even thrown out of school. Muggeridge and Mad magazine flourished in an atmosphere which was gradually, perhaps intentionally, becoming more tolerant. Joe McCarthy was censured and rapidly faded. Muggeridge attacked the accents and style of British royalty. The Monarchy did not fall, and minor Muggeridges flourished. With the Christine Keeler scandal the B.B.C.'s cabaret programme (TWTWTW) hit the high spots of hilarity at the expense of the conservative Establishment. Meanwhile the western world was becoming more affluent—and, more important, more optimistic about the permanence of affluence. After the mid 1950's there began for France, Germany and Italy those economic miracles (even Austria had one) which would flood Europe with consumer goods, which produced (for some) American style living[2] (apart from car sizes) and made many German workers pro-establishment. Rates of economic growth in Europe embarrassed the older capitalist countries of Britain and the U.S.A.

Throughout the 1950's European and American youth were politi-

---

[1] See M. Muggeridge, "The Queen and I", *Encounter*, July 1961.
[2] See M. Beloff, "Letter from Germany", *Encounter*, July 1968.

cally uncommitted.[1] In America the big corporations recruited happily on the campuses. The "Organisation Man" (and his wife) seemed to be the logical and far from unhappy product (for the swelling middle class) of the economic system. It might be that other men lived as part of the "lonely crowd" but even for them their standards of living, their education, their entertainment seemed assured. In Britain and the U.S. religion and conservatism were thought to be in the upswing—the Conservatives' third consecutive Election victory in 1959 seemed to be part confirmation—as was the re-election of Eisenhower in 1956.

When youth began to break away from conventional political attitudes in the late 1950's it came in Britain, France[2] and America because of war or the fear of war. In Britain (and to a much smaller extent in the U.S.) the Ban the Bomb movement (Campaign for Nuclear Disarmanent, C.N.D.) was the first drift of youth leftward out of apathy. C.N.D. became *the* activity for the children of bourgeois radicals. It had great appeal; it was non-party; it marched, camped out overnight, was very well but quite unofficiously organized, its message was simple, it was rather joyful (usually the British left is sad) and its protest was against those adults who sought peace through nuclear destruction. If C.N.D. was naive it was not much more so than were some of the adult nuclear warriors. C.N.D. was a British middle class movement which some sections of the British Labour movement could not ignore, for it appealed to Labour's ingrained pacifism and to the anti-Americanism of the semi-Marxist left. In Britain the Communist Party was not wholly behind C.N.D., and the C.N.D. "leadership" adopted a *campaign type* organization (eschewing rule books and membership dues) which made a C.P. take over of C.N.D. impossible. The C.N.D. emblem and the Ban the Bomb marches spread out from England to Europe and the U.S.A. Middle class it may have been at the outset. But "class" was as hateful to most of its adherents as war. C.N.D. got on the whole a good press in Britain. The severest critics were those who pointed to the sloppy dress of the C.N.D. marchers. But jeans, T-shirts and guitars were overtaking the square or the "Edwardian" fashions of the early '50's.[3]

---

[1] D. Riesman, "The Uncommitted Generation", *Encounter*, Nov. 1960.

[2] On France see P. Williams, "Vietnam. America's Algeria" in *Wars, Plots and Scandals in Post War France* and on the French student scene generally P. Seale and M. McConville, "French Revolution 1968", and H. Lefebvre, "The Explosion", Editions Anthropos 1969.

[3] T. R. Fyvel, "The Teddy Boy International", *Encounter*, Aug. 1961.

Another British export to the U.S.A. was some ideas for a "New Left". Suez and the Soviet suppression of the Hungarian uprising uprooted a few more British Stalinists and caused some Labour moderates to consider again whether British imperialism was in fact dead. Some results of this disillusion were the appareance in 1956 of "The Universities and Left Review" (Oxford-London) and the "New Reasoner" (Leeds-Hull)—journals with considerable (and scholarly) polemical punch produced by talented Marxists. In their view Marxism did not need "revision";—it needed to be learnt as it had stood before Stalin, and to be developed for the purpose of explaining the condition in which the working classes now found themselves. These British journals (which were written mainly by historians) were not without interest for radical intellectuals on the non-Stalinist left in America. Simultaneously some faculty and graduate students at the University of Wisconsin produced "Studies on the Left".

Though it was to be the Negro and civil rights[1] which in the 1960's gave cause for most concern and activity on American campuses the original stimulus was the peace issue.[2] In France too the first serious manifestations of disobedience by students came during the Algerian troubles when French students refused to break off relations with Algerian student bodies and devised ways and means of avoiding military service in Algeria.[3]

Not having their own countries at war by no means absolved (in their own eyes) British and German students from concern with wars. C.N.D. continued until the victory of the Labour Party in 1964 made its role somewhat less clear—the Nassau "agreement" and MLF proposal befogged the whole discussion in the Labour Party. In Germany one of the first big flare ups came at the Free University of Berlin where students refused to obey the dictates of the cold war—they insisted on inviting a speaker from East Germany to the campus. When their University authorities sought to forbid it, the "free speech" issue was raised—as at Berkeley in the beginning.

It would be quite unfair to suggest that the older side of the generation gap was unconcerned with the state of the world—or with youth

---

[1] For an excellent review of where it all began see John H. Schaar and Sheldon S. Wolin, "Where We are Now", *New York Review of Books*, 7 May 1970.

[2] The *Student Peace Union* was formed in 1960, but by 1964 it had virtually disappeared. C.O.R.E. and S.N.C.C. had absorbed youth's reforming energies in the U.S.A.

[3] P. Williams, op. cit., p. 211.

and its problems. The post war western world was analysed and found deficient in many—but not many fundamental— respects. In *Encounter* magazine in 1954 Herbert Luthy was writing about the state of France with its "immobilisme", its "plus ça change" characteristics. Max Beloff was deploring the overwhelming power of constitutional executives and disciplined parties—an old theme but still not quite irrelevant, while Daniel Boorstin was pointing to the persistence in America of what would later be known as Goldwater concepts of liberty. The death of Stalin and the rise of Kruschev were traumatic for some on the left, but not for the youth, who knew and cared little for Soviet communism—that was their parents' problem, if their parents were leftists. Until 1960 it was the middle-aged, organized, political left which was troubled—by Hungary, Suez, Poland, Algeria and the continuing success of Conservative governments in England and the U.S.A. Mark Abrams (U.K.), Daniel Bell (U.S.A.), and Anthony Crosland (U.K.), wrote in the May 1960 *"Encounter"* on the "Future of the Left", and in 1960 Abrams and Richard Rose produced the slim but highly influential paperback "Must Labour Lose". C.N.D. was flourishing, but the "natural" socialist in C.N.D.'s ranks seemed to have little interest in the socialism of the British Labour Party. In America by 1960 nothing much was yet afoot—but there were beginnings. S.N.C.C. was started in 1960—(financed in part by the liberalism of the Chase Manhattan Bank). The Student Peace Union was formed in 1960, S.D.S. in 1961. The Student Peace Union soon collapsed as student idealists in increasing numbers decided that civil rights work in the South and elsewhere was of more immediate importance. C.O.R.E. and S.N.C.C. grew. The March on Washington (1963) drew 250,000 and the Communist Party of the U.S.A. came onto the youth scene with the Du Bois clubs in the same year. (1963).

By 1960 "Youth" had established itself as a social category in the western world. It had tastes, spending power and vaguely political leanings. It was becoming increasingly classless in sentiment, and to that extent likely to support under-dog causes and to ridicule bourgeois values. Young people of all classes were more inclined than their elders to encourage individuality, to applaud it even when it became "outrageous". This made for confusion when *political* causes were discussed.

In 1960 the older generation were impressed by the youthful vigour of J. F. Kennedy and his team (Kennedy was 43). Youth liked his style perhaps but Kennedy was far too old to be considered a part of their culture. In November 1960 David Riesman could still talk of the "Uncommitted Generation" in the U.S.A. (Encounter, November, 1960).

Kennedy's election created a new atmosphere in the U.S.A. McCarthyism was at last dead. New ideas could blossom even if the design and implementation of new social policies ran up against old political and administrative obstacles. The euphoria was not to last. Racial discrimination, Cuba, and then Vietnam became the rallying points for those young Americans who were already (with the assistance of mass circulation authors like Galbraith, Wright Mills and Vance Packard) beginning to question both the practice and the theory of American private enterprise.

Why is *American* experience regarded as so important in the whole of this survey? The answer must be that both pro- and anti-Americans, pro- and anti-capitalists, pro- and anti-militarists took as their model (for exposition or for emulation) the United States of post World War II. It was the civilization which, allowing for a few crudities and the inevitable frictions, was rapidly developing as one which produced the material benefits of "the welfare state" along with "non-socialist", "non-bureaucratic" personal freedom, and which by its adherence to private enterprise experienced ever expanding economic activity which both enriched the individual and provided the material basis for essential activities in the public sector. Much of this, most of this picture was true. It was America's misfortune that it came to see itself too self consciously as *the* model. The imperfections, the frictions were too often denied or ignored. Publicists became burdened with illustrations of the beneficence of capitalism which the evidence did not wholly support. It became difficult for others to admit that anything was right with the U.S.A. Radicals in Europe could not help being impressed by American affluence, so far ahead was America in the mid 1960's. Traditionalist Labour leaders in Europe may not have felt drawn to the U.S.A. but European working class opinion was not strongly anti-American—it never had been.[1] Liberals, Conservatives, and some Socialists advocated development on American lines— socialism was unlikely in the U.S.A. but working men were treated decently there and if unionized, vastly rewarded.

Youth values are today surprisingly international—youth's political

---

[1] The highly educated classes in Europe had some intellectual links with the U.S.A.; the working classes had family links—it was their kind who had emigrated.

preferences, and demands, seem to bear little relationship—and to make few concessions, to national differences. Unlike the leftwing agitation of the 1930's todays student rebels in the U.S.A. seem to have nothing to say about American values except to condemn them. In the 1930's Jefferson and Lincoln were cast by Communists in the roles of prematurely wise sympathizers with the 1930's political line of the American C.P. British leftists, (and French too) exploited the radical-revolutionary traditions to be discovered in their countries. Not so today.[1]

In Britain student leftists even when they congregate in social science departments show little interest in the problems and in the history and development of British government and politics. Their world of ideas is political, but only very loosely geared into the politics of their own country. In the U.S.A. the brief flourish of activity in the cause of Eugene McCarthy must of course be noted—but it was both *brief* and *important*. If student activists were about their business in Britain's 1970 General Election they were not very noticeable—except perhaps as a counter productive element in the Liberal Party.

It may seem unfair to accuse student politicos of failure to immerse themselves in todays national politics. It could be pointed out that they did march at Aldermaston, they did (a small minority) *concern* themselves with the Algerian problem, they did in considerable numbers dedicate themselves to registering voters, and giving political aid and comfort to blacks in the South. But they didn't do it for long.

The *student based* civil rights movement—for that is what it was—S.N.C.C.—was the seed bed for the *anti war movement* (1960) and the anti-University movement (Berkeley 1964). The career of Marshall Bloom may perhaps illustrate in extreme and tragic form radical student activity and disillusion in the 1960's. Civil rights and race relations work and research in the south, while at Amherst; 1966 at L.S.E. as a graduate student[2] who masterminded there the first real student trouble in Britain; returned to the U.S. in summer of 1967,

---

[1] It is a matter for genuine intellectual regret that the "New Left" in the U.S.A. has not advanced much further than the Populist writers of the 1880's and 1890's in its appreciation of the quality of American history, or in its analysis of the mechanisms of American capitalism. Distaste, on aesthetic grounds, for American society seems to be the burden of its message.

[2] See Colin Crouch, *The Student Revolt*, 1970. Crouch (who was chairman of the Labour Society at LSE in 1966) is a talented young sociologist whose book is essential to the understanding of the British student revolt.

ran a radical "underground" press agency, then went to a hippy farm community for the simple life, followed by suicide in 1969.

Apart from the ritual pilgrimage to Havana where do the European and U.S. student rebels throw themselves into battle? Outside U.S. Embassies sometimes, but not in North Vietnam or South America, or even much today in the Southern States of the U.S.A. Now that white U.S. students no longer take the bus to Alabama, no longer (since the S.N.C.C. change in 1967) work closely with black students (or with other radical groups) there seems to be an increasing similarity of task or outlook between European and U.S. student militants. The task seems to be to exploit the weaknesses (or foolishness) of "Authority" to raise the political consciousness of increasingly large numbers of young people for the purpose of—this is where the sentence and the idea run out.

The inability of the "student movement" to formulate a programme (or develop a theory) of political action is its most striking *international* characteristic. While this assertion would be contested by some student militants (particularly in Italy[1] and perhaps in France) many would agree, and would point out that the absence of theory and the insistence upon the unreality of most political programmes conceived in advance of events, were the really novel and attractive aspects of their movement. And it is arguable that the movement is up to the minute in its view that conventional learning—and learning methods—are increasingly irrelevant. Computers will do the sums, and store the information and outline the operational solutions which heretofore had been tasks for the human mind—hence courses, examinations, and book learning are not necessary for the mass of humanity in the western world.

The student revolutionary however, both accepts and vehemently rejects this picture of the future—leaving himself open to the criticism that he is obtuse, dishonest and/or merely unwilling, if he can avoid them, to take tests of his acquired learning.

Student leaders are only rarely successful in mobilizing student

---

[1] Italian students seem to be better geared to the radical politics of Italy than e.g. French students are to the left in France—which means the French C.P. (The difference is the difference between the Italian and the French Communist parties within their respective national politics. See e.g. on students in Rome Gordon J. Di Renzo "Student Politics and Student Movements". Paper presented to VIII World Congress of the International Political Science Association. Munich Sept. 1970.

followers.[1] Most of the time meetings are hardly attended at all; despair in the movement is far more usual than joy. But given a good cause much concern and activity can be generated. What is a good cause will depend on local/national circumstances. (Cynics have pointed out that the Kent State (white) shootings were such a cause while Jackson State (black) deaths aroused very few protests in the North). The police at Nanterre—and later around the Sorbonne were a good cause. Middle class parents (and Nanterre students' parents were unusually affluent and successful) love the French police as little as does the Paris proletariat.[2] Free speech in Berlin, the new Director (ex Rhodesia) of L.S.E. skillfully libelled in an anonymous publication, industrialists pressured at Warwick University plus the persistent agitation about the immorality of Universities having Rhodesian and South African investments (Edinburgh)—it seems that only simple "liberal" issues can be exploited effectively. They are successfully exploited, for in Universities in Europe the young political conservative is liberal in sentiment and only the extremist conservative believes in *not* questioning the bona fides of those in authority. Students want all the time to know *who* has authority, and *why*?[3]

American students have been involved in a series of American experiences, against a background of American history and institutions which have presented them with opportunities and challenges not available to European militants. The Castro revolution, the Bay of Pigs, the bus boycott in the South, Greensboro N.C. lunch counters, Alabama, Oxford Mississippi. All these events have been pushed together to provide the materials for the fundamental criticism now levelled at U.S. society by student leaders the world over. This is the price that is paid for being the richest, most powerful (and best equipped with mass media) country in the world today.

The "frictions" in the system of American capitalism are seen by the dissenters to be its essential mechanisms; racism, police brutality,

---

[1] In 1965 student opinion in the USA was strongly in favour of American activity in Vietnam see S. M. Lipset, "Student Opposition in the USA" (*Government and Opposition*, Vol. I 1965) also Lipset and Altbach in S.M. Lipset (ed.) *Student Politics*.

[2] Nanterre students backgrounds were decidedly more affluent than those of Sorbonne students. P. Seale and M. McConville, op. cit., p. 26.

[3] This questioning has led to internal reforms of a mild and useful character in many British Universities, and to more drastic reforming in French Universities. (America has too many colleges and Universities for any generalization to be made with confidence).

poverty, militaristic thinking at home and imperialist aggression abroad—if any one of these parts were removed the machine would collapse. The consequence of this train of thought is the belief—so naive that few could be accused of taking it quite seriously—that an attack on any part of the sytem will inevitably weaken the whole. Probably the majority of student rebels do not believe this; they fall back on the more conventional revolutionary theme that *any* struggle can be used to arouse the political consciousness of the participants who will then be better prepared for the final battle.

The beliefs of student leftists are not easily fitted into any ideological pattern—at least not into any pattern save the simplest opposition to "capitalism" and its accompanying bureaucracy, but "who are the students rebels" is a question to which sociological research has produced clear answers. In the U.S.A., the U.K. and Europe student rebels are the offspring of bourgeois liberal parents who do not wholeheartedly disapprove of the views and activities of their sons and daughters. There is no doubt a serious "generation gap" between the hard hats and the militant young gentlemen of the Ivy League, between L.S.E. militants[1] and Barbican site building workers, between Daniel Cohn Bendit and the middle aged "Stalinist filth" of the French C.P. (Bendit's phrase) who brought up the rear of Bendit's victory parade. But between parents and their politically active children the gap is not qualitatively significant—though it may be that what is true of Britain, France and the U.S.A. is not so true of German speaking countries. (Certain studies suggest that in the latter countries higher educational levels do not correlate with greater liberalism on moral and social questions as they do in the former.[2]) The places where student activism has occurred have always so far been the colleges and Universities housing students of above average intellectual attainment from above average affluent backgrounds. In Paris Nanterre, which can claim to have started it off in France, houses, in grim new buildings in a characterless part of the city's periphery (the "bled") a large quantity of youth of the upper middle class. Stanford, Berkeley, Michigan, Harvard, Columbia, even Yale and Princeton have all shown political concern. In the U.K. where 25% of students now come from working

---

[1] For a detailed study of LSE students see *Students in Conflict. LSE in 1967* by T. Blackstone, K. Gales, R. Hadley and W. Lewis. LSE. Research Monographs. 5.

[2] See Allerbeck, op cit. and for Vienna. D. Kramer et al. "Viennese Apprentices and Grammar School Students" IPSA paper VIII World Congress Sept. 1970.

class homes—the highest percentage in Europe—it is not the "working class" universities like Strathclyde in Glasgow which have been turbulent but the middle class colleges, like L.S.E. which have given the lead.

The student left faces a serious dilemma. To the extent that they are Marxist revolutionaries an alliance with the working class should be an essential part of their strategy. The working class is however seriously underrepresented in the student population, and those who are in the student world have aspirations to use its advantages to leave the working class. Moreover one of the triumphs of capitalism, perhaps its greatest triumph in the last 25 years, has been to produce a segment of skilled and highly paid workers whose interest in the perpetuation of the system is as great, if not greater, than that of the legal owners of the means of production. Given skilful union leadership they can do better out of the system than any mere shareholder. Many student theorists recognize these facts of life, but a clear appreciation of the situation does not automatically provide the solution to the problem. For some the urban working class has been corrupted beyond redemption. Revolutionary spirit must be sought (and created) amongst the less corrupt—the exploited peasantry. If your own country has no peasants all that is left is admiration for a dimly perceived Che Guevara in the mountains of South America. (But some French theorists have had a better idea—the positing of the young technologists as the seminal, creative "new proletariat" of French revolution).

In their own immediate environment, the Universities, it would be churlish and inaccurate to state that students have sought all the wrong solutions and have achieved nothing. They have often had the right ideas about Universities and Universities have responded and in most cases but not in all have survived the testing time. Certainly British Universities have not been seriously damaged by the few reforms they have been obliged to introduce; they have probably been improved. Whether one would say the same for all French Universities may be less certain and perhaps too for some American colleges and Universities. But it would be wrong to suppose, (and perhaps at this late date trite to say) that student rebels "attacking" Universities were primarily interested in University reform. They were protesting at some of the gross deficiencies and solemn crimes committed in the name of progress, democracy, G.N.P. or national security. It is most "unsporting" to attack a C.I.A. "agency" or a C.& B.W, "activity" or shout down a director of Barclays Bank. This line of thought may lead to the conclusion that it would have been "better" morally to have assassinated the Commander in Chief or blown up Barclays Head Office. Most students would not agree that the latter activity would be "better". They have been brought up in a world where symbols denote "reality"; no generation is more convinced of the importance of this than the present. A demo is "better" in every way if covered by T.V. When Universities are attacked they are attacked not so much for their known deficiencies as because they are there, as living symbols of a culture which was not the creation of todays students.

Another line of speculation about the causes of the student condition has been stressed by Professor Berger of the University of California in *Student Unrest and Prolonged Adolescence*.[1] He does not wish to praise or blame ideologies or particular institutional practices but seeks for an explanation in societal conditions characteristic of modern affluent nations. His clue to the problem is prolonged adolescence. Modern youth are physically and educationally better equipped than ever before in mans history. Two hundred years ago a young man at 18 with the education (and physique) of many today would have been governing a district in India or running a family business or leading companies of soldiers. As it is our 18 year old of the 1970's looks forward to perhaps another 10 years in de facto statu pupillari, and, as Professor Berger grimly indicates, even after that he may be dependent for many more years upon an academic or business superior before he can call himself truly his own master. Moreover a part of the (adult) cult of youth is a yearning for its simplicity, its innocence, its carefree foolishness—all of which will be tolerated even encouraged, for anything is better than a seriously committed youth. So twenty year olds are expected, within reason, to behave like kids and well bred hooligans and are given footballs and fraternity houses to fool about with, when they are in fact capable of a great deal more both physically and intellectually.

The political orientations[2] of U.S. and U.K. and European students are, I believe, strikingly similar. Contrasts between the U.S.A. and Europe are in this area far less striking than similarities, common reference points, common "objectives" (largely personal in character) common heroes and bogeymen. French, American, British history all

---

[1] In *Dialogue* Vol. 3. 1970 No 4. (U.S.I.A. Washington D.C.).
[2] See in particular Crouch, op. cit., Ch. I "Political Orientations".

are equally irrelevant. Youth in the world suffers from the same adult imperfections, the same capitalist and militarist excesses, and a thin Marxist type materialist interpretation provides the analysis,—and less adequately, much less, suggests solutions.

For those who think about these matters Soviet Communism is no more successful than capitalism in making man's lot bearable, though fascination with Lenin, Trotsky and the early Bolsheviks gives the U.S.S.R. a somewhat better romantic rating than the U.S.A. Social Democracy has no drama and can point only to its steady improvement of (and acclimatization to) the capitalist system. If Social Democracy (or Labourism) has monuments they will be, in many cases, the students' own parents.

A common disillusion with Soviet Communism and Social Democracy produces in the student left a strong sympathy for the localist, community oriented self administration in which the "local control" aspect is seen as far more important than the old socialist shibboleth of legal ownership. Cohn Bendit was particularly scathing about the "obsolete Communism" that aspired to C.P. control of the economic bureaucracy. It is a matter for regret however, that the new student left has not produced yet any compelling arguments to support the important principles of localism and participation— in particular arguments which would support (or refute) the objection that localism, in particular places in particular circumstances, may be indistinguishable from racial (or social) segregation.[1]

There are no certain conclusions to be drawn. The student revolt against Universities could disappear as speedily as it arose. This is unlikely but not impossible; not impossible for the general condition of any one student as a student does not depend upon what he can do about his condition whilst he is a student; but unlikely because it would be expecting something not so far experienced—total student political apathy and conformism. The gravest long term problem of serious student politics is the theoretical and practical difficulty of reliable allies outside the Universities. The student body will probably become more socially mixed in future, not less, and this could well reduce the coherence of the student movement. The student movement has not yet produced its own student heroes. It has martyrs, notably

---

[1] "Localism" and "Community" are also values of the Right. See D. R. Schwertzer and J. M. Elden, "Convergence of Opposition from Left and Right". Paper presented to VIII World Congress I. P.S.A. Munich Sept. 1970.

in the U.S.A. but heroes and prophets have not been forthcoming. The adult world has designated Herbert Marcuse as the movements ideologue, but it's the adult intellectual who reads him, not the student activist. Theory and seriously meditated ideology is as alien to the younger generation as is (to their once radical parents) the adulation accorded to Che the failed guerilla leader. The reaction, by some of the children, to the Talmudic Marxism of their parents can be easily understood, but to wander about in a haze of "good" feelings can offend the rationalism of those whose education and experience have taught them to distrust all feelings not directed by hard facts, reason and argument.

MALCOLM BRADBURY

THE ART OF NOVEL WRITING, 1945-1970

At another American Studies conference earlier this year, Marcus Cunliffe reported on a nightmare of Professor Harry Levin's: the door-bell rings, there are voices in the hall, and someone comes to him to say: "The men are here to compare the literatures." The men are, indeed, here to compare the literatures. For though my title is a general one, "The Art of Novel Writing," the assumption of this meeting is that I shall be distinguishing between the ways in which American writers have set about their task, and the ways in which English and European writers have set about theirs. We have long taken it to be the case that there is a distinction; and that American writers, like Scott Fitzgerald's rich, are different from us, in nature and in circumstances. Many of the familiar theses about the nature of the American novel-tradition—for instance, Richard Chase's in *The American Novel and Its Tradition;* Leslie Fiedler's in *Love and Death in the American Novel*; and Richard Poirier's in *A World Elsewhere*—depend upon this assumption. If one wanted to reduce a general argument from all of these books, then it would run something like this. The American novel is different from the European in matter of genre, mode, subject-matter and style. In genre, because it has tended toward the romance rather than the realistic line in the novel, concerning itself less with manners and mores and action within society, and more with the fabulous and metaphysical action of the self outside society. In mode, because being more disposed to fabulation, invention and symbolic action, it has taken on the attributes of the Gothic, drifting toward isolation, mystery and death. In subject-matter, because it has been concerned with themes about man confronting directly and with little social intervention the problem of his nature, with lonely heroes and the expanding frontiers of society and spirit. And where critics like Chase, Fiedler and Lewis see distinctive genres, modes, and themes, Richard Poirier has added the notion that the American novelist has a distinctive *style:* the American writer tends to use literary style as a personal implement with which to build up special verbal universes of his own, analogous to independent societies, outside the familiar orders of linguistic as well as social community.[1]

To all this, we might add the recurrent assumption that much of this distinctiveness is the product of the fact that the American writer, as compared with the European, has occupied an odd and equivocal position in his society. He was, as Hawthorne and Melville felt themselves to be, a cultural stranger: a man lacking not only those materials in society and manners which had enlarged the growth of the nineteenth-century novel in Europe, but also lacking the social acceptance, the national prestige or function, that his more fortunate European confrères possessed. Hence then not only his stylistic isolation and uncertainty, but also his nay-saying vein, his power of blackness, his sense of internalized tragedy. Now for the view that the American novel has had its own way, there are many justifications: many have been given by the American novelists themselves. Repeatedly, the American novelist has sought to suggest that, in his novel social circumstances, he is undertaking a special task, that of creating a national species of fiction; and frequently he has attempted to define that task against the different practices of Europe, and to assert that his own work is made otherwise, out of local materials on native grounds. The desire to make a declaration of literary independence runs through American writing; and it is inevitable that the independence declared must be either from England, or from Europe generally.[2] Of course there is no doubt that a distinctive body of American styles and modes, distinctive patterns of authorial life, distinctive areas of experience and species of sensibility, do come out of American writing. Equally there is no doubt that we are left with a small paradox: for if almost every American writer feels he has contributed to a particularly American tradition, why then is there *still* a complex fate for the American

---

[1] Richard Chase, *The American Novel and Its Tradition*, New York and London, 1957; Leslie Fiedler, *Love and Death in the American Novel*, New York, 1960; London, 1967; R. W. B. Lewis, *The American Adam*, Chicago and London, 1955; Richard Poirier, *A World Elsewhere*, New York, 1966; London, 1967.

[2] From many classic instances, one might pick out just one—Melville's comment in his essay, "Hawthorne and His Mosses," first published in the *Literary World* in 1850:

"But it is not meant that all American writers should studiously cleave to nationality in their writings; only this, no American writer should write like an Englishman or a Frenchman; let him write like a man, for then he will be sure to write like an American. Let us away with this leaven of literary flunkeyism towards England. If either must play the flunkey in this thing, let England do it, not us."

writer, why does he need to *repeat* the claim of Americanness, why does the fight against the European embrace go on into the present century? No doubt the answer is that the superstitious valuation of Europe is not so easily escaped; the main movements of European fiction can never be entirely overlooked; the differences have always been relative rather than complete. But that is only one of the difficulties we have in talking about a distinctive American way; there are others too. For example, the judgments of critics like Chase, Fiedler and Poirier are highly illuminating if we are talking about the differences between the *nineteenth*-century American and European novel—and especially those between the nineteenth-century American and *English* novel. The sense of creative isolation; the myth and romance elements; the concern with confrontation with the natural environment; the nay-saying vein of protest and blackness—such things are indeed there in the classic American novel, and they help us see a distinctive American temper. But the model of the European novel as a kind of grandly social novel, quite antithetical, was never quite accurate. And certainly by the twentieth century, as D. H. Lawrence pointed out, many of the qualities that we see in American novels are very much present in the leading European ones. A distinction founded on this basis works less well for this century; and it works less and less well the nearer one gets to the present.

As for my own concern, it is not with the nineteenth-century novel, nor with the twentieth century novel as this is still classified in many universities, at least in England (where the modern novel often ends in 1939 or 1945), but with the contemporary or rather the postwar novel. It is in this area of time, between 1945 and the present, that I want to explore contrasts that are of a different order and kind from those great antitheses to which I have already referred. My line of approach I ought to define a little. For someone who is, in one of his roles, a writer, there is a temptation to make a personal statement; to say what seems different about the way in which an American writer goes about his task from the way I go about mine. This is a difference I am always very aware of when I go to America or talk to American writers. They live in different environments, they meet and talk to one another in different circumstances and in different ways, they are financed differently, they have more and better typewriters, they achieve their reputation through different channels and their careers have a different feel. In many respects the literary life in America seems more attractive and better endowed than that in England; the opportunities for living in a writers' colony or as the literary hermit on campus are greater; and the possibility of using the writer's life as a species of action and enquiry in the United States are larger, than they ever were. On the attractions of the American literary life I have written elsewhere, and it is not my main theme here.[1] For someone who is, in another of his roles, a critic, there is another kind of temptation; this is to offer some form of total analysis which explains on historical and stylistic grounds the differences between modern American and modern European writing. This again is not really my aim; I am most concerned to look at some of the literary tactics and aesthetic discussions which prevail in America and then in Europe, and to see the similarities and the differences.

I am sure there *are* differences, and I am going to suggest some of them. But one point must be stressed, and that is that in certain respects the situation of all modern writers, or postwar writers, is similar. We all live in a tumultuous world in which change is an active force; and we live in that world with much greater awareness than ever before about how others are responding to it. In that world the balance of power has shifted, culturally as well as politically; and American writing has ceased to be a marginal literature or a provincial literature, worried about what distinguishes it as un-European and hence as American. American writing has become vastly more important for people in many countries than it used to be. Gore Vidal has just offered us an explanation of this fact; writers in powerful countries get a credit beyond that which they deserve, and modern American writing is wildly overpraised. This has a profound truth in it, though of course it is not the whole truth. The writing of a nation can engage us through our sense of the interest, for good or ill, of what that nation is doing, doing amongst other things to us; it can also engage us because its experience seems to be the experience of a type of the modern to which we ourselves well may come. It has the advance-guardism of the nation advanced in process or history. Fortunately, as it happens, I think that America has in fact produced writers who are by any standards important writers, and they have come to notice not simply because they carry with them the force of a powerful culture, but also because they have been able to distil, order and shape the experience deriving from it. Equally it is true that other literatures seem to have lost ground in the international balance of cultural power: postwar

---

[1] See, for instance, Bryan Wilson and Malcolm Bradbury, "Why Young Writers Emigrate: The Away Game," *Twentieth Century*, 169 (January, 1961), pp. 69-80.

English writing is just such a case in point. Here again the matter is to some extent a matter of unfortunate cultural discriminations but also in part a matter of just deserts; it is, I think, true that England in the postwar period, though it has produced many interesting writers, has produced only a handful that one would think of as actually or nearly first-rate. I even suspect—not being an utterly uncritical fan of the French nouveau roman—that something the same is true of France; it may be true of Germany as well. That suggests one type of caution; we must remember, when we talk of the Americanness of American literature, that we are no longer contemplating a situation where the American writer feels compelled to assert his independence of a vastly more powerful and "advanced" European literature—feels compelled, that is, to recognize its dominant existence and then do different.

Nor, indeed, are we talking of a situation in which national traditions in literature can be seen as entirely distinct. The notion that there was a "European mind" in literature, which was somehow different from the "American mind", persisted in some quarters right up to the war; one of those who spoke of it most in England was in fact an American, T. S. Eliot. But today European-American cross-fertilization has become so intense that it is possible to conceive of writers in their different European countries looking across the Atlantic to America and taking their own influences, in their different ways, from there rather than from each other. In England, for instance, many young writers are for the first time vastly more aware of what is going on in American writing than they are of what is going on in French or German writing. Not only does this make it hard to think of a distinct European way; it also has the result that I, as an English writer and critic, do not find it easy to speak of European practice, and my judgments in what follows are likely to have a highly Anglocentric or Anglo-American cast. This means that, in the paper that follows, I feel it best to concentrate on the practice of a certain number of selected American writers whose work seems to me important, and who have, I think, found forms and structures for contemporary experience of a significant kind, and then allow most of the contrasts and similarities with European practice to be a matter for general consideration and discussion. I will hazard some words about what European writers are doing now, but they will be tentative words, mostly about English fiction, and I can only leave it to others, better equipped, to extend discussion further.

II

I have said that all postwar writers, whether American, English or European, seem to me to share a situation in common, and I would like to begin by talking about what it is. Lately, reading through a fair amount of criticism of the contemporary novel, I have been struck, and somewhat baffled, by one remarkable emphasis; there is, in much of this criticism, a presiding assumption that the postwar novel cannot theoretically exist. It would appear that for many critics there is reliable, indeed scientific, evidence that the novel died as a form somewhere around 1939 or 1941 or 1945. For its death there are several sound historical—or rather *historicist*—reasons. The novel was a liberal-bourgeois form; and we have left liberal-bourgeois society behind. It depended on a communal language, a shared notion of "reality" and value which we can now unmask as a conspiratorial theory about the nature of the world of persons and objects, causes and effects, chronicity and sequence. It depended on a notion of character founded on the ideal of the rounded, individuated, autonomous self; and on plot as a derivative from recognizable, logical sequences both in time and in the development of people and of societies. And all of these things have gone into question; reality is in question. The modernist novel at the beginning of the century showed us that, and held the novel-form in suspension at the very point of its ultimate exhaustion. But now modernism, as a stylistic phase, has ceased—leaving the writer with nothing to go forward from, and nothing to go back *to*. Not until we get a new reality will we get a new novel; and the new reality may not sanction the novel-form at all. Hence the Death of the Novel. Fortunately we know that, as with Mark Twain's reported death, the rumours have proved greatly exaggerated; despite the funerals and the wakes, the novel has continued. I have made the doctrine sound implausible, which it is; but it does suggest something essential to my argument, which is that the modern writer has had to face the difficult problem of his relation to modernism, which is now as much a feature of literary history as it is of present creative practice.

"Periods end when we are not looking...," wrote Cyril Connolly in *Horizon* in 1941, "The last two years have been a turning point; an epidemic of dying has ended many movements." The same sense of stylistic transition is present in many of the western literatures, in some cases for clear historical reasons. One can find them too in

America—as, for instance, in John Aldridge's *After the Lost Generation* (1954) (though I shall suggest in a moment that there the situation had certain interesting differences). Indeed there seems to have been a general feeling, as a postwar generation of writers emerged in different countries, that the great conventions of modern literary radicalism were weakening (in some cases, of course, they were actually historically discredited), and that the modernist-experimental tendency was joining other tendencies of the past as one of the available traditions. But on the other hand no positive new style seemed to be emerging; and postwar fiction has come to us in a bewildering variety of modes, radical and realistic, naturalistic and symbolist, highly physical and highly metaphysical. I shall be suggesting that to some extent an aesthetic debate *has* emerged in the postwar novel, and that it is not very different in America and in Europe; but what I think most postwar writers in the different countries felt in common was a kind of uncertainty about where to go next. But what also seems clear is that in some countries the sense of relationship to proceeding movements and tendencies was greater than in others. And paradoxically—since if anything is obvious about postwar American writing it is that it has come from more or less new sources in the culture, from the efflorescence of Jewish and now of black writers, from the urban chaos and the slums and the climate of anguished uncertainty that marks our era of rapid and accelerating change—it would seem that in America this continuity was particularly strongly felt. What is more, this sense of continuity apparently derived from the conviction, which seems to me marked in the postwar generation in the American novel, that the novel was a very possible form in the United States. It was, so to speak, a form close to its beginnings. Whereas in Europe the contributions of the new writers appeared, often, as a contribution to the tail-end of a great tradition of creation in the "burgher epic," as the novel has been called, the American novel was only just beginning to acquire a distinctive momentum.

For this greater confidence one may suggest several reasons. One I have already proposed is the important presence in the American line in the novel of that great generation of experimentalists which distilled itself in the 1920s and was extended and amended in the 1930s: the generation of Ernest Hemingway, Sherwood Anderson, Sinclair Lewis, William Faulkner, John Dos Passos, John Steinbeck and Nathanael West. By 1945 this great generation of American writers—the writers who were in fact the "modernist" generation in the twentieth-century

American novel—was coming toward the end of its production. Some of them had indeed faded both from critical and popular attention, though they were to come back remarkably into notice in the early 1950s. And thus, where in Europe the great "modern" generation seemed to lie back at some distance, and to belong, very largely, to the early years of the century—in England, for instance, there was the "intervening" generation of Evelyn Waugh, Aldous Huxley, Graham Greene, Joyce Cary, and so on; and in the postwar period a marked questioning of modernist experiment—in America the continuity was more direct. As a result, these writers gave their successors a conviction that the novel was a fresh and developing form which had only just begun to chart the complexities of modern American experience; they conveyed to them at least the belief that the American novel was a distinct and viable modern species. Their writing, a distinctively post-World War I writing, appealed to a novelty of experience that seemed manifest in American life. The spare, tough, hardshell heroes of Hemingway, encountering a nihilistic universe and redeeming it by style in life and style in art; the lost heroes and heroines of Scott Fitzgerald, pressing towards a species of desperate emancipation through modern history which was also a profound and febrile psychological experience; the central figures of Faulkner, complexes of difficult consciousness seeking moral value amidst the chaos of cultural transition in the south and the nation at large; the interfused world of Dos Passos, where character was presented against the city, reality, history and amidst an accelerating American transition in which country gave way to city, clear national character to melting pot, idealistic dream to tawdry reality; in all of these writers one could feel the presence of a distinctively modern, indeed contemporary experience, feel the enormity of America's modern development, and also feel the possibility for coping with these in an art that contained epicality, grandeur and the formal consolations of style. For if these writers were experimental, they did not contain the "formal desperation" which marks many of the works of European modernism; it is not the sense of crisis in fiction but the sense of the nature of modern consciousness that produced, say, the rhetoric and experimentalism of Faulkner. "Faulkner's style," says Norman Mailer in *Advertisements for Myself*, in which he also credits his debt to Hemingway,—which fs to say, his vision—was to haunt my later themes like the ghost of some undiscovered mansion in my mind." And in addition to such credited debts, and to such obvious links as nakedly exist between say Faulkner and the postwar explosion of Southern Gothic (Flannery O'Connor, Truman Capote, Eudora Welty, Reynolds Price, etc.), or between the post-World War I and the post-World War II groups of war-novels, there is a basic continuity of theme and technique which serves as a bridge over the obvious differences between the two generations: differences of ethnic composition and basic social experience, of moral emphasis and cultural assessment, which fund the American novel afresh in the 1950s and 1960s. Where the European novel is, I think, touched with a sense of purposes lost, purposes which need to be regained, the American novel already seemed to have established patterns of response to modern experience which to many Europeans gave it a striking dimension of difference and of interest.

In short, then, the American writers of the postwar period appear to have inherited from the twin American traditions of naturalism and formal aestheticism a very varied body of means for dealing with the transition into a new phase of American experience that follows the war. Of course what they got from their predecessors is only part of the story. The great writers of the earlier period might have led the way into a distinctive mode—or set of modes—for dealing with American experience by recognizing both its availability and modernity, by adjusting their sense of artistic experiment to their awareness of the forces burgeoning in American history. But they had not become engrossed to the same degree in the urban, anonymous, rapidly accelerating world that was to form the essential context and the essential area of exploration of the postwar writers. Theirs was a world of mass society and of the insidious claims of conformity; of vast technological thrust and commercial expansion; of ethnic heterogenity and rapid social change. The dominant landscape was inevitably much more urban and technological, the dominant culture more cosmopolitan, the images surrounding them much more powerful, the dominant politics much more alien and unreal. The cultural alternatives that had existed for many writers of the 1920s, in an agrarian world or in the world of a more cultured Europe, were appropriately diminished. The artist himself was afforded less chance to be an heroic individual separatist but had to define his position from a world much more crowded and intrusive. Appropriately enough, then, we recognize in the writing of this period qualities of despair and alienation and absurdity that run in many variations across much of contemporary western literature. The themes themselves derive from several logics: an aesthetic or post-romantic logic; a philosophical logic; a historical or cultural logic. They are, of course, in no sense absolute; one of the things that distinguishes postwar writing is not only its plurality of modes but its plurality of assumptions about the present human condition. Various attempts have been made by critics to characterize the nature and preoccupations of the recent American novel, in books like Ihab Hassan's *Radical Innocence* or Leslie Fiedler's *Waiting for the End;* the task is a difficult one and well beyond my present purpose.[1] But what is clear is that the modern American writer has gone well beyond not only his predecessors but also probably his European contemporaries in his concern with the notion of man's living in an utterly transformed world, and in an experience of amorphousness, unreality and solitude. Yet despite the fact that, as a result, American postwar fiction has been a fiction of alienation and solitude, anomie and human plight, it has also been often a fiction of epical gestures and social expansiveness. What, then, seems striking to me about the modern American novel, and what I think explains a lot of its fascination, is the presence in most of its works and in its general spirit of two characteristics. The first is that it is, on the whole, deeply founded in contemporary American experience and very much evolved with the evolution of American society, which is to say that it is not so much an aesthetic fiction as one designed to be infinitely accessible to history; and the second is that it is remarkably ebullient in its stylistic vigour and general mood, that it wears its desperation lightly, and hence seems open to large forays of creative inventiveness.

III

Some years back, in an article called "Some Notes on Recent American Fiction," Saul Bellow spoke of the fascination that modern American novels had for their European readers. Remarking that many modern French novels and plays are derived from "definite theories which make a historical reckoning of the human condition and are peculiarly responsive to new physical, psychological, and philosophical theories," he went on:

> American writers, when they are moved by a similar spirit to reject and despise the Self, are seldom encumbered by such intellectual baggage,

---

[1] Ihab Hassan, *Radical Innocence: The Contemporary American Novel*, Princeton and London, 1961; Leslie Fiedler, *Waiting for the End*, New York, 1964; London, 1965. See also Marcus Klein (ed.), *The American Novel Since World War II*, New York, 1969.

and this fact pleases their European contemporaries, who find in them a natural, that is, a brutal or violent acceptance of the new universal truth by minds free from intellectual preconceptions.[1]

Bellow's point is that their fascination for, and their difference from, some of their European contemporaries lies not only in their formal attributes but in the kind of universe behind them with which they think it proper to deal. And indeed it is the fact that this fiction has been created out of an expanding, technologized, post-industrial society that gives it a kind of automatic modernity. For if the postwar American writer has been aware of anything it is that he lives in a world that is onerously modern, an accelerating environment in which moral and aesthetic perspective becomes extremely difficult to create, and where the energy for action and style derives from that context of proliferating change. In a social order that has acquired an amorphousness, solitude and rapidity never felt in American society before, it is perhaps inevitable that one should recognize in these writings that actuality itself, American actuality, is a kind of metaphor for all of us. As R. W. B. Lewis has put it: "It is as though these novelists, and the characters they create, had been shaken loose by the amount and the violence of the history America had passed through (America, it must be remembered, has until late been unaccustomed to history)".[2] The new species of man, the new versions of consciousness, the spectacular context of surreal history, which inhabit many modern American novels are less fictions and fantasies or philosophically mounted enquiries into the status of modern self and society than responses to dominant conditions. As Philip Roth put it in an article of 1962 called "Writing American Fiction":

> ...the American writer in the middle of the 20th century has his hands full in trying to understand, and then describe, and then make *credible* much of the American reality. It stupefies, it sickens, it infuriates, and finally it is even a kind of embarrassment to one's own meager imagination. The actuality is continually outdoing our talents, and the culture tosses up figures almost daily that are the envy of any novelist. Who, for example, could have invented Charles Van Doren? Roy Cohn and David Schine? Sherman Adams and Bernard Goldfine?...
>
> The daily newspapers then fill one with wonder and awe; is it possible? Is it happening? And of course with sickness and despair.

---

[1] Saul Bellow, "Some Notes on Recent American Fiction," *Encounter*, XXI, 5 (November, 1963), pp. 22-29.

[2] R. W. B. Lewis, *Recent Fiction: Picaro and Pilgrim*, Washington, D. C., Forum Lectures Series 14, n.d.

The fixes, the scandals, the insanities, the treacheries, the idiocies, the lies, the pieties, the noise... Recently, in *Commentary*, Benjamin DeMott wrote that the "deeply lodged suspicion of the times [is] namely, that events and individuals are unreal, and that power to alter the course of the age, of my life and your life, is actually vested elsewhere." There seems to be, said DeMott, a kind of "universal descent into unreality..."[1]

What Roth is saying is that it is extremely difficult for the contemporary novelist to write about current American experience as a *normal* experience, to document it as it stands or invent versions of it that outshine or even catch the real thing. In that particular article, he suggests that this has a disabling effect on American fiction, and that it tends to encourage writers to think of themselves as actors in this particular culture. He especially cites Norman Mailer, who is, he suggests, trying to act within the absurd event rather than distil it or outrun it. And indeed there is perhaps something understandable and characteristic in the fact that Mailer should, after beginning with high aesthetic ambitions (and for instance planning an eight-novel sequence in the Faulknerian manner with elaborate strategies of point-of-view and box-within-box structure) have shaped his career by advertising himself rather than his work, by offering the struggles of his consciousness rather than the total and completed products of his craft, and by moving toward a complex interfusion of fiction and documentary. But of course to take what Mailer is doing, even at his most documentary, as a species of journalistic report would be to mistake the case. For Mailer's writing, whether documentary or fabulatory, is the product of a particular kind of Freudo-Marxian historiography, a version of the interfusion of crisis in self and crisis in society, which has much to do with the potent epicality of his writing and that of a number of his contemporaries. But by containing the crisis of apocalyptic sensibility[2] within the self as well as within the

---

[1] Philip Roth, "Writing American Fiction", *Commentary* (March, 1961); reprinted in *The Commentary Reader*, ed. Norman Podhoretz, New York, 1966, pp. 595-609.

[2] It is not hard to find instances of apocalyptic sensibility in American writing today; it is paramount through Mailer's work, and one might take as an instance the passage in *The Deer Park* where Marion Faye looks towards the atomic testing grounds:

> So let it come Faye thought, let this explosion come, and then another and all the others until the sun God burned the earth. Let it come, he thought, looking into the East at Mecca where the bombs ticked while he stood on the tiny rise of ground trying to see one hundred, two hundred, three hundred

society, by making alliances between the psychology of the individual and the state of social affairs, by relating man to his times, many modern American writers have produced a highly complex art of distinct aesthetic as well as reportorial fascination.

I am arguing that the American writer has been highly conscious of the fact that the novel is, as a form, highly exposed to the force of change in society; that he has felt the obligation to reach forward into new experiences, into futures, dreams, frontiers of sensation; but that in doing all this he has created both a complex and an ebullient art. We are well used to the idea that today's American writer is alienated. (I always find it striking, for instance, by the syndrome of cultural relationships that emerge whenever I visit the United States and take part in those recurrent panels of international writers with the title of *The Writer: Alienation, Commitment, or Conformity?* which are staple fare in universities and at writers' conferences. It is usually the American writers who are most confident in the role of men of gut-plight; it is also they who seem particularly well-endowed and well-placed, and who, on the strength of that plight, are able to get a Guggenheim grant or a State Department tour, a Creative Writing fellowship or a publishers' advance. My own immediate response it that the English writer's plight is more modest; he finds it hard to make a living. Nonetheless, it is the fact that the plight is so publicly credited that makes it into a viable, creative literary possibility; it is possible to play it out with considerable grandeur and on considerable scale.) What is more remarkable, perhaps, is the fact that out of his, or the human situation, he has succeeded in creating complex literary strategies and designs; that the paucity or deprivation he confronts invokes large artistic structures. For the spectacle that engages us in reading contemporary American literature is not a modernist attenuation of language or plots; we hear today a lot about the withdrawal of writers toward silence, but the American silence is a highly vocal one. Indeed it is hard *not* to remark—as Bernard Bergonzi observes in his book *The Situation of the Novel*—on the enormous stylistic energy of American writing.[1] Bergonzi suggests that one difference between much

---

miles across the desert. Let it come, Faye begged, like a man praying for rain, let it come and clear the rot and the stink and the stench, let it come for all of everywhere, just so it comes and the world stands clear in the white dead dawn.

[1] Bernard Bergonzi, *The Situation of the Novel*, London, 1970. And for another discussion of the same kind, suggesting not only the stylistic energy but also the

English writing and American writing is that the English writer still is able to conceive of a public literary language; in America, he says, each book has the air of being made anew in its own linguistic mode. This, perhaps, misses a certain conventionality in American spontaneity (after a period of reading a lot of American writers one realizes that many devices of spontaneity are remarkably widely shared); nonetheless there is an element of innovative extravagance, a desire for freewheeling expression, and above all an area of psychological and subconscious reference which distinguishes the American from the English way with a common language. Equally one is likely to be struck by the fertile imagination, the metaphysical freewheeling, of the fictional structure; I offer as brief instances Bellow's *Henderson the Rain King* and Richard Brautigan's *Trout-Fishing in America*. Perhaps it is because the American 'absurd is such a practical, such a historically and socially rooted, absurd that its quality strikes one as quite different from, say, the French enterprises in the genre. Where they tend to undertake a philosophical quest in the metaphysical evolution of one man, carried with inexorable logic to its conclusion, as in *L'Étranger*, or where they provide a coherently minimal verbal world, as in the nouveau roman, the American variant is vastly more empirical; contrast, say, *La Nausée* with John Barth's *The Floating Opera*, where the perception of the meaninglessness and contingency of the universe is comically resolved by recognizing that if there is no reason for continuing living there is no reason for suicide either. Consider the mixture of desperation and ebullience that exists in the world of Jewish-American writers like Saul Bellow, Bernard Malamud, Philip Roth, or Herbert Gold—writers in whose work an elaborate running comic-metaphysical rhetoric sustains a creative action beyond all its moments of negation. Or consider, finally, the way in which much American fiction since the war has depended on pastiche and parody of popular literary forms, and has produced—in the black humour writers, for example—a tactic of absurd collage that sustains both the pleasurable contingency and the threatening ridiculousness of human life.

IV

One of the points I have been trying to stress in this argument is the point that the American novelist since the war has sought inter-

---

stylistic ingenuity of recent American fiction, see Tony Tanner's striking new study *The City of Words*, London, 1971.

estingly to mediate between the contrary claims of form and those of time. In an era of great change and new experience, there is always a temptation upon the writer to feel that the history he has been passing through is his real subject-matter, and takes precedence over his means and arts for shaping and ordering it. But for the serious writer there is an inevitable need to produce the fine and finished work of art, absolute and independent within its own completeness, or be accountable to that possibility. Characteristically the great writer contains within his work, and interests us by, a creative adjustment of both these claims upon him. But the ways in which he does this are apt to change with time, and I think one can sense a considerable change at work in American writing over the period about which I am talking. The American writing of the fifties showed a considerable tendency toward an aesthetic compactness, and with that a distinctive moral preoccupation, a concern with maintaining the purity of self and of human relationships within the deteriorating environment of a society of impersonality, abstraction and conformity; the novel formally distilled virtue out of the chaos of a massified and urban world. The emergence of that complex thread of moral responsibility that links Leventhal and Albee in Saul Bellow's *The Victim* or the central characters in Malamud's *The Assistant*; the distillation of the fragile, redemptive aim of Holden Caulfield in *The Catcher in the Rye;* the quest beyond exposure to immediacy and solitude in Updike's *Rabbit, Run*—all of these themes serve to cohere and consolidate the centre of these novels, to turn them into meaningful fables about human action. But increasingly we have seen, with the sixties, the coming of much looser fictions, concerned with surreal and freewheeling invention, carrying large pastiche elements, floating with history or that dream-world of sex and violence that Norman Mailer has said underlies the world of normal politics and day-to-day facts. Instead of the controlling humanism of many of the fifties writers, their concern with redeeming or substantiating individual life, we have seen an art which has followed Mailer's preference for allying his consciousness with the anarchy and disorder of the human psyche, itself working ambiguously either toward destruction or renewal. We have seen, in fact, a marked dehumanization of art, and a drift in two directions: toward reporting the fantastic factuality of the times, as in Truman Capote's "non-fiction" novel *In Cold Blood* or Mailer's history-as-fiction, fiction-as-history structure for *Armies of the Night*; or toward a new surrealism or fantasy, as in Burrough's *The Naked Lunch* or

Mailer's *American Dream*, the box-within-box science-fiction novels of Kurt Vonnegut or Joseph Heller's *Catch-22*.

One consequence of this has been the creation of a much more formless and open-ended kind of art, an art of contingency rather than containment. We might cite as an example the evolving career of Philip Roth, whose earlier fiction possesses a marked formal and moral control, in many respects consciously Jamesian; *Goodbye, Columbus* and *Letting Go* are eminently socio-moral novels, asserting the realistic judgment of the narrator over the material. But his *Portnoy's Complaint* and his more recent story *On the Air* are a flagrant casting aside of the earlier mode; they are looser and slacker in structure, the looseness deriving apparently from the impossibility of shaping the materials morally. *Portnoy's Complaint* is precisely a psychiatric confession, a psycho-social recollection which is given its narrative freedom through the joke that the Jew's subconscious is all on the surface. So Portnoy can articulate and shape his problems, offer them in the form of a kind of freewheeling art, until the last page of the book—where the language ceases in a shrill scream and the psychiatrist comes in with a reassuring realism to offer another order, a therapeutic one, to the material. Nonetheless the material *is* shaped, sectionalized, divided into stories; the novelist is present in a double persona, as the first-person narrative complainer *and* the shaper of his complaint into a socio-Freudian version of modern history. The insecurities of form that are present in the book, the obvious lack of control and shaping, are there in the interest of allowing the stuff of need and desire to well forth in a, so to speak, unedited form. But the design of the story comes from the feeling that past history and society have inhibited some essential flow of sexual identity and community that Portnoy *ought* to have; the book is the flow of the perverted consciousness on the way towards becoming true. The same map of desire is present in Norman Mailer's sex-and-power fantasy, *An American Dream*, in which the ultimate aim is a dominance over consciousness so complete that both the forces of society and extra-terrestrial forces of salvation and damnation are mastered and tapped. In both cases there is a great loosening of traditional forms of moral and aesthetic control in order to let material well forth; in both cases there is also a high sense of artistic endeavour and accomplishment, but focussed on a loose species of creative flow rather than a tight one. And instead of a crisis of form there is a crisis of self; a loss of the moral independence of the humanist centre of fiction.

I have spoken of the fact that the contemporary American writer seems to have been led toward two different kinds of aesthetic attitude. One of these is an emphasis on the autobiographical or documentary aspects of a fiction, and the continuity of fiction and other forms of systematic but ordered discourse like sociology, history or journalism. At one time it was thought that sociology and psychology might between them kill the novel; today we can see an attempt on the part of novelists to subsume not only the enormities of modern history but the accredited structures for describing and assessing them within the novel form. The other attitude is ostensibly the reverse of this: a great interest in what Robert Scholes has called "fabulation," with free and speculative invention, fantasy and surreality.[1] With this has gone an enormous fascination with the "fictiveness" of fiction, an intense internal speculation about the means by which the fictional act is performed, a game-like self-mockery of the sort that invests the work of John Barth, Thomas Pynchon, Vladimir Nabokov or the later Salinger. Both of these tendencies tend to encourage the formal looseness of which I have been speaking; and both emphazise the apparent contingency of fictional craft. Indeed they have yet more in common. For one senses running through the self-consciousness of much modern American writing a profound conviction that all narratives, whether they are those of journalists or sociologists or fictionalists, are of the same order; they are impositions of language on the utter contingency of events and experiences. Hence all narrative is co-existent, is a constructional game; the classical distinction between "truth" and "fiction" becomes aborted; and the novelist becomes the exemplary expert in the means by which all fictions (which is to say *any* linguistic narration) are made. *In Cold Blood* is a non-fiction *novel* because it contains an expert query about the truth of all document; *The Armies of the Night* is history as fiction because it poses the problem of placing any "objective" grid over the detail of the march on the Pentagon. In Kurt Vonnegut's *Slaughterhouse-5* a fantastic and horrifying historical moment, the bombing of Dresden during the war, is surrounded by a vast web of fictions expanding into galactic space and indeed into all of Vonnegut's earlier novels to date. Where in the past the novelist who turned to history or realism was attempting to *objectify* his materials, to give them the guarantee of the real, today the writer functioning as historian is concerned with giving both history itself

---

[1] Robert Scholes, *The Fabulators*, New York, 1969.

and the narratives that record or analyse it the character of a fiction. Enormous powers operate the forces at work in the modern world, and they may encompass or limit man, make him the victim of psychological or cultural conditioning or of some abstract system. They may produce the end of the novel, because the novel finds itself incapable to cope with the enormity of surrounding experience. The novelist, and not only the American novelist, has lost, in the force of history, some of his power to create in fiction a meaningful society or a meaningful, effective and logical human being. But the novelist has sought to deny a complete incompetence in the face of such challenges; and he has found his answers in what looks like a desperate and apocalyptic historicism. His newer metaphors of man are much more determinist metaphors, yet they deny the totality of the Freudian truth or the Marxian truth. Consciousness may be locked indissolubly with history or force, but its resources then become a species of internal struggle in which all the external powers compete for the man within. The novelist may make his compact with time, but not by taking the world of the real, the world of events and process, as real and ultimate. These chaotic inner contests can be viewed as a matter for intense irony, as they are in Saul Bellow's *Mr. Sammler's Planet;* they may be seen half-approvingly as the emergence of a dehumanized machine-man, as in William Burroughs's *The Naked Lunch;* they may involve a perplexing compounded alliance between the inner consciousness and the violence and fantastic nature of the world outside, as in Norman Mailer's *An American Dream.* But the continuity between the fantasies of self and those of the historical process, while it loosens fictional control and produces artistic dehumanization, also leads to a new imaginative infusion into the novel form, which simultaneously invents and yields itself up to a universe of multi-directional plots contesting for dominant expression.

V

From the emergence of the novel in Europe on, the debate about the double propensity of the novel—towards realism, documentary and contingency on the one side; toward poetic making and aesthetic compactness on the other—has persisted. At various stages in its development, one or another emphasis has dominated, and the terms of the debate have changed as systems of causality and explanations of the nature of the universe and of the character of man have altered.

Today we seem to be in an era of redifinition, though within the old terms. We live in a time when all forms of "structure" are matters for scepticism, and when the notion of "reality" as a shared and public concept is very much in doubt. What I have been describing is a set of contemporary terms in that debate; and if we now turn back to Europe again I think we shall find that, with whatever differences of emphasis and degree, we today are enclosed in much the same aesthetic field. The great socio-moral tradition that runs through European fiction did come into question in the early part of this century, and since that period of questioning we have seen a wide variety of tendencies emerging. In England, since the war, there was a marked renewal of documentary realism which has been described in some quarters as a "reaction against experiment," though this is to deny its interesting humanism and also to limit its peculiar achievements and the possibilities it has created for extension in the world of writers like Iris Murdoch and Muriel Spark, where the continuum that links the symbolizing or self-universalizing power of fiction to the contingent world of life has become, within their writing, a matter for much speculation. In France, in the nouveau roman there emerged another version of realistic objectivity, another sacrifice of the person to force, here based on the desire to distil "things" uncluttered by metaphor or pathetic fallacy or by commitment to chronological causality or moral explanation. In Germany, in the works of Günther Grass and others, we have seen a concern to clarify the surrealism of history and its links with the lives of persons—and to redefine it as yet another fictive structure. These tendencies are, I would suggest, very much of a piece, in their different ways, with what is happening in contemporary American writing. Whether the effect of contemporary versions of reality is to produce a kind of miniaturization of the matter of fiction, as it has done in Beckett and some of the French writers, or whether it is to produce a much looser and more undesigned and fantastic kind of fictional structure as it has done in Grass, the species of aesthetic speculation behind all this is not radically at odds. One thing that is undoubtedly happening is a turning of the novel away from a symbolist and formalist separatism, *and* from a humanist moralism, and back to its sources in the things of time and history. But the result of this has not been an unexamined realism; rather, indeed, an intense speculation about what the relation between reality and fictions is. I do not see the differences between the American and European novel as great; but I do, as I have said, *see* differences. They are not differences of radically different aesthetics, but rather of energy and speculative power. The distinctiveness of the American novel perhaps lies finally in the way in which the crises of the present have been resolved with a higher degree of energy and style. It is quite simply in that stylistic energy and verbal inventiveness of which I have already spoken that one senses the peculiarly *American* contribution to that still highly profitable and expansive form, the contemporary novel.

R. HAAS

SOME COMPARATIVE OBSERVATIONS ON THE
SENSE OF THE TRAGIC IN EUROPEAN AND
AMERICAN LITERATURE

I

The title "The Sense of the Tragic in European and American
Literature" is so complex and at the same time so hopelessly comprehensive and general that your speaker, trying to tackle his topic, feels
very much reminded of the first question of the famous Chinese
examination: "Write all you know!" It is quite obvious that our
discussion of the theme can only be selective. There is no "absolute"
and precise description of the so-called "tragic"—even if we include
the most representative definitions from Aristotle to Karl Jaspers.
The word "tragic" itself has broadened and levelled its meaning to a
tremendous scope, ranging from colloquial connotations to philosophical terms and theses. Considerable differences and shades of
meaning have developed in the different languages. In many areas the
word has become a sort of counter, used in a time of terminological
inflation and no longer covered by the gold standard of real meaning.
But our problem is even more complicated. It is virtually impossible
to cover the different traditions in a way which would entitle us to
talk of the "sense of the tragic in European and American literature"—
each of these many literatures being a pluralistic universe in terms
of reflected experience of reality, of philosophy of life, of different
genres, periods, styles. To force such a dynamic multitude of documents of language charged with individual meaning into the rigid
framework of a theme like ours would result in a considerable number
of simplifications, and thus demonstrate the tragic irony which is
necessarily one characteristic of our frustrating experiment—an experiment which can only be successful if we take into account not
only the sociological aspects influencing the different concepts of
"the tragic" in human life but also the environmental factors which
condition them to a very large degree. We might remember Franklin's
interpretation of that very fact in the *Pennsylvania Gazette* of May 9,

1751,[1] where he expresses the colonists' strong disapproval of the British practice of selling English convicts for service in America instead of punishing them in England, justifying it on the grounds that these criminals might change their natures with a change in climate. Franklin rather sarcastically suggested that Americans who objected to the brutal killing of rattlesnakes might send them to England in the hope that the change of climate might render them harmless—an anecdotal hint at the problem that every interpretation of the tragic as well as its representation in literature is influenced by Taine's "race, milieu, moment".

II

May I begin by just sketching a brief outline of method and perspective:

a) As I do not believe in a manageable description of this term that could possibly cover all the variations of the theme in European and American literature, it would be futile to start with a "basic" definition of "the tragic".

b) I shall, however, try to analyze significant material selected from different literatures in a comparative way. From these literary patterns corresponding forms and variants of the so-called "sense of the tragic" may be consequently derived and described, working in terms of multiperspective.

c) The models will be taken from different genres. It would be too one-sided to focus our attention on the classical form in which the so-called "sense of the tragic" has always expressed itself most dramatically: tragedy itself. Popular traditions, fiction and drama will be our main areas of interest.

d) The principle of selection and arrangement will, again, not only be a chronological one, thematic aspects playing an important rôle.

e) As far as the balance of material is concerned, American literature will be given somewhat more attention, European literature having rather background than foreground function.

f) The models selected ought to be seen in the context of sociological, historical and environmental factors without, however, being reduced to mere reflections of socio-economic constellations.

---

[1] Benjamin Franklin—*The Autobiography and Selections from His Other Writings*, ed. H. W. Schneider, New York, 1952, Note 28, p. 214 f. (*The American Heritage Series*[2]).

g) Differences will be worked out as carefully as possible, but not simplified to plain patterns of contrasting generalizations.

h) Occasionally it might be necessary to refer to "great" traditional interpretations (or negations) of the so-called "tragic", providing a broader horizon in terms of the simultaneous presence of important literary traditions in European and American culture.

i) Contacts between Europe and the United States and mutual influences in the field of literary representations of the "tragic" deserve our special attention. They play an important rôle in the area of traditional and literary ballads, in the phase of O'Neill's fascination by European writers, and on the contemporary European stage. The influence of modern American fiction on the changing concept of the "tragic" in some European countries must also be taken into consideration.

k) At the same time, we ought to be aware of the fact that there may be common interpretations of the tragic on both sides of the Atlantic due to archetypal layers in human experience and psychology.

l) I shall, according to these points and perspectives, organize my lecture as follows:

1. I shall begin with a few general remarks, keeping them within the limits of an introductory description rather than of a definition, including some remarks on the problems of variants in the ballad tradition.
2. In a second part, we shall focus our attention on some aspects of the novel.
3. A third approach will be characterized by a comparative analysis of the sense of the tragic in European and American drama.
4. In a final summary I try to offer a number of theses.

III

Starting with some initial remarks, I refer to one of the most interesting European thinkers in the field, Miguel de Unamuno, who, in *The Tragic Sense of Life*[1] carefully avoids to simplify his subject by limiting it to Aeschylus, Sophocles, Euripides and Shakespeare, rather amplifying it by calling this "tragic sense" a complex of attitudes, ideas and feeling. Avoiding the slightly too pathetic term "tragic vision", I should like to agree with Unamuno's broader description and apply

---

[1] Cf. the English translation by J. E. C. Flinch, London, 1921.

it to our topic. Sophisticated and interesting as it may sound, Walpole's general and at the same time too polarized remark to Horace Mann on December 31, 1769,—on the other hand—would not carry us very far although it may be worth quoting: "I have often said and oftener think that this world is a comedy to those who think, a tragedy to those who feel—a solution of why Democritus laughed and Heraclitus wept."[1] Three significant attitudes show in this statement: the somewhat simplifying differentiation between comedy and tragedy, the relation of the sense of the comic to ratiocination and of the sense of the tragic to emotion, and—last not least—the recurring illustration of both philosophies by Greek tradition. Looking more closely into the American situation, however, we get a much more differentiated and complex picture. It seems possible to draw at least a few lines:

a) When American literature came to life and even of age, the Greek tradition of the tragic which had been so important for the development of European drama was no longer as powerful as in the 16th and 17th centuries. American literature has never participated in the close attachment to the Greek heritage. Emerson, of course, was familiar with it; Thoreau read and admired its texts and authors. But between the "American Renaissance" around 1850 and the renewed interest in the Greeks in the 20th century—when Jig Cook in Provincetown cultivated a neo-Greek feeling, O'Neill used Greek themes and motifs, Pound studied Greek literature thoroughly, Eliot revived it in his later plays, Lee Masters was inspired by Greek poetry when writing the *Spoon River Anthology* and Updike applied Greek mythology to his *Centaur*—there is what one might call a gap in the reception of Greek concepts of the tragic, and even Baker in his *Workshop 47* never specialized in this area.

b) The Puritan tradition in North America was not only hostile to the theatre and—to a certain extent—to literature as a whole. It also proved to be essentially non-tragic .The key-word "providence" excludes the fatal fall of man into the abyss of negation and annihilation. Whenever man falls, he cannot fall out of the hands of God. The sense of the tragic as the Greeks developed it does not know grace. The position of man in tragedy has always been conditioned by religion, but not by its Christian form. Aeschylos talks of the "dike" of Zeus and of the justice of the Gods. Sophocles sees man as a guilt-

---

[1] Quoted from Richard B. Sewall's very instructive *The Vision of Tragedy*, New Haven, 1959, p. 150.

less victim in a tragedy of errors. Euripides interprets man's loneliness and sympathizes with him as a plaything of "tyche". Cotton Mather and Wigglesworth knew the horror of not being a member of the "massa selecta" and belonging—from the very beginning of creation— to the "massa damnata". But they accepted this fate not as blind tragedy but as a part of a "wonderworking" providence in terms of the "Magnalia Christi Americana" in a teleological, divine process of salvation and damnation which made *The Day of Doom*—terrible as Wigglesworth described it in 1662—not the fifth act of a cosmic tragedy but the dramatic climax of a *Divina Commedia*. A man like Bryant admires providence even in the flight of a homing waterfowl.

c) Enlightenment—again untragic in its basic attitude—has always been a strong influence in America. "The pursuit of happiness"—as Franklin put it—does not favour a tragic interpretation of life. Pope's "whatever is is right" takes up the basic idea of Leibniz' *Theodicée*, that brilliant justification of the world and its creator—whoever he may be. It is significant that James Nelson Barker called his dramatic treatment of the Salem witch trials—1826—*The Tragedy of Superstition*. And Franklin's famous

> "Early to bed and early to rise
> Makes a man healthy, wealthy and wise"

stands for a whole and basically untragic philosophy of life, which, by the way, James Thurber has ironized in his brilliant fable of the chipmunk and the shrike, turning it into

> "Early to rise and early to bed
> makes a man healthy, wealthy and dead."

d) More than German philosophy and Russian mysticism, American philosophy and literature have always been "pragmatic" and rather limited in their metaphysical aspirations. The dynamic reality of American life proved a permanent challenge to man; action was more important than reflection. The atmosphere of the frontier did not provide—at least not on the surface—a climate for tragedy.

e) Pragmatism, then, as developed by Peirce, William James and Dewey more or less eliminates the tragic aspects of life by its concept of "meliorism" which implies the possibility of endlessly improving the state of society and the world. Pragmatism and optimism form at least one significant pattern in American intellectual history.

f) Commercialized American theatre has always preferred comedy to tragedy. If Aristotle[1] saw tragedy in terms of serious plot, high social standing of protagonists, elevated level of speech as a still ritualized play forcing its audience to identification with the suffering heroes or victims, creating cathartic consequences by evoking fear and pity, the "sawdust realism"—as O'Neill called the "Monte Christo" effects of his father's performances—of Broadway looked to different structures and results. Calvin Coolidge's very conscious coinage "The business of America is business" still covers a broad area of literary commercialism in the United States. In *The Last Puritan*, Santayana has his Oliver Alden, returning from Europe, say: "What a relief to be innocently, foolishly, perpetually busy."[2] Sociology and history account for one of the basic differences between America and European countries in the field of the dramatic representation of the tragic. The feudal residences provided a number of cultural and theatrical centres on the old continent where the great traditions of tragedy and new experiments could be realized in a sort of non-commercial way: London and the Globe Theatre, Paris, Weimar, Mannheim, Munich, Dresden, Hamburg, Berlin, St. Petersburg, Stockholm—where most of the late O'Neill plays were first performed—,Rome and Milan, to mention only a few European names. The development of the sense of the tragic in American literature—compared to Europe—has been conditioned if not handicapped by commercialization and concentration.

g) Europe does not share the American experience of the frontier. The exploration and opening of Siberia by the Stroganows in Russia and the following process of settlement and civilization did not create similar problems and themes in literature as they became obvious in America. The sense of the tragic, as reflected in American writing, has obviously been conditioned by the unique frontier experience.

h) Throughout long periods America appeared to the immigrants—but also to her inhabitants—as a land of utopian quality. The permanent tension between "the American dream" and its "realization" as a sort of pragmatic verification and, at the same time, its inevitable reduction to a problematic materialization creates a field of literary

---

[1] Cf. *poet.* 6, 1449 b 24-28.

[2] P. 399. See also Santayana's interesting remark in *Character and Opinion in the United States*, New York, 1920, p. 168: "To be an American is of itself almost a moral condition."

reflection in which we also find typical variables of the sense of the tragic.

i) In the area of the development of tragic concepts, the rôle of subcultures should not be neglected: the importance of the Irish influx for the popular culture of melodramatic broadsides, the function of the Jewish group in the field of the novel, the position of the black writers in modern American literature. In no European culture do we find a similarly dynamic mixture of different origins, trends, forms and attitudes.

k) More than in Europe, the big city—and now-a-days "megalopolis"—has developed as a thematic field of tragic aspects in American literature. At the same time, the elemental forces of the country have challenged its writers again and again to interpret them as powerful factors in a tragic constellation. Nobody who likes his Hawthorne will forget the gloomy forests of New England which are so different from Cooper's primeval woods. It might be relevant to look for similar aspects in European literature.

l) Let me add one more perspective. Again and again, Americans have turned or re-turned to Europe. The "tragic" undertones of this European experience and the impact of the "re-entrance" problem on American writers will also be taken into account.

IV

Let me now try to analyze a first layer of literature which provides some interesting material for our discussion. How can we discern and describe elements of the tragic in the basic stratum of popular balladry?

Comparing the about 65 living American versions of Child's 305 traditional ballads[1] with their English and Scottish, i.e. European origins, and trying to discover significant differences in the interpretation of "the tragic", one feels that in America a number of variants tend to become less "tragic". By "tragic" I mean the radical confrontation with evil, the "hopeless hope" of man trying to reverse elemental processes, the deadly frustration of young lovers by circumstances, the vulcanic power of human emotions destroying innocence, the

---

[1] I owe excellent information and a number of aspects to G. Malcolm Laws, Jr., "Stories Told in Song: The Ballads of America", in: *American Folklore*, ed. by Tristram Coffin, III, Voice of America Forum Lectures, 1968, pp. 93-103.

dramatic representation of what Lear calls "the mystery of things" without explaining or euphemizing it or turning plot and fate into a didactic pattern. In many cases the social level changes. The "Two Sisters" are no longer princesses. Lord Randall becomes Johnny Randall. The sadness of domestic tragedy appears in less heroic and more sentimental colours. The magic element tends to fade out of the picture. Quantity replaces intensity and polarization: the two sisters multiply to four in an American variant. Local colour comes in: the lover's gift is no longer precious jewelry but a beaver hat. The jealous girl does not kill her more beautiful younger sister herself; it is the miller who pushes her into the water, thus giving the plot an additional melodramatic and at the same time trivial touch. But these examples rather belong to a pseudo-tragic layer. *The Wife of Usher's Well*, however, deals with the tragic theme of a mother sending her three sons to the sea and losing them all, trying to conjure them back to life. They return from paradise and stay one night. Then, in spite of their mother's loving spell—she is a "carline wife"—they have to go back to the dead. The short piece is great literature, reminding one immediately of Synge's *Riders to the Sea* and of a number of genuine "revenant" ballads. In an American version the tragic constellation is reduced to a more sentimental and didactic story. The boys are sent to school "to learn the grammaree"; they die of an epidemic; they return, after the night at home, to Christ, their saviour, telling their mother not to indulge in sadness. Even in an American translation of Bürger's *Lenore* the unhappy ending is bowdlerized to a didactic and harmonizing finale: Lenore is taught not to curse God again, but this time she gets away with it. The ghostly ride was just a dream.

On the broadside level, we meet a number of genuinely American interpretations of "the tragic". In the mirror of these popular forms, occupational catastrophes appear as occupational tragedies. The collective suffering and death of the trapped miners in *The Avondale Disaster* in 1869 is "tragic" in a general and vague way. A lumberman, being killed while breaking a log jam, becomes a "tragic" hero, and a cowboy's fate, dying in a stampede, is "tragic". A recurring American theme crystallizes in balladry when the conflict between man and machine becomes more and more symptomatic. The ballad of *John Henry* offers a "tragic" model in miniature: the powerful and good John Henry working against the steam drill, winning the contest, losing his life, preserving his integrity. Similar themes spring up in fiction and drama: in Norris' *The Octopus*, in Dos Passos' machine imagery in *Three Soldiers*, in Sinclair's *The Jungle*, in O' Neill's *The Hairy Ape*.

Let me round up this aspect by pointing to the Michael Kohlhaas syndrome and its American variants. In Kleist's novella, Kohlhaas turns into a criminal because justice was denied to him and he took it with his own hands. The frontier outlaw who believes in his right and restores order by violence because the legal institutions are unable to do so appears as a "tragic" popular hero, even if his name is Billy the Kid. In a movie like *Chisum* the tension between spontaneous jurisdiction at gun point and institutional order by law and the slow process of civilization appears on a higher and at the same time broader level. The sense of the tragic, implied in this constellation, has, however, in most cases been blurred by moralizing interpretations of this significant frontier topic which, in its local colour, is genuinely American as we realize when we read Crane's *The Blue Hotel* or *The Bride Comes to Yellow Sky*.

V

Leslie Fiedler calls the novel a "non-tragic" form[1] and characterizes the situation of the American novelist as follows: "...indeed, a chief technical problem for American novelists has been the adaptation of non-tragic forms to tragic ends."[2] It would probably take a book even more voluminous than *Moby Dick* or Fiedler's *Love and Death in the American Novel* to discuss the problem of the sense of the tragic in European and American fiction in a substantial way. I limit this part of my lecture to five aspects which I try to treat on a comparative basis, starting from the fact that the novel is the most powerful, comprehensive and adequate medium of literary expression in America— in a country which lacks the archetypal concepts of epic tragedy as they appear in the conflict of kinship and love, loyalty and revenge in the German *Nibelungenlied*, in the gloomy end of *Beowulf* who dies forsaken by his friends, and in the perishing of the hero in the *Chanson de Roland*.

I shall first speak of the tragic interpretation of elemental forces in European and American fiction. In a second aspect, I differentiate between "eros" and "thanatos" novels in Europe and the United

---

[1] In *Love and Death in the American Novel*, New York, 1960, 1966 (new, revised edition), Laurel Edition, p. 8.
[2] *Ibid.*

States. Tragic aspects of the frontier problem shall form a third point, while in a fourth step I compare tragic undertones in American and European city novels. The European experience as mirrored in American fiction provides one more point of view.

a) Looking for some tragic aspects of the elemental forces in human life as represented in European and American prose, Thoreau's *Walden*, of course, impresses us as a non-tragical interpretation of the natural beauty and solitude of the primeval woods—1854—while Vladimir Korolenko in his *Les sumit—The Murmuring Forest*—1886— uses the great forests of Bjelo Russia as a dramatic background for human guilt and punishment. In Alexis Kiwi's *The Seven Brothers*, the endless forests of Finland are taken as a non-tragic, epic element in the saga of the seven brothers. In Stifter's *Der Hochwald*—1841—nature appears as a questionable sanctuary for suffering man; after the catastrophe, the protagonists withdraw to a lonely life in the Bohemian woods, which provide a most perfect backdrop for the sombre interpretation of human existence as Stifter always gave it. Thomas Hardy, of course, must be mentioned. In *The Return of the Native*, Egdon Heath turns into a stage where—always under the aspects of Greek tragedy—the different fates of human beings are played out. The dying of the mother on her endless way back through Egdon Heath is certainly tragic, and the representation of a gloomy landscape— reminding one of Munch's art—in terms of contours and colours is quite fascinating. As far as I can see, Jean Giono in France, Ernst Jünger in Germany, Carlo Levi in Italy have succeeded in integrating nature to a similar extent into a concept of the world changing in its tragic outlook. In American fiction, Hawthorne seems to see the primeval forests mainly as areas of darkness and evil. Youg Goodman Brown comes back from the nocturnal adventure in the forests as a different man. We ought, however, to take into account Hawthorne's "ambiguity" whenever we try to define his attitude in this field. Cooper, of course, provides a more idyllic interpretation of the great American forests. The woods as protection and shelter even re-appear in a very convincing representation in Arnold Zweig's *Der Streit um den Sergeanten Grischa*, one of the most significant German novels on World War I. For Melville, evil as an elemental and still anonymous force is represented in the huge whiteness of Moby Dick. Ahab eventually fails to solve "the mystery of things". The tragic irony in his fate becomes obvious when he hits the whale and—forever connected with his metaphysical quarry— is drawn into the abyss of a tragic world which we can never fully explain. Melville's novel—in its tragic concept of the enigma of creation and in its rhapsodic power of covering the elemental infinity of the prairies of the ocean—appears to me as one of the most genuine American documents in the field, unsurpassed by any European novel. Frank Norris moves along the boundary of the melodramatic when McTeague, chained to the enemy he killed, dies in the alkali desert. To him, to Dreiser and to Crane— we remember the initiation into the basic cruelty of life Henry Fleming experiences in the heart of the woods—the elemental forces are unfeeling powers of cruelty hostile to man. There is also a definitely tragic concept in Hemingway's representation of nature in *The Old Man and the Sea*. As Santiago, man will never be able to land his prey safely in the harbour. The first drop of blood alarms the sharks, drawing them up from the depths of the sea. The shark imagery as an emblematic representation of evil becomes obvious in Crane's *The Open Boat*, O'Neill's early one act play *Thirst*, Hemingway's *For Whom the Bell Tolls* where the German bombers are identified with sharks in the blue ocean of the Spanish sky. In Mailer's *The Naked and the Dead* Mount Anaka stands for the anonymous natural forces which—at the moment when the hornets and bees attack the platoon—turn all human aspirations and passions and the whole hierarchic military system into a grotesque and chaotic farce. It seems to me that the function of nature in the representation of the tragic has been more developed and given more significance in American than in European fiction—a fact certainly also due to the environmental power of unbroken and endless American nature.

b) As in Europe, many American novelists end their stories with the death of the hero. All in all they write more "thanatos" than "eros" novels. In *War and Peace* life, in the long run, conquers death. Natascha and Marie become happy mothers. Thus, in "Woina *y* Mir", the little word "and" stands for the eternal rhythm of life, even in terms of "seasons" in human and personal history. "Eros"—in this broader sense—carries the day in this basically non-tragic novel. But in Hemingway's *A Farewell to Arms* Catherine dies in childbirth, "eros" bringing in "thanatos": tragic irony! Maria and Robert anticipate the process of dying in "la petite mort" of their love. Cantwell, in *Across the River and Into the Trees*, finds no re-birth in "Renata", but his own "death in Venice". Hemingway is a writer of "thanatos" novels, fascinated by a tragic pattern in life which permits man only to die in a sort of ritualized and heroic Promethean attitude. In Hemingway and other American writers, including Melville and, among the moderns, Bowles, the death theme has been developed in a broader and stronger way than in European fiction, even if we admit that in Julien Sorel's death in *Le rouge et le noir* the "thanatos" element shows rather strongly, and that in Mann's *Death in Venice* as well as in L.P. Hartley's brilliant short story *Per far l'amore* "eros", similarly as in *A Farewell to Arms*, evokes "thanatos" in the old Italian city of death. The close interrelation between both phenomena accounts for one of the most interesting aspects of the tragic in Europe and America, before Freud and even in *The Scarlet Letter*.

c) In Cooper—and in *The Prairie* above all—we discover another tragic concept genuinely American: Natty Bumppo dies, looking to the West, eventually a victim of the antagonism between the advancing regulations of law and order of Eastern civilization and the spontaneity of the frontiersmen without which this civilization would not have been possible. McTeague disintegrates under the shock that his "frontier licence" is no longer valid; regulation versus experiment and open frontier again! The tragic conflict between the necessary progress of civilization and the indispensible and re-vitalizing power of the elemental forces of a frontier America has found its most striking image in Ike McCaslin's hunt for Big Ben.

d) Comparing Dos Passos and Dreiser with Döblin and his representation of the big city in *Berlin Alexanderplatz*, we might describe another constellation of "tragic" elements in Dreiser's Chicago novels. His social Darwinism is more pseudo-scientific than tragic; still, he sees man as a set of chemisms whose free will is pretty limited. In *An American Tragedy* Esta, when introduced by a first description, responds to "those ... chemisms upon which all the morality or unmorality of the world is based." (p. 33, Chapter 3). The city appears as a magnetic field into which man is drawn for better or worse—a tragic constellation in spite of the idea—which Dreiser accepted—of the survival of the fittest. Döblin is more complex. He also shows Franz Biberkopf as a victim of evil, but in a deeper sense, adding ironic undertones to his interpretation of the sufferings of an ex-convict who can never readjust to society. In *Last Exit to Brooklyn* Selby paints an even gloomier picture of suffering in the big metropolis. His figures are victims of their eugenic set and the environmental forces surrounding them. They suffer without being guilty, and in the last "gothic" and horrible scene, the anti-hero of the novel appears as crucified. In *The Burthen of Niniveh,* Dos Passos describes the vision of megalopolis destroyed in a moment on the doomsday of modern civilization—certainly an apocalyptic if not tragic view of the big city in our modern time, a big city which, in the "valley-of-ashes" passage in Fitzgerald's *The Great Gatsby,* is depicted as a "waste city", reminding the reader of Eliot's *Waste Land.*

e) In a number of American novels and stories dealing with the crucial moment of Americans "returning" to Europe the element of tragedy dominates again. In Malamud's *The Lady of the Lake* we have the tragic story of a Jew who wants to forget his Jewish complex in Europe and by this very attitude loses the girl of his life, who is Jewish and wants to marry a Jew. *The Roman Spring of Mrs. Stone* is as tragic as Mann's *Die Betrogene—The Black Swan.* In both stories, the two cultures meet under the auspices of a late, frustrated love: Williams shows us the catastrophe of an ageing American woman in Rome, Mann the ironic and grotesque tragedy of an elderly European lady, falling in love with a young American.

VI

After this brief discussion of some aspects of the novel in the two areas, let me now turn to drama. Here America is indeed younger than Europe. The influence of French traditions has always been limited. Schiller's concept of tragedy—great and terrible fate leading man to the heights of intelligible freedom in the very moment of his destruction—never became popular, as Coleridge's *Wallenstein* translation did never cut much ice in England either–Scandinavian determinism, however, proved to be much more significant. From Strindberg O'Neill took that phantastic constellation of festive celebration and catastrophe, as we find it in *Fröken Julie.* In *Abortion* he works with similar effects. Ibsen fascinated him by his representation of the mortgage of personal biography, by his idea of the life-lie and by his concept that writing poems and dramas is nothing but bringing one's own and one's family's past before the jury of poetry: *Long Day's Journey Into Night!* Nietzsche's theory of tragedy, but mainly his early aphoristic philosophy in *Thus Spoke Zarathustra* impressed him for life. Let me point to a few aspects which stand out in O'Neill's concept of "tragedy": a pathetic agnosticism in a cruel world full of mysteries, the image of the poet as a great sufferer, the idea that God is dead, life cruel and man doomed to suffering. In a number of plays O'Neill uses mythology to underline this concept. Harry Hope's Bar becomes a *Nobiskrug* in the limbo between life and death, Josie Hogan turns into a "terra mater" who can heal our wounds for a night but never cure the world's disease: "A virgin who bears a dead child in the night, and the dawn finds her still a virgin." In the "stammering eloquence of us fog-people" O'Neill tells of a world in which we are all doomed to "hopeless hope", an oxymoron reminding us of baroque tragedies. In *Mourning Becomes Electra* he "translates" the Greek tradition into a New England atmosphere. The Eumenides are replaced by the chromosomes; archaic emotions turn into modern neuroses. There is no escape: Orin and Lavinia return from the happy island only to die and to withdraw into the gloomy temple of guilt, the house of the Mannons. To O'Neill—whose sense of the tragic had always been conditioned by his trying to grasp the essence of the relation man-god—"our lives are merely strange dark interludes in the electrical display of God the Father". In his Dion Anthony he combines the elements of Dionysos and Apollo as Nietzsche saw them. The tragedy of American history as a self-destruction of the American dream he called significantly—and that is the collective title of his great dramatic fragment and frustration—*A Tale of Possessors Self-Dispossessed*.

Certainly Lüdeke's appreciation of O'Neill "... in der Vollständigkeit seines dramatischen Erlebens...liegt wohl der Schlüssel seines überwältigenden Zaubers, der ihn siegreich über alle nörgelnde Kritik, über alle Hinweise auf seine unleugbaren Schwächen, über alle Hemmungen eines vom Drama übersättigten Zeitalters zu einem der großen Bühnendichter englischer Zunge, zum größten Tragiker seit den Tagen Shakespeares gemacht hat"[1] comes closer to his significance for our theme than the rather simplifying statement in an essay of the *Times Literary Supplement* in which O'Neill is compared with Aeschylus and Shakespeare: "The most obvious difference between Aeschylus, Shakespeare and Mr. O'Neill is that the two former loved mankind, but the last feels only contemptuous pity for it... There is no sign of nobility in the characters who populate his plays. Not one of them has been made in the image of God. All of them bear the mark of the beast ..." and "All his plays are contemptuous of people and denunciatory of human existence; a commination service without a hymn ..."[2] What he kept trying to do throughout his

---

[1] Henry Lüdeke, *Geschichte der amerikanischen Literatur*[2], Bern/München 1963, p. 477.
[2] Counsels of Despair, 10 April, 1948.

career was to use and assimilate European forms and influences to find a medium for what he would have called the dramatic expression of some typically American aspects of the "tragic"—including, of course, his "universal" theme of "Man and God".

Turning from O'Neill to Tennessee Williams, we recognize at least one aspect of his "sense of the tragic" in his preface to *Cat on a Hot Tin Roof* where he calls poetry and his dramatic art as "personal lyricism" the "... outcry of prisoner to prisoner from the cell in solitary where each is confined for the duration of his life." This sounds very much like a negative version of Max Stirner's "solipsism" in *Ego and His Own—Der Einzige und sein Eigentum*—a book that influenced O'Neill very deeply in his formative period. Using "theatricality" as his most developed medium, he tries to "dramatize" American life beneath the social middle-class level as a particularly dynamic stratum not only of human vitality but of human suffering. *Camino Real*, a modern pageant organized in "blocks" and representing the simultaneous existence of literary traditions, impresses us again as a "waste land" where "the spring of humanity has gone dry". But that "tragic" end-of-the-line situation—dominated by Gutman, claustrophobia and nightmarish visions—is not the author's last word. For Kilroy— who represents almost another "American myth"—the "inferno" turns into a "purgatorio". From his golden heart and vicarious suffering springs salvation: "The violets in the mountains have broken the rocks." Accompanied by Don Quixote he breaks out of Camino Real and enters the land of poetic freedom and new adventures, thus overcoming the lethargy of modern American life by the old "European" tradition of the quest and human peregrination. Aware of the "tragic" transitoriness of life and art, Williams wants "to snatch the eternal out of the desperately fleeting" (preface to *The Rose Tattoo*), even by translating Ibsen's symbolism (*The Wild Duck* etc.) to the level of erotic and sexual allusions and connotations.

While an author like Wilder appears as a more or less "non-tragic" playwright—we might recall the famous Joyce passage in *Our Town* which implies again that we are all safely "programmed" in the mind of God—Arthur Miller uses the "landscape of the mind" as scenery for the dramatization of tragic aspects of American life. Miller's world is a world "after the fall", a world in which Willy Loman loses his identity, a victim of his own "unrelatedness" in a competitive society. Having failed to "realize" the opportunities of the "American dream", he also fails to recognize its limitations and to see behind the façade of his own life-lies. Still, Miller believes in the creative commitment of the playwright, in a "prophetic" theatre which also—in Quentin in *After the Fall*—demonstrates man's responsibility not only for his individual life but for humanity. As a "social dramatist", Miller still believes in the development of a freer society, a world of "decontrol", acting out in his plays the tension between the "death-dealing" and "life-giving" drives in man and interpreting his own rôle as a spokesman of the human condition in terms of a diagnostic but not utterly pessimistic attitude.

Albee—again influenced by European traditions and modern writers, including Pinter—varies the "sense of the tragic" in a number of ways. The "American dream" and its negation prove to be a recurring constellation in his non-affirmative plays. Not only in *The American Dream* proper but also in *Who's Afraid of Virginia Woolf?* the "killing" of the son by his parents turns into a vicarious metaphor for the death of an illusion which has become a collective life-lie in the development of American self-interpretation. In *A Delicate Balance* Albee characterizes the tragic "boundary situation" of the individual, significant groups and mankind by dramatizing at least in seven variations the subtle equilibrium of "reality" and "annihilation" so easily disturbed. He shows man as a creature whose mind can always lose its "delicate balance" and turn into madness. He analyses the frail harmony of marriage. He develops the theme of the complex and always strained relation between parents and children. He exposes the true character of the American cult of sociability, neighbourhood and friendship. He reveals the morbid rhythm of alcoholic "lucidity" and euphoria and escape from depression in the figure of Claire. He differentiates between clichés and truth in the stratified area of human communication. Last not least, he indicates that the "tragic" element of basic insecurity in modern life and our permanent need of evasive and euphemistic attitudes are deeply rooted in the "delicate equilibrium" of the two atomic powers: every day we pay for the balance of terror with the terror of balance. Two more aspects of the "sense of the tragic" are evident in Albee's latest play, *Box-Mao-Box*. Here he unfolds the "Lear theme" of parents rejected by their children on two social levels, and he points to the "emptiness" of contemporary life and culture in the variations of the "box" image.

VII

Summing up, we might condense our selected observations into a number of theses:

1. The "sense of the tragic" in American literature cannot be reduced to a formula; it remains pluralistic in spite of its showing a number of typical American variables as described in this lecture.

2. After 1945, the representation of the "sense of the tragic" seems to me to be somewhat more genuine and vigorous in the American models I have tried to compare to some selected European patterns.

3. The strongest and most comprehensive stratum of significant aspects of "the tragic" in American literature I find in American fiction and not in American drama.

4. At least one area of "popular culture", however, also provides a considerable amount of material in ballads, broadsides, comics, movies, dime novels and television scripts a closer analysis of which would yield additional and interesting results.

5. In modern American plays, European influence, "filtered" through the medium of American experience, returns to Europe in a cyclic process, re-influencing and even reshaping European dramatizations of the "sense of the tragic". One of these "cyclic effects" might be described by the keywords Stirner—Nietzsche—Strindberg—Ibsen—O'Neill and the reception of O'Neill's posthumous plays on European stages.

6. We ought to add that in Faulkner's Nobel Prize acceptance speech we hear an additional American undertone referring to man's position in this world of ours. Faulkner verbalizes a new "humanism" in his pessimistic but not tragic image of man and his power "to prevail" even after an atomic war.

7. What we could offer, of course, was just a fragmentary contribution to a theme which will always remain infinite and unfinished, whether we limit it to *An American Tragedy*, see it as a *Strange Interlude*, take it just as part of the *Comédie humaine* or accept it as one aspect of the *Divina Commedia*.

TONY TANNER

NOTES FOR A COMPARISON BETWEEN
AMERICAN AND EUROPEAN ROMANTICISM*

The subject is clearly too vast to admit of definitive treatment in this space, and the essay should accordingly be regarded as no more than a tentative exploration of the topic. As my method relies extensively on allusions and short quotations it seemed undesirable to over-burden this printed version of my paper read to the conference of the EAAS at Rome, September 1967, with footnotes locating precisely the source of every such reference. I have instead indicated in the text wherever possible the title of the work cited, and it may be helpful to add here that the essays of Emerson on which I have mainly drawn are these: "Nature" (1836), "The Transcendentalist" (1843), and "The Poet' (1844).

I

Animals have often provided Romantic writers with important images. Blake's tiger and Melville's whale are both used to focus on the awesome and ambiguous energies at the heart of creation. Insects, too, have often been invoked for the purposes of emulation or identification. Wordsworth gathers visual pleasures "like a bee among the flowers"; Emerson admires the "Humble-Bee" in his "sunny solitudes":

> Sailor of the atmosphere;
> Swimmer through the waves of air;
> Voyager of light and noon;

Emily Dickinson cries "Oh, for a bee's experience/Of clovers and of noon"; Rilke writes "We are the bees of the Invisible. Nous butinons éperdument le miel du Visible pour l'accumuler dans la grande

---

* First published in the Journal of American Studies, vol. 2 no. 1 (April 1968). Reprinted by permission of the Editors of the Journal and of the Cambridge University Press.

ruche d'or de l'invisible."[1] It is an attractive and understandable image for any Romantic writer who seeks to assimilate the pollen of perception in order to transmute it into the honey of his art. But more unusual perhaps is the attraction which the spider has held for American writers from Jonathan Edwards to Robert Lowell. Thus Edwards starts one of his earliest pieces of writing, "Of Insects": "Of all Insects no one is more wonderfull than the Spider especially with Respect to their sagacity and admirable way of working." Edwards was particularly struck to see spiders apparently "swimming in the air" (like Emerson's bee), and he describes how he watched and experimented to see how they managed to sustain themselves in space. The secret, the marvel, was the way they "put out a web at their tails" which was so light that the wind took it, and held up the spider at the same time; then

> If the further End Of it happens to catch by a tree or anything, why there's a web for him to Go over upon and the Spider immediately perceives it and feels when it touches, much after the same manner as the soul in the brain immediately Perceives when any of those little nervous strings that Proceed from it are in the Least Jarrd by External things.

Pausing to notice how the Puritan imagination effortlessly makes the external fact emblematic of an inner process, I want to juxtapose Whitman's poem on "A Noiseless Patient Spider" where the spider's emblematic significance is fully developed:

> A Noiseless patient spider,
> I mark'd where on a little promontory it stood isolated,
> Mark'd how to explore the vacant vast surrounding,
> It launched forth filament, filament, filament, out of itself,
> Ever unreeling them, ever tirelessly speeding them.
>
> And you O my soul where you stand,
> Surrounded, detached, in measureless oceans of space,
> Ceaselessly musing, venturing, throwing, seeking the spheres to connect them,
> Till the bridge you will need be form'd, till the ductile anchor hold,
> Till the gossamer thread you fling catch somewhere, O my soul.

We could scarcely hope to find a better image of the American Romantic writer, which is almost to say the American writer, than this. Isolated and secreting filament, filament, filament (think of Whitman's

---

[1] As quoted and translated by Erich Heller in *The Artist's Journey into the Interior*, London, 1966, p. 153.

constantly renewed stream of notations and enumerations) to explore, to relate to, and to fill "the vacant vast surrounding". America is the "measureless oceans of space"; the web is the private creation of the writer, constructed with a view of attaching himself somehow to reality, a world of his own making in which he can live on his own terms, assimilating and transforming what the outside world brings his way. Emily Dickinson, too, obviously saw something of her own poetic activity in the movements of the spider, as in the famous poem which starts:

> A spider sewed at night
> Without a light
> Upon an arc of white.

And in other poems, for example, "The spider...—dancing softly to Himself/His Coil of Pearl—unwinds." She elsewhere calls the spider an artist of "surpassing merit" whose tapestries, wrought in an hour, are "Continents of Light"; but also very ephemeral. "He plies from Nought to Nought/In insubstantial Trade." A not dissimilar image occurs to Henry Adams in the crucial chapter in his *Education* on "A Dynamic Theory of History":

> For convenience as an image, the theory may liken man to a spider in its web, watching for chance prey. Forces of nature dance like flies before the new, and the spider pounces on them when it can... The spider-mind acquires a faculty of memory, and, with it, a singular skill of analysis and synthesis, taking apart and putting together in different relations the meshes of its trap.

And in a comparably important statement in Henry James's essay "The Art of Fiction" the work of the spider receives perhaps its finest transformation:

> Experience is never limited, and it is never complete; it is an immense sensibility, a kind of huge spider-web of the finest silken threads suspended in the chamber of consciousness, and catching every air-borne particle in its tissue. It is the very atmosphere of the mind; and when the mind is imaginative...it takes to itself the faintest hints of life, it converts the very pulses of the air into revelations.

The emblem has become a metaphor; the web has been internalized and experience has become the atmosphere of the mind.

Now it is a truism that one of the recurrent features of Romantic art is the elevation of inner activity over external reality. Hegel's is

only the most sweeping of many such generalizations, when he says
in the Introduction to the *Philosophy of Art:*

> In brief, the essence of Romantic art lies in the artistic object's being
> free, concrete, and the spiritual idea in its very essence—all this revealed
> to the inner rather than to the outer eye...This inner world is the con-
> tent of Romantic art; Romantic art must seek its embodiment in
> precisely such an inner life or some reflection of it. Thus the inner life
> shall triumph over the outer world...

But since for Hegel Romantic art included nearly everything since
Classical art, this panoramic view of the internalization or subjectiviza-
tion of reality (examined brilliantly and at length by Erich Heller in
The Artist's Journey into the Interior) will not help us very much in an
attempt to suggest some of the differences between American and
European Romanticism. This analogy between the American writer
and the spider may at least provide a specific point of departure.

II

One of the formative experiences of all those early American
writers was of a sense of space, of vast unpeopled solitudes such as no
European Romantic could have imagined. As the hero of Chateaubriand's *René* says to his American auditors: "Europeans constantly
in a turmoil are forced to build their own solitudes." The reverse
was true for the American Romantic. Solitude was all but imposed
on him. Nothing seemed easier for him than to take a few steps to
find himself confronting and caught up in those measureless oceans
of space where Whitman found his soul both surrounded and detached. This gravitation towards empty space is a constant in American
literature, even if it appears only in glimpses, as for instance when
the narrator of *The Sacred Fount* turns away from the crowded house
of Newmarch and staring up at the sky finds the night air "a sudden
corrective to the grossness of our lustres and the thickness of our
medium"; or when the narrator of *The Last Tycoon* says "It's startling
to you sometimes—just air, unobstructed, uncomplicated air." Charles
Olson is justified in starting his book on Melville (*Call me Ishmael*)
with the emphatic announcement: "I take SPACE to be the central
fact to man born in America, from Folsom cave to now. I spell it large
because it comes large here. Large, and without mercy." But like
those spiders who came under Jonathan Edwards's formidable scrutiny, the American artist, once he found himself at sea in space, had

to do something to maintain himself, and one instinctive response was to expand into the surrounding space. William Cullen Bryant writes of "The Prairies": "I behold them from the first,/And my heart swells, while the dilated sight/Takes in the encircling vastness"; Whitman claims "I chant the chant of dilation"; Emerson records how "the heart refuses to be imprisoned; in its first and narrowest pulses it already tends outward with a vast force and to immense and innumerable expansions...there is no outside, no inclosing wall, no circumference to us". Emerson's eye, and his mind after it, was continually drawn to the remotest horizons; the only true encirclement to a man obsessed with circles was earth's vanishing point, the very perimeter of the visible world where sight lost itself in space. When he writes about "The Poet" and his attraction to narcotics of all kinds Emerson says: "These are auxiliaries to the centrifugal tendency of a man, to his passage out into free space, and they help him to escape the custody of that body in which he is pent up, and of that jail-yard of individual relations in which he is enclosed." (That could have been written in San Francisco this year!) Near the end of *Walden* Thoreau has some marvellous lines about the "ethereal flight" of a hawk which sported alone "in the fields of air". "It appeared to have no companion in the universe...and to need none but the morning and the ether with which it played." Thoreau ends the book, appropriately enough, with the parable of the bug which hatches out in on old table and breaks free into "beautiful and winged life", and Whitman at the end of *Song of Myself* literally feels himself diffused back into the elements: "I depart as air..." In these three seminal American Romantics we find a similar "centrifugal tendency"; a dilation of self, which can become an abandoning of self, into the surrounding vastness. But of course if this were all we would have had no record of the movement since words are not carefully strung together by a man in the process of being metamorphosed into the circumambient air, as Emerson seems to recognize in a letter to Samuel Gray Ward: "Can you not save me, dip me into ice water, find me some girding belt, that I glide not away into a stream or a gas, and decease in infinite diffusion?" Like those spiders swimming in the air, the American writer throws out filament, filament, filament, and weaves a web to sustain himself in the vastness. Paradoxically these webs are often notable for being composed of many very concrete particulars and empirically perceived facts (thus Thoreau is also one of the earthiest of writers); it is as though these solid details offered some anchoring attachment. When Frost described a poem as a stay against confusion, he might have more accurately phrased it, for the American writer, as a stay against diffusion.

The web is the writer's style; the concrete details are the nourishing particles which the web ensnares and transforms. And what extraordinary webs the American Romantics (and indeed post-Romantics) have spun: Emerson's essays for instance, which often seem to tremble and blur with the very vertigo they were written to counteract, of *Walden* and *Moby Dick* which, although they seem to repeat stock Romantic themes—the return to nature, the voyage—are of a stylistic idiosyncrasy which can scarcely be paralleled in European writing. And much of that style is not being used to explore self or environment so much as to fill in the spaces between self and environment. Again, *Song of Myself* might at first glance appear to have much in common with *The Prelude*, and the phrase "egotistical sublime" which Keats applied to Wordsworth could certainly be extended to Whitman. And yet the sense of harmonious reciprocities between mind and landscape, that "intimate communion" which, says Wordsworth, "our hearts/Maintain with the minuter properties/Of objects which already are belov'd", is absent from Whitman's more desperate and sometimes hysterical ecstasies. "My voice goes after what my eyes cannot reach,/ With the twirl of my tongue I encompass worlds and volumes of worlds." This verbal and visual pursuit of objects and worlds to fill up his void is somewhat different from the serene stealth with which, for Wordsworth, "the visible scene/Would enter unawares into his mind/With all its solemn imagery".

Among American Romantics there is an unusual stress on a visual relationship with nature. "I am become a transparent eyeball; I am nothing; I see all"—Emerson's famous formulation is relevant for much subsequent American writing. Thoreau, whose other senses were active enough, puts the emphasis on sight: "We are as much as we see." Whitman asks himself "What do you see Walt Whitman?" in "Salut au Monde" and answers literally and copiously, using the phrase "I see" eighty-three times. Obviously new habits of attention, recovered visual intimacies with nature, were crucial for European Romantics as well (and Ruskin was to make of sight an instrument arguably more sensitive than anything to be found in American writing). But more often than in America, the English Romantic's response was also auditory. Keats listening darkling to his nightingale is only one of the many English Romantic poets whose ears were highly receptive to any vibrations or music that reached them. "With what strange utterance did the loud dry wind/Blow through my ears", "I heard among the solitary hills/...sounds/of undistinguishable motion", "Then sometime, in that silence, while he hung/Listening, a gentle shock of mild surprise/ Has carried far into the heart the voice/Of mountain torrents"—these examples from Wordsworth of the voices and utterances of landscape may be readily multiplied, perhaps the most famous being "The Solitary Reaper", where the sound of the woman's song provides lasting nourishment for the poet:

> The music in my heart I bore,
> Long after it was heard no more.

The American Romantics do not give the impression of valuing auditory responses in quite this way. More to the point, for the English Romantics a purely visual relationship to the outside world betokened a state of deprivation, a loss of intimacy, a failure of poetic vision. Coleridge's "Dejection: an Ode' hinges on this severance between self and surrounding things: "I see them all so excellently fair,/I see, not feel, how beautiful they are!" and Shelley's "Stanzas Written in Dejection", by lamenting the absence of some other "heart" to "share in my emotion" as he looks at the scene in front of him, is also asserting the insufficiency of mere sight. A purely or predominantly visual relationship with nature in fact can indicate a state of alienation or detachment from it. An auditory response suggests that the sounds of the environment mean something to the hearer, something within becomes alert to something without which seems to speak a comprehensible language. This suggests at least the possibility of communication, of significant relationship, perhaps even of a kind of dialogue. To be linked to a thing only by sight is at the same time to be severed from it, if only because the act of purely visual appropriation implies a definite space between the eye and the object. And American writers have been predominantly watchers. Thoreau, supposedly so immersed in his environment, can still use this strange image: "I enter some glade in the woods...and it is as if I had come to an open window. I see out and around myself". Having left man-made dwellings behind him, he reintroduces part of their architecture to describe his feelings. To be in the midst of nature and yet to see it as through an open window is surely in some way also to feel cut off from it. Emerson often refers to the world as "spectacle" and is extremely sensitive to all shades of visual experience, as when he says it is enough to take a coach ride to have the surrounding world "wholly detached from all relation to the observer". He said of the soul: "It is a watcher more than a doer, and it is a doer, only that it may the better watch." This in turn anticipates James, whose central figures are all great watchers, thereby excluded from participation in the world they survey—like James himself, leaning intently out of one of the many windows in his house of fiction. Again, in Hemingway's characters their visual alertness and acuity is in part a symptom of their alienation.

Those American writers we associate with the New England Renaissance (and many subsequently) most typically felt themselves to be swimming in space; not, certainly, tied fast into any society, nor really attached very firmly to the vast natural environment. In many ways this state was cherished and preferred; to sport in fields of air could be the ultimate ecstasy. On the other hand there was the danger of, as it were, vanishing or diffusing altogether. The emergent strategy, variously developed by different writers, was to spin out a web which could hold them in place, which would occupy the space around them, and from which they could look out into the world. But even when they scrutinized their environment with extreme care, and took over many of its details to weave into their webs of art, they were seldom in any genuine communion with nature. European Romantics, on the other hand, do seem to have enjoyed moments of reciprocal relationship with nature and could speak truly of what they "half perceive and half create". With Wordsworth they could consider "man and nature as essentially adapted to each other". In discovering nature they were at the same time discovering themselves; in internalizing what was around them they were at the same time externalizing what was within, as Coleridge often described. "The forms/Of Nature have a passion in themselves/That intermingles with those works of man/To which she summons him." That is Wordsworth, and it is just that sort of fruitful *intermingling* of Nature's and Man's creative potencies that is absent from American Romantic writing, which tends, rather, to testify that Nature holds off from man's approaches. Nature is indeed seen, seen with intense clarity through the intervening air, but it leaves precisely that intervening space to be filled by the writer's own filament. That marriage between subject and object, mind and nature, which is an abiding Romantic dream, is seldom consummated in the work of the American Romantics. When Emerson speaks of "the cool disengaged air of natural objects" he is pointing to a perceptual experience which makes for important differences in American Romanticism.

Of course it would be an unacceptable simplification of Emerson's strangely fluid writing to fix on any one of his descriptions of nature as his definitive attitude. But in his first famous essay on "Nature" we find a conception of nature markedly different from any to be found in any comparable European documents. Above all it is the fluidity, the insubstantiality, the transparency of nature which is stressed. Emerson may sound like Wordsworth when he talks of "that wonderful congruity which subsists between man and the world"— so much was a stock Romantic piety, or hope. But what a strange congruity Emerson's is. To the poet, he says, "the refractory world is ductile and flexible". When a poetic mind contemplates nature, matter is "dissolved by a thought". The Transcendentalist, says Emerson, (and Transcendentalism was pertinently described as "that outbreak of Romanticism on Puritan ground" by James Elliot Cabot[1]) has only to ask certain questions "to find his solid universe growing dim and impalpable". The "poet turns the world to glass"; when he looks at nature he sees "the flowing or the Metamorphosis". "The Universe is fluid and volatile": "this surface on which we now stand is not fixed, but sliding." If there is any "fixture or stability" on all this sliding, dissolving, melting world, it is "in the soul". "We are not built like a ship to be tossed, but like a house to stand," says Emerson. Since his Nature is distinctly watery, and the "ethereal tides" seem at times almost to inundate him as he opens himself to them, we may wonder what will be the origin of this stable house of self which can stand firm in the flowing flux of Existence.

Although Emerson is sometimes very specific about individual facts and perceptions, the nature he refers to has no autonomy and very little local identity. It is a mental fabrication. We look in vain for the specificity of all those place-names which are so common in European Romanticism, whether it is Tintern Abbey or Mont Blanc or "Lines Composed while Climbing the Left Ascent of Brockley Coome, Somersetshire, May 1795" (Coleridge). Emerson says that America's "ample geography dazzles the imagination" and a dazzled imagination may respond in unusual ways. His own response, more often than not, is to treat nature as a flimsy, flowing tissue of appearances. He is concerned either to see through it, or withdraw from it. It is indeed

---

[1] Quoted by Henry James in his essay "Emerson", reprinted in *The American Essays of Henry James*, ed. Leon Edel, New York, 1956, p. 70.

a source of emblems, but he tends only to assert this emblematical quality. Perhaps the difference between an emblem and a metaphor is that an emblem is a sign existing at a definite remove from what it signifies and composed of different material; while a metaphor merges the sign and the thing signified. For Emerson Nature was more a matter of emblems than metaphors; it provided no final resting place, no home, for the mind. Here, perhaps, we can detect vestiges of the old Puritan suspicion of matter as fallen, flawed, and misleading—despite Emerson's programmatic optimism about the essential benevolence of all creation. However it is, Emerson's Nature lacks the substantiality, the local external reality, to be found in many European Romantic writers. In Emerson Nature may be a symbol for the mind, or a manifestation of the invisible Over-Soul. What it tends not to be is its own solid self. Children, said Emerson, "believe in the external world". When we grow older we realize that it "appears only". Perhaps Emerson found no more dramatic phrase for his concept of Nature than when he suggested it might be "the apocalypse of the mind".

What Emerson has done is to interpose his version of a ductile, transparent, fluid, apparitional nature between himself and the hard, opaque, refractory (and dazzling) otherness of the real American landscape. This way he makes Nature amenable to himself and his purposes. It is notable how often he talks of playing with Nature as if it were a collection of baubles and toys. The genius, he writes in his journal, "can upheave and balance and toss every object in Nature for his metaphor"; we must be like Shakespeare, he says, who "tosses the creation like a bauble from hand to hand". Anything less tossable from hand to hand, less bauble-like, than the American landscape in the mid-nineteenth century would be hard to think of. But Emerson is swimming in air; and this Nature, this flowing stream of soft transparent playthings, is the web he has created to keep himself afloat. By contrast Wordsworth's or Keats's poetic Nature is, if not the apocalypse of reality, at least its consecration. More recent American writers have not found themselves in exactly the same vast otherness as the mid-nineteenth-century writers. If anything they have to deal with a congestion which would squash them rather than an emptiness which might swallow them, though of course there is a kind of crowdedness which feels like a vacancy. But when Wallace Stevens says that "resistance to the pressure of ominous and destructive circumstance consists of its conversion, so far as possible, into a different, an explicable, an amenable circumstance",[1] he seems to be placing the emphasis in a way which is typical of the American Romantic attitude, which has so often "converted" the given environment into something amenable, not necessarily benevolent if we think of Poe, Hawthorne, Melville, but amenable—ductile to the weavings of their art.

III

Emerson tells his American poet-figure "Thou shalt leave the world", adding: "the impressions of the actual world shall fall like summer rain, copious, but not troublesome to thy invulnerable essence". Reality becomes something like a light shower, easily disregarded. In its place, as he says at the end of "Nature", "Every spirit builds itself a house". This is the house (or the web) which we have already seen the American artist constructing for his own stability, sustenance and unhindered development. "Build therefore your own world", Emerson goes on to admonish his readers in a phrase which has given Richard Poirier a starting-point for his exciting book *A World Elsewhere*. Poirier's more fully developed ideas, as in such a passage as the following, corroborate my suggestion that the creation of a verbal web, safe for habitation and the expansion of consciousness, is a major characteristic of American Romanticism:

> The books which in my view constitute a distinctive American tradition within English literature are early, very often clumsy examples of a modernist impulse in fiction: they resist within their pages the forces of environment that otherwise dominate the world. Their styles have an eccentricity of defiance, even if the defiance shows sometimes as carelessness. Cooper, Emerson, Thoreau, Melville, Hawthorne, Mark Twain, James—they both resemble and serve their heroes by trying to create an environment of "freedom", though as writers their efforts must be wholly in language. American books are often written as if historical forces cannot possibly provide such environment, as if history can give no life to "freedom", and as if only language can create the liberated place.

Elaborating on the Emersonian image of the house, Poirier comments: "*Walden* is only one of the examples of something like an obsession in American literature with plans and efforts to build houses, to appro-

---

[1] "The Irrational Element in Poetry", in *Opus Posthumous*, London, 1959, p. 225.

priate space to one's desires"; he mentions the houses in Cooper, Mark Twain, *The House of the Seven Gables*, Fawns in *The Golden Bowl*, Sutpen's Hundred, Silas Lapham's house, Gatsby's estate, even Herzog's country house, and of course the work of crucial architects like Frank Lloyd Wright, and he adds "the building of a house is an extension and an expansion of the self, an act by which the self possesses environment otherwise dominated by nature". It is certainly a way of interposing your world between yourself and the given world and obviously of particular importance in America where the unparalleled freedom, and need, to erect habitations of one's own design has produced unique architectural and literary structures alike. Poirier could have developed his point further. When Emily Dickinson says "I dwell in Possibility—a Fairer House than Prose' we can see that it is also the house of her own style. Similarly all those extremely ornate and cunningly decorated, coloured and upholstered interiors in Poe's stories (which Baudelaire commented on enthusiastically) are surely images of his own pure art style which he so defiantly opposed to the unpoetical barrennes of contemporary America. (One might note in passing Edith Wharton's enthusiastic writing on house decoration which preceded her fictional works.) The opening stanza of Wallace Steven's "Architecture" (in *Opus Posthumous*) admirably evokes this whole attitude:

> What manner of building shall we build?
> Let us design a chastel de chasteté.
> De pensée…
> Never cease to deploy the structure.
> Keep the laborers shouldering plinths.
> Pass the whole of life hearing the clink of the
> Chisels of the stone-cutters cutting the stones.

Let us build a castle of thought (just as James speaks of "a palace of thought"), what is more, let us build it of any materials we please, arranged in any fashion that pleases us. The suggestion is that for these and comparable writers, art is a continuous building of a private edifice; and the process of building—of playing with the available materials, as Emerson's poet plays with the baubles of nature, as Stevens plays with rare exotic things and words (like chastel)—is perhaps more important than the product. Build therefore your own world, or weave your own web—here is a key cry of the American writer, particularly those writers we designate as being in one way or another Romantic. The same sort of idea is of course also to be found in Europe, in Coleridge's "stately pleasure-dome", and Tennyson's "Palace of Art" for instance. But these are different sorts of building, built for a different purpose (to explore the world of the creative unconscious among other things), and in both cases the edifices represent dreams from which there has to be a waking.

A good visual example of this sort of private "architecture" in American art is provided by an amazing picture by Erastus Field called "Historical Monument of the American Republic".[1] It shows the most extraordinary mélange of heterogeneous architectural styles of building from various cultures and various ages, all connected up at the top by tenuous little bridges—filaments, really, of the painter's fantasy. The result is that although the various specific contents of the work are public and historical, the over-all effect is private and fanciful. Field is building his own world and its relation to the actual world is more apparent than real. Among poets, Stevens can be such an architect. Pound and Eliot likewise use fragments of the world's past and disparate cultures to build their own private worlds. This sort of relatively unfettered eclecticism when dealing with the past is peculiarly American and an utterly different thing from the European writer's sense of the past. If anything it negates the historical sense— Pound plays with the cultures of the past, tossing pieces from hand to hand, just as Emerson played wich images of Nature. The results and new juxtapositions can be brilliant, breathtakingly original, and very un-European. As in Field's painting, images of the real past are dislodged and reassembled at the whim of the poet as he spins out his web. And there is another aspect to this almost forceful gathering together of human culture into one web through the sheer effort of style. Faulkner often repeats a sentiment that "I'm trying to say it all in one sentence, between one Cap and one period...I don't know how to do it. All I know is to keep on trying in a new way".[2] This ambition to "put all mankind's history in one sentence" partly explains some of the Gargantuan qualities to be found in many American writers—for example, an unprecedented omnivorousness which effects syntax as well as length. Wallace Stevens reveals his own tendency towards this when he writes in a letter "for me the important

---

[1] Reproductions of this picture may be consulted in, for example, Oliver Larkin, *Art and Life in America*, New York, 1949, p. 230, and Henri Dorra, *The American Muse*, London, 1961, p. 160.

[2] *The Faulkner-Cowley File: Letters and Memories, 1944-1962*, London, 1967, p. 14.

thing is to realize poetry...it is simply the desire to contain the world wholly within one's own perception of it".[1] This pre-empting of the world and history, this making it over on your own terms, is necessarily a condition of much art anywhere. But nowhere do you find this will to reconstitute and contain the world and the past in the web of an individual style more strong than in certain American writers.

A final point about this private house of the American Romantic, again from Emerson: "It is awful to look into the mind of man and see how free we are...Outside, among your fellows, among strangers, you must preserve appearances, a hundred things you cannot do; but inside, the terrible freedom." The notion that the house which the spirit builds for itself may become a place of terror is deftly conceded by Emily Dickinson with her trenchant economy:

> One need not be a chamber to be haunted,
> One need not be a house;
> The brain has corridors surpassing
> Material place.

Robert Frost's "Bereft" suggests similar terrors, when the wind turns threatening and the leaves hiss at him:

> Something sinister in the tone,
> Told me my secret must be known:
> Word I was in the house alone
> Somehow must have gotten abroad,
> Word I was in my life alone,
> Word I had no one left but God.

The horrors which take place in Poe's secluded rooms also emphasize how often the American writer is to be found sitting alone in the house which his soul has made for him and which is so often and so singularly haunted.

Alone in his house or sporting in fields of air alone, the American writer seems to have taken his cue from Emerson's axiom "Alone is heaven". The word, and the aspiration, recur constantly, and it is most apt that the first sentence of Emerson's first major essay should define the conditions for the procurement of solitude: "To go into solitude, a man needs to retire as much from his chamber as from society." As Emily Dickinson puts it, "The soul selects her own

---

[1] *Letters of Wallace Stevens*, ed. Holly Stevens, New York and London, 1966, p. 501.

society/Then shuts the door". No single sentence differentiates Emerson more clearly from a writer like Wordsworth than this (it follows after Emerson has been discussing the grandeur of nature): "Yet this may show us what discord is between man and nature, for you cannot freely admire a noble landscape if laborers are digging in the field hard by. The poet finds something ridiculous in his delight until he is out of the sight of men". But Wordsworth does not. For Wordsworth to encounter the shepherd, the leech-gatherer, the reaper, or anyone else living in intimacy with nature, could be the occasion of an epiphany, a visionary gleam. Emerson reveals a more Oriental streak in the American response to landscape when he emphasizes the discrepancy between tiny man and the vast dissolving grandeur of nature. Indeed, he would even banish those tiny figures which Oriental painters include to remind one of that discrepancy. For Emerson the ideal landscape was the unpeopled landscape. Thoreau does meet people in the woods, yet his instinct is for solitude. "It would be sweet to deal with men more, I imagine, but where dwell they? Not in the fields which I traverse." Whitman seems to reach out to embrace the whole continent; his imagination is crowded with electric tactile contacts. Yet it seems to be more a dream of contact; for the most part he is "out of the game", "apart from the pulling and hauling", looking, peering, beholding, watching—one of those great lonely voyeurs who recur in American literature. At the end of the poem it is his evasive solitariness which we feel as he promises to "stop somewhere waiting for you" and then vanishes without even waiting to close off his poem with a full stop. Carlyle's warning to Emerson could be extended to cover other American writers: "We find you a Speaker indeed, but as it were a Soliloquizer on the eternal mountain-tops only, in vast solitudes where men and their affairs all lie hushed in a very dim remoteness..."[1] By contrast, "The Prelude" starts and ends with an address to "my Friend" (Coleridge, of course).

All Romantics are supposed to be soliloquizers, enraptured by their own potency, yet a good deal of European, certainly of English, Romantic poetry is addressed to friends, or presupposes or involves them. These Romantics cherished company, even if it had to be very select, just as they seem more interested in women than their American counterparts. And the implications of this go beyond the relatively

---

[1] Quoted in *Selections from Ralph Waldo Emerson: An Organic Anthology*, ed. Stephen Whicher, New York, 1957, p. 492.

trivial question of whether the European Romantic had more friends
than the American. It involves a difference in their relative conceptions
of their own role in relation to their societies. "The poet", says
Wordsworth, "binds together by passion and knowledge the vast empire of human society"; poets, says Shelley "are the unacknowledged
legislators of the world". Wordsworth's poet is a "man speaking to
men"; by contrast the American Romantic seems more to be a man
speaking to himself. William Cullen Bryant stands in the American
woods and dreams of a future civilization: [I] "think I hear/The
sound of that advancing multitude/Which soon shall fill these deserts";
but his poem ends "A fresher wind sweeps by, and breaks my dream,/
And I am in the wilderness alone." The European Romantic did not
have to dream of crowds and societies and civilizations, they were
everywhere he turned; and despite the fixed image of the European
Romantics as escapists, most of them were very politically minded
and concerned with the development of society. Ever since Rousseau
had shown that society was an arbitrary man-made structure, the idea
had been gaining ground that man could reshape society according
to the demands and dictates of his imagination. Mental structures
might precede and ordain political structures. The French Revolution
demonstrated both the will and the arbility of men to actively reshape
their society. In a rich and authoritative article on "English Romanticism: The Spirit of the Age"[1] M. H. Abrams demonstrates conclusive-
ly that for the English Romantics the French Revolution was the
single most formative experience of their lives. The great outburst
of social or anti-social energy provoked and encouraged a similar
release of personal creative energy. Millennial hopes and apocalyptic
expectations ran high. The advent of the New Jerusalem or Paradise
on Earth was prophesied. English Romantics argued from the French
Revolution to the Book of Revelation, and prophesied liberating
changes in the "vast empire of human society". The poet's role was
to offer the shaping vision, to produce imaginative constructs which
would provide models for social constructs. Acknowledged or not,
they felt themselves to be, or potentially to be, the legislators of
the world. Most European Romantics were implicitly if not explicitly
revolutionary; as Hazlitt shrewdly commented on the Lake School,
"regular metre was abolished with regular government". Of course,
disillusion with the French Revolution set in, and it is precisely a

---

[1] In *Romanticism Reconsidered*, ed. Northrop Frye, New York, 1963.

part of Professor Abrams's story to show how the English Romantics experienced a loss of hope, gave up their expectations of a specific historical revolution in the near future, and concentrated on what Abrams calls "the apocalypse of imagination". I quote one of his conclusions, concerning this shift of emphasis. "The hope has been shifted from the history of mankind to the mind of a single individual, from militant external action to an imaginative act; and the marriage between the Lamb and the New Jerusalem has been converted into a marriage between subject and object, mind and nature, which creates a new world out of the old world of sense".

In America, the writing of the Transcendentalists, and all those we may wish to consider as Romantics, did not have this revolutionary social dimension. It was not rooted in the energizing conviction that the poet's imaginative visions, in one way or another, could vitally influence and enhance the conditions of life of their fellow men. Whitman certainly talks of the great "en-masse" and has dreams of a harmonious collectivity, yet even here the strongest emphasis is on "the centripetal isolation of a human being in himself". Between that centrifugal tendency into space I mentioned earlier, and this centripetal isolation of the human being in himself, the American artist spins his self-sustaining web, with society usually excluded, ignored, or unenvisaged. Appropriately enough the most famous use of the image of the spider's web in nineteenth-century English literature is in George Eliot's *Middlemarch*, where she uses it to illustrate the complex and ramifying inter-relatedness of all human relationships, that "stealthy convergence of human lots". What in English literature has here provided an image of our unavoidable involvement in the lives of other people, in American literature has typically been the image for the patterns and strategies with which the American artist both fills and preserves his radical solitude. The contrast has at least some parabolic aptness.

IV

While dealing with attitudes towards society and civilization, another point is worth making, which is put clearly in the poem written by Bryant for the painter Thomas Cole as the latter was about to leave for Europe. First Bryant reminds Cole of the wonderful wild and savage landscapes which he has painted (and which indeed he loved), then he warns him of what he will see in Europe:

Fair scenes shall greet thee where thou goest—fair,
But different—everywhere the trace of men,
Paths, homes, graves, ruins, from the lowest glen
To where life shrinks from the fierce Alpine air—
Gaze on them, till the tears shall dim thy sight,
But keep that earlier, wilder image bright.

In Europe, "everywhere the trace of men": in America, "that wilder image". Bryant himself is clearly appreciative of both, but he more particularly wants to retain "that wilder image" which the as-yet uncivilized landscape of America can provide. The wildness of this landscape was felt to have values and provide spiritual nourishment not available in Europe. "We need the tonic of wildness", says Thoreau, while Cole, in his "Essay on American Scenery" (1835), insists that "the wilderness is YET a fitting place to speak of God". Against those who prefer Europe, Cole argues that "the most impressive characteristic of American scenery is its wildness", while in "civilized Europe the primitive features of scenery have long since been destroyed or modified". He instances some of the splendid wildnesses of America, for example Niagara: "in gazing on it we feel as though a great void had been filled in our mind—our conceptions expand—we become a part of what we behold". (It is amusing to recall that when Chateaubriand first saw Niagara he was so overwhelmed that he wanted to throw himself in, and indeed did nearly fall over the edge—a pregnant Romantic anecdote. And it was in the wild American woods Chateaubriand says a new, an "unknown muse appeared to me". Such wildness, he felt, would provoke a new poetry.) At the same time anyone writing in America then was aware that the rapid "improvements of cultivation" were inevitably replacing "the sublimity of the wilderness". Here was a difficulty. The American wilderness was a course of visionary exaltation. Unlike Europe, the land was not scarred and stained by the intolerably crimes of history: "You see no ruined tower to tell of outrage—no gorgeous temple to speak of ostentation". But if American landscape was not suffused with a sense of the past it was full of what Cole calls "associations...of the present and future". "And in looking over the yet uncultivated scene, the mind's eye shall see far into futurity. Where the wolf roams, the plough shall glisten; on the gray crag shall rise temple and tower..." There is a problem for the American Romantic. Blessedly, there are no man-made towers marring the American landscape; but happily there will soon be towers springing up. The wonder and richness of America is its wildness, but wonderfully, the wildness will soon be put to the plough. As soon as Cole has outlined his optimistic vision of a civilized society living in a domesticated landscape, he goes on "yet I cannot but express my sorrow that the beauties of such landscapes are quickly passing away—the ravages of the axe are daily increasing—the most noble scenes are made desolate and oftentimes with a wantonness and barbarism scarcely credible in a civilized nation". Where the European Romantic, used to the "traces of men", might look forward to an imagined millennium for human society, the American was very aware of increasing depredations of the precious wildness. He might cling to images of idealized pastoral domesticity, or indulge in pieties about manifest destiny or the melting-pot, but his strategy on the whole was to seek out that solitude, those unpeopled landscapes, prescribed by Emerson—in reality, or in art. That is why while European Romanticism characteristically looks to the past and to the future, American Romanticism seeks to move out of time altogether, out of time and into some sort of space. For time means history, and history means "traces of men" and society, and society means not only the loss of "that wilder image" but also the spaces it provided and the limitless freedom to sport in air.

"The great discovery of the eighteenth century is the phenomenon of memory," says Georges Poulet,[1] and certainly the attempt to renew contact with one's individual past and the past of society is a decisive factor in the literature of Europe we call Romantic. Chateaubriand's René, who laid down so many of the behaviour patterns for subsequent Romantic poets and heroes, is exemplary in this. Accounting for his melancholy in the depths of the American woods, René recalls his European past. In one early phrase he anticipates many subsequent works: "Memories of these childhood adventures still fill my soul with delight." Another key word is introduced when he describes how the sound of bells in his native land awakens the happiest associations in later life. "All is contained in these delicious reveries into which we are plunged by the sound of our native bells." Revery, first eulogized by Rousseau, is a word which appears very frequently in European nineteenth-century literature, and René's sentiment is echoed by Wordsworth and Proust to mention only the most obvious. To cope with his misery—caused by that favourite Romantic frustration, hopeless incestuous love—René has recourse to the Romantic

---

[1] *Studies in Human Time*, by Georges Poulet, Baltimore, 1956.

antidote of travel. "I went and sat among the ruins of Rome and Greece: countries of strong and productive memory." In particular he favours moon-lit meditations: "Often, by the rays of this star which nourishes our reveries, I thought I saw the Spirit of Memory seated in deep thought by my side." I need hardly point out what a wealth of Romantic iconography is here assembled. And when René cries out "Is it my fault, if I find limits everywhere, if what is finite has no value for me?", and "I lacked something that could fill the emptiness of my existence", he articulates archetypal Romantic feelings. Having left Europe after the death of his sister and come to the depths of the American woods, he does not find anything to fill that emptiness and indeed he is said to die shortly after completing his tale, his recollection. A recollection, not quite in tranquillity, but one which suggests that what meaning and content there was to his life is all in the past. There is nothing emptier than the present. René also affords us an excellent picture of a typical European Romantic as he sits at the edge of the sea when his sister has immolated herself in a convent after confessing her illicit love. René is awaiting his ship, knowing that his life henceforward will always be incomplete, unfilled. As he describes the contrast between the convent behind him and the ocean in front, we can see him hanging between two worlds. On the one side there is the place, the symbol, of infinity, calm, refuge, timeless knowledge, and unfaltering motionless light; on the other, the unceasing tides of Time, the place of storm, of shipwreck, of uncertain navigation, and moving beacon lights which shift and sway with the swell of the sea. And in between, drawn to both, full inhabitant of neither, is the unappeasable, the European, René.

René, it is true, does not find something to fill his inner emptiness in past, present or future. He perhaps qualifies as one of those who, as Georges Poulet puts it, in an effort to create their identities out of the past and present or future time, risk a "double tearing of the self" by finally feeling themselves cut off from both. But if nearly all Romantics have felt what Poulet calls "the infinite deficiency of the present moment", some of them have indeed managed to reconstitute a more lasting self out of remembrance. For memory proved to be one of the major defences against the disintegration of the self and its endless diffusion into innumerable unrelated moments. As Poulet puts it, "all at once the mind is able to feel an entire past reborn within itself. This past, together with the whole train of its emotions, surges up in the moment and endows it with a life that is not momentary."

Instead of being a mere creature of intermittent and discrete sensations, the writer, through this remembering, recapturing, reexperiencing of the past, discovers the miracle of his own duration. It would be out of place and unnecessary to embark on any sketch of the role of memory in European Romanticism; but this deliberate cultivation of an awareness and a sense both of society's historical past and the past of the individual provided the European Romantic with one of his main themes and activities. Let Wordsworth suffice as an obvious example:

> But a sense
> Of what had been here done, and suffer'd here
> Through ages, and was doing, suffering, still
> Weigh'd with me, could support the test of thought,
> Was like the enduring majesty and power
> Of independent nature; and not seldom
> Even individual remembrances,
> By working on the Shapes before my eyes,
> Became like vital functions of the soul;
>
> (*Prelude*, VIII, 781-9)

and again:

> There are in our existence spots of time,
> Which with distinct pre-eminence retain
> A vivifying Virtue, whence...
>   our minds
> Are nourished and invisibly repair'd...
>
> (*Prelude*, XI, 258-65)

In the rediscovery of the Middle Ages in German Romanticism, or in the Hellenism of poets like Shelley and Byron, European Romanticism was as retrospective as it was revolutionary.

A few quotations from Emerson will suggest how radically different was the American Romantic's attitude towards memory and the past. "But why should you keep your head over your shoulder? Why drag about this corpse of your memory...?" "In nature every moment is new; the past is swallowed and forgotten; the coming only is sacred"; "how easily we might walk onward into the opening landscape...until by degrees the recollection of home was crowded out of the mind, all memory obliterated by the tyranny of the present, and we are led in triumph by nature." Emerson described himself as "an endless seeker with no Past at my back", and in his funeral address on Thoreau he said of him "he lived for the day, not cumbered and mortified by his memory". This antipathy to memory, the resolute rejection of the past, is of course connected to America's national growth. For the past was Europe, that old world whose influence America had to escape if it was to discover itself. It is part of the American genius not to be dominated and held back by the inertia of the past, to feel that the future is still full of infinite possibilities, that, as Stevens put it, "the vegetation still abounds with forms"[1]—new forms, not copies of the old forms of the past. However, this denial of memory seems to rob most American writers of any experience of duration. Henry Miller is only an extreme form of the many American writers, Romantic and otherwise, who seem to experience life as an unrelated series of spasmodic "nows". "There is nothing else than now," says the Hemingway hero to himself. The past can certainly be every kind of burden, a real load of nightmare and repression. But to lack any sense of the past can be impoverishing, and to live in a pure present can have its terrors. Certainly it must lead to a much less stable sense of self. As I suggested earlier, the tendency of certain American writers to dilate into the space around them, even to dissolve into their environment, is related to this flight from the past which is a flight out of time. "What scared you all into time"?...come out of time and into space. Forever. There is no thing to fear. There is no thing in space." William Burrough's message to Allen Ginsberg effectively sums up a position held intermittently by American writers over the last hundred years. Of course if the American artist did manage to vanish out of time and into space he would not write anything. First, because, as Burroughs points out, there is no thing in space and you cannot have art without things any more than you can have consciousness without things. Secondly, because it is doubtful whether the pure present, a series of spatial moments utterly cut off from the past, can mean anything at all. Needless to say, Emerson, Whitman and Thoreau did not vanish in this way, and even Burroughs is still writing. But Emerson and Whitman, for example, get very repetitive; indeed at times it seems as if Emerson's prose loses inner direction, as if the words at least had got out of time and into space where they are sporting in air. And the American novelist had to turn to the past before he could find any subjects productive of drama and significance. Hawthorne sitting in the customs house sifting through those old

---

[1] "Lions in Sweden", *Collected Poems of Wallace Stevens*, New York, 1954; London, 1955, pp. 124-5.

papers is the precise image of the American artist looking for some sort of American past which will provide the dynamic for his art. Mark Twain and Melville both looked back for the material of their greatest works, while James's fiction begins and ends with the introduction of an American sense of the present into European territories drenched with the past. Today, young American poets like Ed Dorn are trying to isolate and imaginatively use the figure of the Indian and his culture—the true historic part of America.

For good or bad the American Romantic writers do not have that sense of the past which was so important for their European counterparts. Of course, they faced a landscape devoid of "traces of men"; clean, "dazzling", but humanly speaking empty—potentially alien in a way that the European landscape, so saturated with history, legend, myth, could never be. This perhaps partially explains why the European writer can seem to be more genuinely intimate with his landscape than the American with his, why it offers him so much in the way of suggestions, associations, and consolations, while the American landscape, "that wilder image", tends to hold off from its watcher as pure obdurate fact. Of course there is a whole tradition of sublime writing celebrating nature in American Romantic poetry. Josephine Miles has described it in her excellent *Eras and Modes in English Poetry*, but she also, most interestingly, notes that the whole vocabulary of subtle "psychological discriminations" which was developed by the English Romantics, was not adopted or developed in America. This corresponds to my sense that the American Romantic feels nature to be something so vast as to be almost beyond him; he does not feel that sort of psychological intimacy with his environment, that sense of reciprocities between man and man, man and nature, which marks much European Romantic writing. For Emerson, despite his celebratory euphoria, the actual surrounding world could often seem "an Iceland of negations" from which he would habitually escape into his visions of "infinitude". Similarly Wallace Stevens uses the image of a barren wintry landscape to describe his sense of a world which has not been supplemented and illuminated by some imaginary construct invented by the poet himself. The world unmediated or unmodified by Imagination is perhaps a cold and empty place for most Romantics. But whereas the European seems to draw help from history, legend, memory, from friends (and lovers), from visions of future societies, from the landscape itself, as he strives to fill that emptiness, the American Romantic seems to be thrown back much more on his own resources, the devices and designs of his own style. To consider American Romantic literature from Emerson to Wallace Stevens in this light is to realize anew how very remarkable and inventive those resources are.

That recurrent image of the spider, drawing the filament out of himself alone, weaving his private web, provides an illuminating analogy for the situation, and secretion, of the American writer. His delight (or is it sometimes his desperation?) is to put together his own unique verbal structure; and in this activity, the ingredients which go into the making of each piece of filament are perhaps less important than the fact of the web itself which sustains the writer in the real and imagined spaces of America. The visions of the European Romantic interpenetrated on all sides with their natural and human surroundings. It is just this feeling of *interpenetration* that seems to me to be missing in the work of the American Romantic. If we seek him out we are most likely to find him as Emily Dickinson found her spider—dancing softly to himself, unwinding his coil of Pearl. The wonder is what "continents of light" he thus manages to summon into being.

BERNARD POLI

THE HERO IN FRANCE AND IN AMERICA*

I

Renart the fox, D'Artangan the musketeer, ambitious young men like Rastignac or Julien Sorel are usually described in France as universal types and yet they strike the foreign observer as typically French. Conversely, who could say that Huck Finn, Sister Carrie, Joe Christmas or Frederick Henry are anything but American, though their stories have been read and made emblematic of the human fate in numerous foreign countries? There seem to exist subliminal signals which give readers at home the shock of recognition, and also denote the foreignness of a character when seen from distant shores.

In this paper, limited to a brief study of the French and the American hero, I would like to examine what creates a kinship between the hero and his compatriots, what makes him into a model they will want to imitate. By heroes I mean the demigods, who are not so far from the average man as to live in an empyrean, and whose biographies, real or fictional, embody values which are accepted as such by the community. George Washington or Louis XIV would not be good examples because they somehow descended from heaven and have returned there. I want to focus on this narrow zone where the hero emerges, becomes different from his compatriots, and still remains typical of their own way of projecting themselves.

In France a man becomes a hero when he has gone beyond certain limits set by his social group and has defeated pressures which tend to keep him in his place. From then on he has a right to live isolated and respected. In sports, for instance, in spite of the efforts of the mass media to bring the stars closer to the public, the recognized heroes are always presented with a sort of aura which keeps them away from the crowd. They would practically never be photographed hugging mother or playing ball with the neighbourhood kids, but

* First published in the Journal of American Studies, vol. 2 no. 2 (October 1968). Reprinted by permission of the Editors of the Journal and of the Cambridge University Press.

relaxing in a farm they have just bought, or having a drink in an exclusive place, or giving a kiss to a pretty girl. Even the twelve or thirteen brothers and sisters of a popular singer and her lower-class origin quickly tend to be forgotten. Trips to foreign lands, glamorous or ill-fated love affairs will soon make Cinderella into a princess. It is always Mars and Venus and Mount Olympus. After winning a bicycle race an athlete was asked how it felt to become a national hero. The answer was that, for him, it primarily meant a social promotion.

The French university system has its heroes too: they are the bright members of the middle class who join the ruling class; that is to say an aristocracy of prestige, if not necessarily of money. A selective process based on competitive examinations gives to the successful candidates a privileged status, the right to live in separate buildings, to be taught by special teachers and to take liberties with the system. Later, as high-ranking government employees, their status is not so much denoted by their salaries as by the special privileges they enjoy: reserved seats, reserved parking spaces, no office hours, and privacy! In other words, what counts for these bespectacled heroes of the brain is to join an élite and be separated from the crowd by a clearly defined border-line.

French national heroes, even when they were soldiers, are best remembered as isolated figures, not engaged in action, but rather lost in their thoughts, or communicating with the powers above. Saint Louis is seen acting as a judge under an oak tree, Joan of Arc listening to her voices, Napoleon sombrely brooding at St Helena or receiving the crown, rather than commanding his troops, and General de Gaulle meditating at Colombey rather than marching down the Champs-Elysées.

The French hero, however, is no Cincinnatus who returns to his plough, no Ulysses longing for home, family and peace. His isolation is not based on self-sufficiency but on social recognition. Humble, modest heroes of course exist, as in all folk traditions, but they belong to the realm of abstraction, like the unknown soldier under the Arc de Triomphe in Paris. The hero rises in the eyes of others and reaches a point of no return. The end is an apotheosis, or else a downfall, tragic or ignominious.

A more significant illustration of this pattern can be found in French fiction. For a French writer a hero tends to be a combination of two types: the tragic hero inherited from the Greeks, who occupies a central place in the classical tradition, and the picaresque hero who is a social climber. The former is a nobleman with a noble soul whose career involves supreme glory and a catastrophic ending; the latter rises above his social milieu, from servant to master, from bourgeois to aristocrat, and he then has to fight ruthlessly in order to preserve his position. He is also likely to stumble upon some unforeseen obstacle which will hurl him into an abyss of humiliation. The hero is a demigod or a monster, sometimes a combination of the two, but, in any event, an individual who has cut himself off from the average man. If d'Artagnan on his nag looks like an unpromising character in Dumas' novel, it is only to make more striking his admittance into the company of three recognized heroes of the aristocracy, the famous musketeers. Rastignac becomes rich and powerful when he learns how to play with the weaknesses of men and begins to despise them. Renart the fox has no friends, no ally; he is feared and respected so long as he proves more clever than other animals, but defeat and shame constantly threaten him. Julien Sorel and Fabrice del Dongo find love and glory before they are defeated by their *hubris*. Love, wealth, power, or a combination of these elements make up a dream world in which a few manage to survive and from which many fall into despair, death, or worse, humiliation.

The best example is perhaps that of Balzac's Louis Lambert, because his biography is described as an "intellectual history" and will thus better reveal the fundamental structure of the hero's destiny. At school, Louis lives away from the world and from his parents; he has only one friend (the narrator), while teachers and pupils as well make him into an outcast and a victim. With his only companion he keeps aloof, lives "like a rat" and is the only real aristocrat. Later, he will gain the love of a beautiful and rich girl, the badge of complete triumph for a picaresque hero, but his visionary genius will suddenly bring him to complete insanity, so that he will later be found again, under the care of his beloved, living in complete isolation, full of contempt for a crawling humanity.

Though heroes of nineteenth-century novels owe much to the Romantic picture of solitary geniuses, popularized by Chateaubriand or Byron, they are also probably derived from a deeper pattern which can be illustrated, as early as the seventeenth century, by the behaviour of Madame de Clèves who, because of a very aristocratic feeling of self-respect, and, as she puts it in very unromantic terms, "dans l'intérêt de mon repos", decides not to be carried away by her passion. In twentieth-century fiction, Meursault in Camus' *L'Etranger* probably stands out as the most striking and the most representative character in a long period. Though he is by no means an aristocrat in his social life, what makes him a hero by French standards is his fundamental isolation, his obstinate refusal to be like other people, and the higher level of lucidity to which he rises in his prison cell. In Sartre's play, *Les Mains sales*, a hero like Hoederer who is, by definition, a man of the people, reaches his real stature when his intellectual superiority becomes most striking. The love of a beautiful girl and an absurd death will be the rewards of this lonesome and clear-sighted hero.

The important factor in this analysis is not, of course, that the hero should be seen as exceptional by a person who loves him (a platitude in all love stories) or by himself (a Romantic feature), but that the author should manipulate his story in such a way that the hero objectively comes out as "different". A French hero is one who has succeeded in joining a social or an intellectual aristocracy (moral values have little to do with this promotion), is keenly aware of his own superiority, keeps far from the crowd and pursues his aim in a straight line. In other words, the archetype of this hero is the picture Descartes gives of himself in *Le Discours de la méthode*.

The *Discours*, Descartes said, is merely a story, or a fable, meant to stimulate the mind of his readers. We should therefore have no misgivings about using the narrator as the hero of a philosophical tale. What is most significant, first of all, is that Descartes selected a period of conflict to shut himself up and do some calm and leisurely thinking. He constantly insists on this pattern of distance between his superior isolated self and chaos around him: he is a man walking in the dark, he lives alone, as in a desert, in the middle of the crowd, but still with all the amenities of the city, and he is now building a temporary but comfortable house for himself to wait until his philosophical system has been reconstructed. His philosophy, he says, is meant for a very small élite, while the rest of the world should hold on to traditions. Now, this privileged position is not, he realizes, an entirely secure one. The hero of the *Discours* fears attacks from all sides: under the constant threat of unnamed enemies, bound to be the victim of perfidious interpretations, he protects himself in order to enjoy the privilege of leisure and solitude. From then on he will quietly set about his business of reconstruction, walk with confidence and always follow a straight path towards the truth. But the first battle he had to win was a battle against the crowd.

The hero thus described is fundamentally French, and looks like the type condemned by Emerson as useless in America:

> It is bad enough that our geniuses cannot do anything useful, but it is worse that no man is fit for society who has fine traits. He is admired at a distance, but he cannot come near without appearing a cripple. The men of fine parts protect themselves by solitude, or by courtesy, or by satire, or by an acid worldly manner, each concealing, as he best can, his incapacity for useful association, but they want either love or self-reliance.
>
> Our native love of reality joins with the experience to teach us a little reserve, and to dissuade a too sudden surrender to the brilliant qualities of persons.[1]

II

The paradox of the hero in the United States is that he must be a common man, or at least look like a common man, or pretend he looks like a common man. The French are always puzzled by American champions who say they never learnt how to race or fight, or, for that matter, by a writer like Faulkner who claimed he was only a farmer. This sort of tall tale, of course, belongs to the tradition of the American folk hero, of the squatter who beats up the dandy and of Californian jumping frogs. The hero is a man of the people. Tom Wolfe's essays, for instance, contain a picture of Cassius Clay enjoying the company of the crowd around him, joking with strangers, playing his part with great gusto. Wolfe also explains that in auto-racing famous men in America are not *grand prix* drivers, but stock-car drivers like Junior Johnson. If these men have become idols of the people, it is because the people like to have them available, to slap them on the back occasionally, to call them by their first names, to remind them that they were born in Brooklyn or in Prairie City.

One could go on to show that higher posts in America are not filled by competitive examinations, but through a process of selection, characterized as "natural", based on a mental image of growth and development. The elimination of mediocre men is not supposed to be brutal and arbitrary, as when a line is drawn at the bottom of a list, but is achieved in a spontaneous way, the best being pushed forward by reserves of stored energy. In a way, every succesful American "grows up with the country", or with his firm, or with the organiza-

---

[1] "Nominalists and Realists", *Essays*, Everyman Library edition, pp. 325-6.

tion he belongs to. One knows only too well how this goes with the cherished myths of humble (and if possible rural) origins and of a classless society. "Ben" Franklin arrived in Philadelphia with two loaves of bread under his arms (and under the mocking smile of a young girl); "Tom" Jefferson tied his horse to a post before being inaugurated president.

The fact that a "power élite" now exists in America goes strongly against an American tradition, but the new heroes who hold the key to real power enjoy none of the privileges of the old humanist élite, since their power is not individual, leaves them no leisure and forces them to reshape their own public image according to the advice of public relations consultants. Furthermore, these new heroes of American society do not even get the reward of the kiss of Venus, for, like Vulcan, they are dull and hardworking husbands. Psychologically, at least, if not socially or economically, no one is expected to rise too high, to become too different.

If we try to analyse the American success story of the nineteenth century, and see in what sense it is different from its French version, we notice that in the "rags to riches" myth there are, after all, no insurmountable obstacles for the hero to overcome. Instead of becoming different, he remains true to himself and to his aspirations; no one tries to keep him in his place since he has no set place in American society, and there lies one of the reasons which make the American social novel so mediocre. What has happened to the hero who has reached success? Nothing. Tom Sawyer cannot grow up, Carrie, at the end of her career, moodily reads books in her old rocking-chair and has only a glimpse of the superior artist she might have become, had she turned to comedy-drama. The fact that American heroes never rise to join an élite or find a protected island to enjoy their leisure (and not merely their money) is not due to economic and social circumstances only, but is part of a deeper tradition (probably a reaction against European aristocracy) whereby the commonness of the hero, his fundamental identity with other men, should be underlined. Huck Finn describes himself as "lowdown and ornery", Ishmael is a plain sailor on the *Pequod*, Leatherstocking is a scout, Uncle Tom is a slave. Frank Cowperwood, apparently an exception, is indeed a Titan: he has everything he wants, money, power, women, all obtained through unscrupulous methods, and, as such, he is very close to many of Balzac's heroes, but his story never becomes a destiny because it brings him neither to an eventual membership in a stable élite nor to a catastrophic ending. Like *Tom Sawyer* or *Sister Carrie*, *The Titan* has, strictly speaking, no ending.

The real American story is, paradoxically, composed of two elements, the spirit of enterprise of the success story and the lack of a legitimate goal which would justify the hero's ambition. There must always be a "territory ahead" to look forward to, or the log cabin of an irrevocably lost childhood. Between the two poles the hero cannot aim at material success but at spiritual improvement. The American hero is, in fact, Emerson's American scholar, a man with a noble mind, enterprising, full of self-trust, looking towards the future, and also inwards, towards the inner self, towards what is low and common and shared by everybody. "I embrace the common, I explore and sit at the feet of the familiar, the low". Socially, the American scholar has no promotion to expect; his experience is not that of a protected individual because he has to take in and embrace the multiple elements which make up his country. He wil not even enjoy privileges of individual superiority, for, according to Emerson, "character is higher than intellect". Is there even such a man as the American hero?

> We not only affirm that we have few great men, but, absolutely speaking, that we have none...The saints and demigods whom history worships, we are constrained to accept with a grain of allowance. Though in our lonely hours we draw a new strength out of their memory, yet pressed on our attention, as they are by the thoughtless and customary, they fatigue and invade.[1]

This is, after all, Huck's reaction when the raft was "invaded" by the Duke and the Dauphin. In fact, for Emerson, the hero is only "the extreme of individual nature"; that is to say, an exceptional person and a common man; in other words, a "natural born" hero.

III

If we now return to this obscure zone where the ordinary man becomes a hero, we are confronted with two opposite problems in France and in America. In France, what is after all not explained is the continuity of the hero's development, the permanence of his self. In America, on the contrary no real change can be accounted for. These two unsatisfactory patterns of transition will be revealed more strikingly if we examine them in the light of national traditions.

---

[1] "The Over-Soul", *op. cit.* p. 166.

French pupils, who study the history of France as the biography of a heroine, are used to a view of their national past broken up into periods which memorable dates clearly define: 1789, 1848, 1870, and so on, down to the last watershed, 1958. Dates, of course, must have symbolic value in any national history, but, more than any other, French history appears as a series of revolutions and radical political changes, to the extent that even Marianne, on postage stamps, undergoes a process of rejuvenation with each new Republic. The same applies to a study of French literature: it begins with the " *Serment de Strasbourg*"; then, with the "*Défense et illustration de la langue française*", the Renaissance started. For Classicism, wait until 1660, and for Romanticism until 1830; in between, Neo-Classicism and Pre-Romanticism will provide neat categories: two camps arraigned against one another with the inevitable victory of the Moderns seen as a turning-point. It is almost true to say that, in order to understand French literature, a good knowledge of famous prefaces and manifestoes wil be more useful than reading the works themselves.

The biography of a French hero is usually seen in a comparable light: a normal child, or an average person, suddenly changes. It seems that the stroke of a magic wand is required to make an ordinary man into a hero. Joan of Arc, a plain shepherdess, hears voices from heaven and becomes a general; Bonaparte and Napoleon are two different men. One day Molière wrote *Les Précieuses ridicules* and became a classic. The same remark applies to heroes of fiction: in a famous scene Julien Sorel decides to hold Madame de Rénal's hand and is transformed into a different man. After Goriot's burial, Rastignac turns towards Paris and utters the famous "A nous deux maintenant!" while Vautrin, a man of great experience, points out to him the importance of the decision he will make: "Voila le carrefour de la vie, jeune homme, choisissez." In French classical tragedies, the crux of the plot is often a momentous decision a character has to make, or a choice which will change the whole course of his life and make him into a hero. This applies to Rodrigue as well as to Titus or Phèdre. Molière's comedies are built after the same model in reverse: a man makes the wrong choice about the conduct of his life and about the husband his daughter ought to marry; he is a buffoon because he is no longer, and perhaps temporarily only, the sensible person he used to be. This pattern is also clearly found in Descartes' *Discours*. The author decides that he has wasted enough time and begins a new life; the philosophical attitude he advocates is a task of complete reconstruction, and the advice he gives his readers is to walk straight ahead in order to get out of the woods. Whatever aspect of French thought we explore we find dividing lines, radical changes, watersheds, sudden decisions.

If we now return to the American hero, we notice that he has always lived in a country where continuity, unity, and, more recently, consensus, were key words. In spite of sectional conflicts, everything must converge, and the dominant image is that of the process of accretion through which the country was created, the constant addition of new states into the Union with complete equality of rights. In periods of crisis—when Lincoln, Wilson, Franklin D. Roosevelt were inaugurated—radical political changes were not part of a revolution but of a task of restoration. The Civil War was fought in order to preserve "the Union". Even the greatest "break" of all in American history, the War of Independence, was fought for the defence of certain rights, and the continuity between American Colonial history and that of the early years of the Republic is striking.

Major heroes in American fiction are men or women who do not change, sometimes obstinately refuse to change. Hester, in *The Scarlet Letter*, never repents, and we do not know what she was like before her sin; Ahab will not go back on his devilish oath, and though we hear that he had "his humanities", that other period of his life, before his wound, is kept a mystery. A description of Hester's first meeting with Dimmesdale or of Ahab's family life is unthinkable precisely because these characters are endowed with a fundamental unity. There can be no break, no arbitrary choice, in their biography. Huck's departure from St Petersburg is almost accidental, for who could think of Huck's taking the initiative of drifting down the river? On another level, his big decision to save Jim and "go to Hell" is manipulated in such a way that Huck clearly appears true to himself. Silas Lapham's choice to make business arrangements which will ruin him, in accordance with the voice of his conscience, or Lily Bart's resolution not to marry a man she does not love and to pay her debts, are both presented in a perspective of characters who have no real choice and merely preserve their identity.

Even when they use their own biography under a very thin veil of fiction, American novelists find it difficult to describe characters who change, who are different and still the same. William Dean Howells, using Mr. March as the narrator of his story *A Hazard of New Fortunes*, notices that the same Basil March who was the hero of *Their Wedding*

Journey refuses to be handled in the same manner and to be called by his first name. The author is deeply puzzled by the change he finds in himself and sees no way of explaining it. Mark Twain, who wrote so many autobiographical books, never came around to giving an account of major transition periods in his career, how he left childhood behind and became an adolescent, how he gradually gave up his Western style to become an Easterner, how he changed from a humourist to a pompous thinker. *Life on the Mississippi*, a story with a broken back if there is one, perfectly illustrates this hopeless confrontation of mature man and child who hardly recognize each other. In one of his many autobiographical sketches, "The Turning Point of My Life", he humorously enumerates momentous events which "changed" his career, the ultimate effect of this story being precisely that there are no important changes in an individual, and that the personality of a man is an odd combination of permanence and fortuitous events. Like many of his contemporaries he was worried by deterministic theories and wondered how far back one would have to go in order to find this centre which a man calls "I". Except for James, so admirably able to describe a character who changed and remained the same (like Isabel Archer or Strether, for instance), American writers who try to give us a continuous picture of a character undergoing a major evolution will most of the time fall back on the story of the quest for an impossible ideal. In his effort to reach self-fulfilment or an ill-defined and elusive goal, a character remains fundamentally the same. Thomas Wolfe, Jack Kerouac, Saul Bellow have their heroes roam the American continent, or even foreign lands, but the quest they are engaged in is not one for a new self but for their own identity.

How, then, is an American author to account for this common human experience, the fact that man does change? How does an ordinary man become a hero? One solution consists in admitting, according to a well-known line, that "growth is only development", but this idea is more easily illustrated poetically or metaphorically than in traditional fiction, where suspense in the evolution of a character is required. In a biography the facts have to be manipulated in such a way that the child, or at least the young man, becomes "the father of the man". The life of "Walt Whitman" as re-told by the author of *Leaves of Grass* represents an effort to make the facts consistent with the fiction, the real man with the *persona*. In the same manner, the biography of Mark Twain has taken the place of that of Samuel

Clemens. Change, then, becomes mere development, a combination of what is fundamental in the self and obscure determinism.

An explanation for this peculiar attitude towards heroes, whether in real life or in fiction, will again be found in the philosophy of Emerson. To him the unity of the self is more than the multiple facets of a man's biography:

> [Heroes] do not, in the record of facts, equal their own fame...This inequality of the reputation to the works or the anecdotes, is not accounted for by saying that the reverberation is longer than the thunder-clap; but somewhat resided in these men which begot an expectation that outran all their performance. The largest part of their power was latent. This is that which we call Character—a reserved force which acts directly by presence, and without means.[1]

Any concept of the life of an individual as a broken line will run counter to this well-established tradition whereby there is an indestructible centre in man—the equivalent of the soul in the Christian tradition.

The only solution left to explain the transformation of an individual or his being made into a hero consists, then, in integrating the decisive events of his life into a larger scheme: they take place at an appointed time, in the normal evolution of a character, of a type, perhaps even of an archetype, and are simultaneously the consequences of circumstances out of his control. Change is brought about by an inner determinism and by outside forces which mysteriously converge. It is symbolic, or part of a ritual. *The Red Badge of Courage* illustrates the use of this literary device perfectly. The "youth" becomes a hero because the time has come for him to reach manhood, and also because his wound has, objectively and perhaps ironically, made him into a hero. The modern novel (or romance rather) makes a constant and conscious use of this device: sex, death and violence are *rites de passage* in Hemingway's novels or stories, as well as in Faulkner's *The Bear*, for instance. But the "change" which can be accounted for in such a way is only a normal change, one which can be expected in the line of growth and evolution of a particular character, or of man in general. At some time or other, any individual is bound to go through the experience of sex, death or violence, and in fact the transformation is merely a revelation.

In other words, the ritual or symbolic event which explains how and

---

[1] "Character", *op. cit.* pp. 252-3.

why a character changed presupposes a perspective of relative continuity in the character, of unity and order in the universe. Once more
this process of transformation will find an explanation in Emerson's
words when he describes the soul:

> The soul's advances are not made by gradation, such as can be re-
> presented by motion in a straight line; but rather by ascension of state,
> such as can be represented by metamorphosis—from the egg to the
> worm, from the worm to the fly. The growths of genius are of a certain
> *total* character, that does not advance the elect individual first over
> John, then Adam, then Richard, and give to each the pain of discovered
> inferiority, but by every throe of growth the man expands there where
> he works, passing, at each pulsation, classes, populations of men.[1]

As opposed to the French hero, the American hero is not different
from what he originally was, and is not superior to other men. One
can only exist in a world of metaphysical discontinuity and of social
hierarchy, the other in a universe of unity and equality.

IV

It should be clearly understood, however, that the two worlds thus
described are not those which an objective analysis would reveal as
existing now, but rather mental patterns inherited from previous centuries, which, because of the very slow evolution of these patterns,
do not correspond to the present social and economic structure of
the two countries. It is obvious, for instance, that nineteenth-century
democratic and egalitarian ideals are still professed in the United
States at a time when social stratification has become an objective fact
of sociological analysis. In the same way, France has inherited aristocratic systems of values, transmitted and adapted by the "bourgeoisie",
which are still part of a society greatly influenced by socialism. This
gap between the way social and economic forces shape men at a
given time, and the old-fashioned, traditional perspective in which a
society sees its heroes or "representative men" explains the permanence
of certain cultural patterns. The modern hero, who is depicted with
all the features that modern society gives our contemporaries, is in
fact seen and reconstructed by those who write about him according
to traditional images which are part of our national culture.

In contemporary French literature, for instance, there are few real

---

[1] "The Over-Soul", *op. cit.* p. 153.

heroes because, according to well-known current analyses, objects have crowded man out of the picture, and all one can do is make an inventory of the things around us. Man is alienated to the point of becoming a complete outsider in a meaningless universe. Pérec's *Les Choses* is a very significant novel in this respect, because it is almost a sociological document on the fascination exerted by desirable objects on a more or less anonymous young couple. In some of Butor's experimental writings, like *Mobile*, there are no heroes, and never has the separation between man and the outside world been so sharply stressed as by Robbe-Grillet. But here again it seems that the way these writers deal with the theme of alienation is peculiarly French in the sense that there is always one privileged hero, the author himself. Goldmann has rather convincingly shown in his *Sociology of the Novel* that the modern novel was bound to be a novel without a hero, and how this started in France with Malraux, but it is a fact that Malraux himself is the hero of his works, as much as Sartre or Simone de Beauvoir, now writing their memoirs, are becoming the heroes of their own literary careers.

With younger writers the same phenomenon will probably take place for it is easier to list members of the "nouveau roman" group than to name any of their characters. What they are trying to do is describe a privileged vision of the world; their adventure is that of an all-seeing eye or of an intellect that is trying to give shape to chaos. From the things, and the world, and others seen as alien, the French writer is thrown back upon his private vision. Butor's *Mobile* is not a rag-bag of notations but an attempt to give shape and meaning to a dazzling kaleidoscopic vision of America, to run order through chaos; but the kind of order which he is looking for is the private pattern of an individual thought, as in *La Modification* or in *L'Emploi du temps*. Butor, as well as Robbe-Grillet or Claude Simon, are looking at the world from a distance; their stylistic experiments are the perspective they take on the world and others. Any effort to reach reality or an objective world, to communicate with others, is once more defeated and brings the writer (the modern hero with a lucid consciousness) back to his private vision. Claude Simon tried to make his last book universal by calling it *Story*, by not giving the name of the town where it takes place, by ending with a question mark about the identity of the narrator, but his narrative is just as personal as that of Tristram Shandy. Contemporary French literature remains in the Cartesian tradition of an isolated self who looks for a method in order to rediscover the world and others while keeping them at a safe distance. This is precisely the reverse of the Emersonian tradition whereby a spiritual intuition puts you directly in contact with an internal and real world. The American answer—Emerson's answer—to the "nouveau roman" is clear and simple: "My prudence consists in avoiding and going without, not in the inventing of means and methods, not in adroit steering, not in gentle repairing."[1] Recently Marshall McLuhan has warned us that we have no use for the Renaissance legacy any more: "The viewer of Renaissance art is systematically placed outside the frame of experience. A piazza for everything and everything in its piazza. The instantaneous world of electric informational media involves all of us, all at once. No detachment or frame is possible."[2] This longing for total involvement is in the great American tradition.

In the United States today the contemporary feeling of alienation experienced by social outcasts as well as by intellectuals and writers is expressed by American novelists who rebel against the prevailing mood of assent and the desire for consensus among their countrymen. The modern American hero is cut off from the rest of the world and lonely. Does this situation bring him closer to French heroes we have described? It is remarkable indeed how few American ancestors this new hero has found; his closest relatives are characters in Kafka's and Dostoevsky's novels, or else in the biographies of writers like Melville or Hawthorne who experienced the same feelings but are by no means considered as heroes. Van Wyck Brooks tried to put Mark Twain in the category of alienated American heroes, but he only created a satisfactory myth for twentieth-century intellectuals. Are we then to believe that the modern American hero is radically different from his predecessors?

In fact, when an American hero in a modern novel goes through this experience of alienation, he does not enjoy it as a way of being different, he is not regarded as a hero by other characters, and the story is manipulated in such a way by the author that somehow the desire for communication with other people, a return to a "normal" situation will be felt to be the most desirable solution. The central character in Bellow's *Seize the Day* discovers that we cannot be separated, and his final burst of sobbing at the funeral of a stranger is a good

---

[1] "Prudence" *op. cit.* p. 125.
[2] *The Medium is the Message*, New York, Bantam Books, p. 53.

illustration of this belief. Herzog is longing for a normal, happy life which he seems to have found at the end of the novel. Augie March or Henderson have, after all, no fundamental quarrel with the world. Malamud, in *The Assistant* or *A New Life*, ends with a picture of reconciliation and even of joyous acceptance of the world as it is. The appeal exerted on the American public by Salinger is not based on the aristocratic feeling of intellectual superiority shared by all members of the Glass family, for that aspect can be related to a combination of the Jewish tradition with the sophisticated tone of the *New Yorker*; his characters are liked because they all have that vague Emersonian ideal of direct communication with an inner world, with God (even if it should be on the telephone), and also, democratically, with the "fat lady".

It is remarkable, too, that, until recently at least, the Negro American literature of protest was not one of dissent. When Baldwin or Ellison, as well as Martin Luther King, gave warning to the Whites, they always did so in the name of American values which they claimed as their own. The "invisible man" wanted to become visible, but not conspicuously different. The drug addict, the Jew, the Negro, the intellectual, all taken to be symbolic of the plight of the American in recent years, are not idolized as heroes; they are even automatically presented, according to an American tradition, as underdogs, but even so, they are not meant to be anti-heroes or rebels who simply refuse to conform. Like frontier heroes they are law givers rather than law breakers. They are still, according to Emerson's definition "extensions of the common man", very much like, on another level, Pogo or Peanuts. What characterizes the modern American hero is still that he is so much like everybody else, trying to reshape the world, without making compromises, without having to change. He may very well be John Barth's goat-boy, the new Grand Tutor:

> "What I believe, certain men are born with a natural talent for the hero-work; they're no more miraculous than great violinists. It's a neutral thing: some people are red-haired, some are hump-backed, some are heroes." And what everyone went through for himself, he went on, more or less profoundly depending on one's character, Grand Tutors went through on the level of the whole student body.[1]

The hero in America is not Captain Ahab who madly defies the universe; he is rather an "Aye sayer", though perhaps an eccentric and

---

[1] *Giles Goat-Boy*, Harmondsworth, Penguin Books, p. 315.

a non-conformist. Even as an outcast, a "misfit", a madman or an idiot he is a genuine common man, at the centre of the concentric circles of the universe. The hero in France is a man who has left his past behind and poses to have his picture taken for posterity. (Think how often the line "Tel qu'en lui-même enfin l'éternité le change" has been quoted!) He wants to get into "Polytechnique", the French Academy or the Panthéon. He believes in his own superior cleverness and little in human nature. Even the modern French hero of complete and uncompromising lucidity, whether he lives in a palace or in a cold-water flat, whether he sees himself as Julien Sorel, Gil Blas or Sisyphus, deep in his heart hopes to be selected as *Time Magazine* man of the year. In a world such as McLuhan described, if instant communication brings us back to the tribal stage, the modern American hero may very well be a quiet little man whose transistor is secretly tuned to a programme of Christmas carols.

T. A. RIESE

THE IDEA OF EVIL IN AMERICAN AND EUROPEAN LITERATURE

To speak on the Idea of Evil in so wide a context as that of American literature may well seem an impossibility. Any attempt to embrace a subject like this can, at the best, only lead to a rough sketch outlining a field of literary thought without truly entering into it. Such an undertaking can hardly hope to reach essentials; all the more so if the task engaged in requires a clarification through confronting American and European literature. By limitation and selection alone a way may perhaps be found which opens a clear view on the subject and can contribute to a better understanding of it.

One basic assumption has to be made and ought to be explained before beginning with a detailed discussion: a concept like the idea of evil, arising from the depth of human experience, from that spiritual sphere where moral and religious attitudes are formed, cannot be understood without recourse to the interpenetration of present and past, for man is a creature of time, of his own as well as of that of his antecedents. The American's encounter with evil, however unique it may seem in each individual case, is nevertheless dominated by forces of history from which a nation of a continental scope like the people of the United States of America has received its cultural identity. The growth of the American mind is widely determined—even unto the complexity of present-day society—by movements active in the early stages of its development: Puritan Protestantism and the optimistic rationalism of the Enlightenment. They gave shape to the nation in the seventeenth and eighteenth centuries and constituted an identity not yet lost. (Though our growing acquaintance with historical sources and the achievement of modern research have shown that what has been called "New England Puritanism" is not so simple a concept as it was once believed to be, that it actually does contain a considerable variety of attitudes, the fact remains that the impetus of Protestantism and the dynamic strength it received from Anglo-Saxon Puritanism engendered a lasting trend in American history and constituted a set of principles for the conduct of life and the understand-

ing of human existence within the temporal and the spiritual spheres.)[1]
It is the prevalence of these forces which gives us the right to speak
of "the Idea of Evil" in American literature. Various and sometimes
contradictory as the attitudes towards the problem of evil are among
American authors, they all retain a connection with the impulses of
Puritanism and Rationalism which permeate American history.

The case is quite otherwise if we look at Europe. Here we find
a variety of widely different intellectual and spiritual traditions which
moulded the nations or groups of nations of our continent. European
history since the decline of the Greco-Roman world has grown on
the cultural and religious basis of a Christianity which early developed
two distinct forms: the orthodox, emerging from the Greek civilisation of the Byzantine Empire and determining the East and South-
East of the continent, and Roman Catholicism, rising on the cultural
traditions of the Western Roman Empire. Since the sixteenth century
the Western church has again been divided by the Protestant Reformation. Therefore Europe has experienced three well defined and
separate cultural spheres against the one in the America of the United
States.

A comparative study confronting cultural phenomena in America
with those in Europe must bear this in mind. In comparing the literary
manifestations of an ontological concept like the idea of evil in
America with European counterparts one has of necessity to restrict
this confrontation to those old world civilisations and literatures with
which America is linked by a common spiritual basis.—Comparative
studies paying no consideration to such a common denominator seem
to me questionable and, often, unprofitable. The common denominator
in our case is Protestantism, and in trying to elucidate the idea of evil
in American literature by a view on European literary counterparts
we shall turn to works which have grown on the spiritual soil of
Protestantism in Scotland and in Germany.

The principle of selection being thus asserted in one respect it has
still to be realized in another. Within the wide range of American
literature attention will be focused only on one phase of its history
in the nineteenth century. The decades from about 1830 to 1860
brought its development to maturity both in spiritual depth and in

---

[1] The enduring influence of Puritanism and of Rationalism in American history
is justly expounded in many of Reinhold Niebuhr's writings, especially in *The
Irony of American History*, 1952.

formal perfection. Much that had been inherent in American thought now came to fruition, and so these years make evident the continuing relevance of the Puritan heritage in a largely secularized world, while at the same time they present a radical calling in doubt of a rationalistic optimism which is yet in full force. Two great authors of this time, Nathaniel Hawthorne and Herman Melville, have repeatedly given imaginative expression to the phenomenon of evil in works of permanent value. For that reason these writers are central to our subject and will demand our chief regard. Beyond them one modern manifestation of the American mind's confrontation with the idea of evil shall be called to witness: a recent poem by Richard Eberhart.

There is no need to emphasize the fundamental importance the problem of evil has within Hawthorne's fiction. It recurs again and again in his novels as well as in the short stories. On account of their concentration in thought and execution the latter show it in an especially impressive and exemplary way. Among them none gives a more comprehensive and at the same time penetrating imaginative realization to the idea of evil than "Young Goodman Brown". This is one of a large number of stories with a definitely historical setting, showing the peculiar frame of mind of early American Puritanism in New England, but transcending the merely historical and revealing something of greater import with respect to human nature regardless of any particular age and region.

The plot and its figures enter into a structural pattern of a parabolic kind. They unfold a meaning which points to a dilemma inherent in American existence as it emerged from its earliest growth in New England Puritanism and remained valid throughout its further development, though modified in the form of its appearance by changing modes of thought and custom. This story of a young man's spiritual adventures, of his voluntary communion with the devil—intended by him as a brief interlude in a life dedicated to God, but turning out as an irretrievable abandonment to darkness and despair—has been a challenge to interpreters.[1] The great varieties of approaches taken by the critics (aiming at the historical, the psychological, the moral, the religious) give proof of the range and depth of Hawthorne's mind

---

[1] A representative selection of different interpretations has been published in "The Merrill Literary Casebook Series": Nathaniel Hawthorne, *Young Goodman Brown*, ed. by Thomas E. Connolly, Columbus, Ohio, 1968.

and of the subtlety of his imagination. As a story of a definitely allegorical type it presents a course of thought which is brought out so strongly that it has been and will be recognized by any interpreter: man in his growth to maturity is confronted with the co-existence of good and evil in this world; this experience is bound to involve him in a spiritual crisis which will decide on his entire future life.

Goodman Brown, the young husband happily wedded to his wife, Faith, does never overcome this crisis. His readiness to have a non-committal intercourse with the devil, to stay away from Faith for one night in the fond hope of returning to her, to "cling to her skirts and follow her to heaven" (a phrasing, by the way, clearly denoting the allegorical character of the wife), this all too careless readiness leads him into an experience of evil which changes his whole existence, so that his relations to the world, to his fellow men and to his wife, Faith, are deeply disturbed.

Evil as it is revealed to the protagonist, as he experiences it in his own behaviour as well as in what he sees and hears of others, is the sin of faithlessness in human fellowship rising from an all pervading doubt, a loss of trust in the power of goodness. (The name "Young Goodman Brown", besides its literal appropriateness, signifying a householder and husband, so gains a decidedly ironic overtone.) As it is fitting for a story about early Puritanism with its obsession by a repressive morality, faithlessness becomes evident to Brown mainly in acts of sexual incontinence. The Goodman himself stays away from his wife for one night; on the scene of his night's adventures he sees "hoary bearded elders of the church," whispering "wanton words to the young maids of their household," women poisoning their husbands to be at liberty for liaisons of their own choice, "fair damsels," secretly doing away with their unwanted children. But beyond this, evil extends to other offences against the fellowship of man. In the gathering of the devil worshippers Brown learns "how beardless youths have made haste to inherit their fathers' wealth."

The full extent of the meaning of evil in this short story is, however, made evident only with the consummation of the tale. Young Goodman Brown is so shocked by what he has experienced with himself and with others that he remains unable for the rest of his life to overcome a sense of man's depravity; from now on to him evil seems to pervade the whole creation. Doubt and distrust destroy his capacity for human intercourse, though he continues to live on to old age together with his wife and family. He never regains a joy in the community of his fellow beings, but remains cut off from them, isolated in spirit, and, as the last words of the story say, "his dying hour was gloom."

So, evil is here much more than man's susceptibility to sinful thoughts and deeds, it is a fundamental inability to accept this world as one where good and bad co-exist, it is the failure to preserve charity and a love of life in face of the depressing awareness of this co-existence.

Two more of Hawthorne's short stories, which may be considered as companion pieces to "Young Goodman Brown", give an additional clarity to this conception of evil: "The Minister's Black Veil" and "Ethan Brand". Parson Hooper in the first of them hides his face behind a black veil in order to typify the secret sin which he believes to be hidden in every human breast. By doing so he estranges his lover, scares his congregation, isolates himself from society. For all his piety and the hold he has over his flock he spreads a faith not of Christian love and joy but rather of fear and trembling. His awareness of evil is so absolute that he has become a stranger to human life, keeping the veil of this awareness between himself and the world unto the hour of his death. Ethan Brand is consumed by the obsession that he must search for the unpardonable sin. Probing for it in the soul of others and by that torturing them spiritually, he at last gains the insight to detect the sin within himself, in his self-righteousness and his intellectual pride. Undeception however comes too late; only suicide can free him from his obsession.

All these embodiments of man's consciousness of evil reflect the intellectual and moral concepts of a Calvinist Puritanism as it reigned in early colonial America and was recreated imaginatively by Hawthorne with an intense and critical insight and in the spirit of an engaged detachment characteristic for this author. The dichotomy in a faith which embraces the notion of man's electness and that of his depravity belongs to all Protestant churches derived from Calvin's reform, and the human dilemma which was bound to rise in a spirit depressed by the apparent incompatibility of this dichotomy can be found anywhere where such a faith is deeply lived. It gained a particular weight in America, where the early settlers, the New England Puritans, firmly believed to have founded a commonwealth based on a purified church and so giving room for a human order free from the corruptions of the Old World. New England as the New Jerusalem, the colonists as the Chosen People, these are conceptions of powerful significance and long enduring effect. They won a new impetus when, with the fading of Puritan orthodoxy, the spirit of an optimistic rationalism became strong, spreading the belief that the American, liberated from the shackles of European "feudalism" and its social injustice, could and did realise a freer, a better, a more humane socio-political order than the Old World.

To such a belief in one's own progressiveness and perfectibility the experience of the power of evil over man would come as a singularly severe shock. The New England Puritan and his spiritual heir, the American of the young republic, who saw in his independence a dispensation of a new perfection, would easily take to the illusion that he had gained the plane of a securely founded order of values, and if the corruptibility of just these values was experienced, if disillusionment was forced upon him, it would be deeper and more painful than that felt by a European who was less in danger of being deluded by a notion of his own society's perfection.

The difference between the American and the European reaction to evil is borne out by a comparison of Hawthorne's presentation of the Puritan mind with European ones of a similar background. The social and religious counterpart nearest to early New England Puritanism is without doubt to be found in late seventeenth century Scotland, the Scotland of the Covenanters. Their Presbyterian church shares its theological roots with American Congregationalism, their social and political ideas are not very far from those of the New England communities. There exists one impressive tale of the power of evil over the Puritan mind by a Scottish writer almost contemporary with Hawthorne, James Hogg's *The Private Memoirs and Confessions of a Justified Sinner*, published in 1824, eleven years before the first printing of "Young Goodman Brown". Hogg's novel exploits a potentiality of Calvinism which repeatedly became evident in the course of its history: antinomianism, the utmost consequence of the doctrine of predestination and election. In Scottish Presbyterianism as well as in New England Puritanism antinomian commotions did break out several times, endangering law and order in church and society. The antinomians held that regenerate man, accepted into the body of the elect by God's grace alone, could not and should not be bound by human laws. No act of his could cause him to fall from the state of grace which had been conferred upon him by God's unalterable will. Much of the ruthless cruelty shown by the Scottish Covenanters in their struggle with the Episcopalians grew out of this spirit.

Hogg based his story on these historical foundations. He shows how a man of unstable character, consumed with envy of his betters, embraces the antinomian doctrine, is corrupted by it and gradually dehumanized. The protagonist, Robert Colwan, is despised by his father, who rightly suspects this younger son not to be his own offspring. An elder brother being preferred, Robert nurses a hatred for father and brother, plots against them, first by petty intrigues, later by bold crimes, and ends in destroying his entire family. His misdeeds growing to enormous dimensions, he is prosecuted by the law, at last tormented by the consciousness of his own moral abnormality, and turns to suicide as his final resort.

There are two traits which infuse this novel with great power, make it indeed into one of the representative works of European Romanticism. One is a far reaching insight into the dark and hidden layers of the human soul, the other the transformation of popular demonology into a personified devil, in which the idea of evil active in the protagonist's mind is embodied. On the day of Robert Colwan's election to the state of grace he encounters a mysterious stranger, a youth resembling himself, who becomes his guide on the way to destruction. It is his second self, gaining possession of his mind and soul as the poison of antinomianism takes its effect.

As a story of human perversion, of the potentiality for evil working in man, this novel is certainly as powerful as "Ethan Brand" or "Young Goodman Brown". It might even be considered more harassing, for it describes the progress of human deterioration as a long drawn-out process. Yet, for all this and all the thematic similarity to the two stories by Hawthorne the effect of Hogg's novel is less sombre, it is not one of unrelieved gloom. There are, of course, aesthetic reasons for this. As a novel *The Private Memoirs and Confessions of a Justified Sinner* has a wider scope, a greater variety of fictional reality. Moreover, it is a tale told twice, from different points of view. The "Confessions" proper, which consist of an autobiographical record by the protagonist, are preceded by the narrative of a chronicler who is an outsider not only to the events but also to the spirit of religious fanaticism evident in them.—But as always in a literary work of perfection the formal difference points to one in spirit. In Hogg's fictional world the spirit of evil as a life destroying, a dehumanizing power has not the absolute sway it possesses in Hawthorne's stories. It is of a very imminent reality, but it exercises its hold only over men of warped character and unbalanced mind. It is understood as a phenomenon of abnormality, not as one of general significance.

This is brought out above all by the totally different interpretations given to the same events by the chronicler's narrative on the one hand and the autobiographical confessions on the other. Even in "Ethan Brand", the one story of Hawthorne's nearest to Hogg, the fundamental difference between the American and the Scottish author remains obvious. Ethan Brand certainly is a person out of the normal, unbalanced by an obsessive idea. He is, besides, perverted by self-righteousness and intellectual pride, and in all this he resembles Hogg's Justified Sinner. But within the story Brand is the one figure of strength and greatness, awe-inspiring and demanding respect, in spite of his monstrosity. The persons with whom he is confronted are beings of low stature: ineffectual and dissipated townspeople and a slow-witted, primitive lime burner. In contrast to this Robert Colwan is set off against men of spirit and of character. Seen within the whole of his human surroundings his own personality appears all the more despicable.

A confrontation of Hawthorne's stories with Hogg's novel seems to me clearly to show a considerable difference in the conception of the idea of evil in American and European literature. In trying to explain this divergence we shall find that it rises from a difference in the spiritual background. For all the power which the consciousness of sin and of human depravity has in Calvinist Europe, evil is here more readily considered in its co-existence with other forces. It is integrated in a view of life which accepts the bewildering intermingling of good and bad in human nature. We should not forget that no European state or society (early Calvinist Geneva, perhaps, excepted) was so exclusively determined by that singleness of mind, that dedication to *one* moral and religious concept, which moulded Puritan New England. Even in the Scotland of the seventeenth century Episcopalian and secular forces were powerful by the side of and against Presbyterianism. And furthermore, none of the European communities were entirely dominated by the idea of having attained a purity and perfection which could generate the illusion of an elimination of evil. It was the peculiar background of American history which led Hawthorne to depict the idea of evil as he did, notwithstanding his personal scepticism against conceptions of total perfection and total depravity, the scepticism of a mind which could see other sides and solutions to the human dilemma over the conflict between good and evil.[1]

---

[1] Both in *The Scarlet Letter* and, still more strongly, in *The House of the Seven Gables* such "other solutions" to the human dilemma over the problem of evil are

To corroborate the findings gained from a comparative view of Hogg and Hawthorne a few German literary embodiments of the idea of evil shall be called to mind. In Germany, as in nineteenth century America, the witchcraft delusion of the seventeenth century had a strong appeal to writers intent on this subject. (It should be remembered that with Hawthorne witchcraft is not only an important motif in stories like "Young Goodman Brown", but that it turns up in his novels as well, particularly in *The Scarlet Letter* and *The House of the Seven Gables*.) In two German novellas of high quality, *Die Bernsteinhexe* (" The Amber Witch") by Wilhelm Meinhold and *Renate* by Theodor Storm, the belief in witchcraft is of central importance. In both stories the evil engendered by this superstition is threatening life and perverting the spirit of humanity, and it is depicted with an awareness of the dark irrationality of human nature. As in Hawthorne and Hogg evil manifests itself as a power benighting the mind of man through suspicion and distrust, and it leads to crimes against the duty to love and respect one's fellow men. But again, as in the Scotsman's novel and in opposition to the American's tale, these German novellas emphasize the limits of the delusion. The heroines in Meinhold's and Storm's stories are not touched by it. Maria Schweidler, the amber witch, keeps her mind clear and is eventually acquitted by trial. Renate, though the suspicion held against her destroys her happiness (her lover turns away because he cannot free himself from superstitious doubts in her), preserves her moral and intellectual integrity unimpaired; she has the strength to carry on life against a world defaming her. In both stories the power of evil is refuted by human beings of superiority in character and intelligence.

Storm especially, if the recurrent strain of the suprarational in his fiction is considered, takes an attitude very different from Hawthorne and reveals a non-Protestant, actually a pre-Christian source of this German writer's thought which has no counterpart in nineteenth century American literature. Storm's latest—and perhaps greatest— novella, *Der Schimmelreiter*, poses a situation comparable to that of *Renate*. The protagonist, Hauke Haien, is a person of exceptional strength of mind and will power much like Renate. His conflict with human mediocrity surrounding him is as unavoidable as hers; in a

---

given, though to a reader of these novels the effect of the long drawn out conflict with the forces of darkness will seem to preponderate over the lighter shades of the redeeming conclusion.

similar way he is threatened by prejudice and superstition which mingle into a malignity marring the efforts by which he as a dike-reeve tries to protect his community against the onslaught of the sea. The forces of evil let loose against him and, in the end, annihilating him physically are conceived as forces of nature, those of the uncontrollable elements (the sea), as well as those rising from the irrational compulsions of human nature. As presented in the story they lie outside the category of moral good and bad. Evil in *Der Schimmelreiter* is understood as the manifestation of an inscrutable fate. The way in which the theme is evolved shows that this novella has grown from an archaic fatalism whose latent potentiality was revived and did intrude in a bourgeois literary world to which for all his paganism Storm belongs. This is less strange than it may seem if one bears in mind that Europe is nearer to the pre-Christian sources of our Western civilization than America whose intellectual basis rests on the negation of these sources by the Protestant Reformation. So a latent paganism is a distinct strain in Storm as it is in Hogg's conception of the devil, but as it is not in Hawthorne.

(A short remark should draw attention to another German author, E. T. A. Hoffmann, master of demonology in the romantic tale. The dark forces let loose in his stories have all the destructive power of absolute evil, they unsettle and often annihilate the human soul. However, at the same time they open up the vision of an experience which lies outside the world of moral good and bad and belongs to an aesthetic ideality. In *Der Elementargeist* Viktor, the high-minded young man who engages in dealings with the devil and is saved only at the last moment by the moral instinct and common sense of his servant, pines away in melancholy for the rest of his life, much as Hawthorne's Young Goodman Brown does. But quite in opposition to Hawthorne's figure Viktor is not unsettled by doubt or remorse, but by the loss of a vision of perfect beauty which had come to him in his communion with the powers of darkness. So to Hoffmann even black magic—and there is no doubt about its activity in *Der Elementargeist*—points to a sphere where the idea of evil is no longer valid.)

Having recognized Hawthorne's conceptions as representative for a strain in the American mind it will not come as a surprise if we find the idea of evil recurring in many a work of nineteenth century American literature. Hawthorne's contemporary and friend, Herman

Melville, an admirer of "the power of blackness"[1] in the New England's creations, gave it, perhaps, the widest scope. To him the sense of "Depravity and Original Sin" as embodied in Hawthorne's writings is a characteristic of man in general:

> ...this great power of blackness in him derives its force from its appeals to that Calvinistic sense of Innate Depravity and Original Sin, from whose visitations, in some shape or other, no deeply thinking mind is always and wholly free. For, in certain moods, no man can weigh this world, without throwing in something, somehow like Original Sin, to strike the uneven balance.[2]

Among Melville's novels *Moby Dick* and *Pierre* show evil as an inscrutable power directing human destiny, remaining hidden to the human understanding behind the ambiguity of appearances. In his tales of the working of evil Melville does not take recourse to the historical phenomenon of early American Puritanism, his spiritual concepts are those of an independent mind of a highly original and self-willed intellectuality. In spite of this the weight of the power of evil and the human dilemma set in motion by it are, in Melville's works, of a kind not far away from Hawthorne's creations in that vein. Two of his shorter tales show this in an exemplary way: *Benito Cereno* and *Billy Budd*. The former may be considered as a confrontation of American innocence with a malignity it cannot deal with because it is not able to realize it. Captain Delano, a typical representative of sound sense and goodwill, tries to help the Spanish captain Benito Cereno and his crew, who suffer from utter exhaustion, but he does not see through the situation and so his well-meant efforts nearly end in disaster. The key figure of the story, the negro Babo, poses as Don Benito's faithful servant, and Delano is entirely taken in by him until Babo makes a murderous assault on his master. When at last undeceived, Delano sees Babo as a figure of absolute evil, to be abhorred and destroyed, but, characteristically, he does not even attempt to consider the reasons which brought about the plot against Cereno and his men: Babo's desire to free the negroes from the slavery into which Cereno's ship was bound to carry them. Moreover, the American captain, though his resoluteness at last saves Cereno from the clutches of his servant, cannot alleviate the Spaniard's spiritual suffering. The consolation of

---

[1] This characterization of Hawthorne as a writer occurs in Melville's famous review, "Hawthorne and His Mosses".

[2] Quoted from *Herman Melville*, ed. by R. W. B. Lewis, New York, 1962, pp. 42/43.

his easy optimism which sees in Cereno's escape a triumph of good over bad and feels the just order of the world restored is lost upon the broken spirit of Don Benito, who pines away and soon dies. To the simplicity of the American captain the mind of his friend who cannot overcome the deadly effect of having been at the mercy of Babo's malignity remains an enigma to the very end.

In *Benito Cereno* Melville makes evident the effect of evil on the American mind under an aspect different from but not less representative than Hawthorne's images of the spiritual gloom engendered in the soul by Puritanism. In his picture of Captain Delano we can recognize the secularized type of man which emerged from the Enlightenment, his common sense and sociability, his optimistic activism ever ready to help but unable to cope with a phenomenon like evil which lies outside his understanding of a rational world. To him evil is the disturbance of an established order which has to be and can be set right again by practical means. He does not see that by his doing so it is only seemingly overcome. The quintessence of *Benito Cereno* is that evil is a phenomenon on an existential level which man may conceive but cannot control.

(It is interesting how this truth, forcefully implied by Melville, is brought out in a modern dramatization of *Benito Cereno*. In his play "Benito Cereno" Robert Lowell, a poet troubled by the manifestations of evil in our present day world, lays the stress on the futility of Delano's proceeding.[1] In saving Cereno and capturing the Spanish ship he becomes involved in a wholesale slaughtering of the negro slaves. Restoring order can be reached only through a brutal assertion of material power.)

If the treatment of evil in Melville's *Benito Cereno* leaves open— at least by implication—the possibility of a more adequate human understanding for this problem and for its integration in a concept of life, his last work, *Billy Budd*, presents Melville's understanding of evil in its ineluctable compulsion, it discloses a view on its workings from the highest level. This story of a guiltless young sailor's entanglement in manslaughter, of his death as a penalty for a crime which he committed in the technical sense but not in intention seems to me to contain the most consummate representation of the idea of evil

---

[1] The play is the last part of the trilogy, *The Old Glory*, published in 1965. It is there preceded by dramatizations of two of Hawthorne's tales, "Endicott and the Red Cross" and "My Kinsman Major Molineux".

in American literature. Billy Budd is innocent man in a fuller sense than Captain Delano in the earlier work. His innocence is not that of a certain cultural and national stage in history, he is innocent man as an image of nature conceived in its absolute purity and beauty. Very appropriately the young sailor impresses his captain like "Adam before the Fall", or like "an Angel of God".[1] Billy is unable to have any conception of malignity as it is practised against him, and he has no means to defend himself against his accuser but the impulsive, speechless reaction of innocence. It is this natural act, the deadly blow of his fist, which makes him a victim of human law and proves that law's inability to deal with evil.

And his adversary, Claggart, the master-at-arms, in his intention to destroy the young innocent, who has never stood in his way, is the personification of evil in a much fuller sense than Babo, the malicious negro. Claggart has none of the latter's motives for his hatred. In spite of the plausibility Melville has given with a few sparing strokes to the master-at-arms' turning unkindly against his subordinates (his haughtiness, his harshness, his ambition), the depth and strength of his fiendish hatred are not explained in human terms. They are presented as the manifestations of irrational evil whose inroads on a world of seeming order and security cannot be withstood. Unobtrusively but unmistakably Melville has given Claggart the insignia of the Satanic as they have been seen since Milton: a pale sombreness, a subdued intensity of passion, the melancholy of one who feels excluded from the world of innocence. As Satan in *Paradise Lost* could love and pity Adam and Eve in beholding them,[2] the master-at-arms' eye sometimes "would have in it a touch of soft yearning, as if Claggart could even have loved Billy but for fate and ban."[3]

The powerful reality of the story gains further weight by its partaking in the essence of the tragic, which is enhanced by Melville giving the representatives of the every day world (Captain Vere and his officers) a sympathetic understanding of Billy's plight and an awareness of their own dilemma as his judges. They realize that under their eyes and with their compliance innocence is made the victim of malignity, that it is martyred by the bare necessities of a worldly justice which does wrong to humanity. The end of Billy, who is

---

[1] Cf. Herman Melville, *Billy Budd, Sailor*, ed. by Harrison Hayford & Martin M. Sealts, Jr., Chicago, 1962, pp. 94, 101.

[2] *Paradise Lost*, IV, pp. 363, 374.

[3] *Billy Budd, Sailor*, p. 88.

executed at the yard-arm of his ship, is not so much his own tragedy, but that of the officers, it is especially the tragedy of Captain Vere, who many years later, at the moment of his own death, turns his thoughts back to Billy Budd's supreme sacrifice.

If we have seen the concept of evil contained in Hawthorne's fiction as the embodiment of an idea peculiar to the American mind, we will find that Melville, for all the difference of his attitude, is still consistent with this idea. In his tales as in those of his elder contemporary life is understood as dominated by a duality, a confrontation of good and bad, unleashing a conflict of extreme intensity, for these forces are realized as absolutes. Melville's representation of the conflict as it is found in *Billy Budd* however reflects a more advanced, one might, perhaps, even say a more mature stage in the development of the concept of this conflict; (the term "more mature", of course, referring to the figures in *Billy Budd*— like Captain Vere—compared with the figures in Hawthorne, but *not* to the mind of Melville as set off against that of his fellow author). Whereas Hawthorne's figures (Goodman Brown, Parson Hooper, Ethan Brand) cannot cope with evil, but are overwhelmed by its absoluteness, the men of insight and judgement in *Billy Budd* find the strength to integrate it in their concept of life. They suffer as Hawthorne's sombre Puritans do, but through their experience they grow to a richer, a truer humanity. The soul in them is not crippled by disillusionment. Melville in his last story has attained a consummation of the tragic as the final test of man's stature, which approaches the spirit of Shakespeare's great tragedies like *King Lear* and *Othello*.

So Hawthorne and Melville, in spite of the dissimilarity of their individualities, have given expression to *one* basic conception of the idea of evil, which leaves the dualism of good and bad unrelieved. The fundamental difference of this American conception from European ones will be recognized if these two authors are confronted with what may be called the classical treatment of the problem of evil in nineteenth century European literature, Goethe's *Faust*. Based on a popular legend which had been the product of the late medieval spirit presenting the struggle between Evil and Good in terms of the traditional Christian faith, Goethe's dramatic poem contains elements of the old dualistic concept. Throughout the story of Faust's earthly course the perversion of all his efforts through the devil's power is emphasized: his way is not one of gradual purification, his works remain entangled in evil from the destruction of Gretchen to the cold-blooded expulsion of Philemon and Baucis, the old couple who stand in the way of Faust's ambition. But in his remoulding of the traditional legend Goethe gave it a trend which resolves the struggle between Good and Bad. In his dramatic poem evil appears as a means of God to lead man through temptation to salvation. In the "Prologue in Heaven" God makes it clear that the devil has a function in the divine plan, that his machinations will eventually contribute to the triumph of Good. In his final words to Mephistopheles the Lord says:

> Man's active nature, flagging, seeks too soon the level;
> Unqualified repose he learns to crave;
> Whence, willingly, the comrade him I gave,
> Who works, excites, and must create as Devil.[1]

In the decisive scene of the drama when Faust is about to conclude the pact with hell, Mephisto admits this himself. To Faust's question "What art thou then?", he answers:

> Part of that Power, not understood,
> Which always wills the Bad, and always works the Good.[2]

This is far away from the American understanding of evil and its working in the world of man, as we met it in Hawthorne's and Melville's tales. Earthly existence in Goethe's drama is not seen as the battleground of two irreconcilable principles. The conflict is resolved, evil is taken up in the harmony of the universe, it does serve as the agent of good. Goethe in contrast to the great American writers considered here represents a spiritual tradition which has preserved the idea of unity in its view of the world and of man as it had come down from classical antiquity and was never entirely lost in the history of the European mind, though called in question by the Protestant Reformation, especially in its Calvinist variety. The American mind, having grown on the ground of just this kind of Protestantism and

---

[1] *Faust*, pp. 340-343, Bayard Taylor's translation. In the original the verses run:
Des Menschen Tätigkeit kann allzu leicht erschlaffen,
Er liebt sich bald die unbedingte Ruh;
Drum geb ich gern ihm den Gesellen zu,
Der reizt und wirkt und muß als Teufel schaffen.
[2] Ibd. pp. 1335/36; in German:
(Faust) Nun gut, wer bist du denn?
(Mephisto) Ein Teil von jener Kraft,
Die stets das Böse will und stets das Gute schafft.

being farther removed from the common roots in classical antiquity, did give up this unity; therefore the idea of evil as conceived and embodied by the American writer does not partake in the sense of unity which inspired Goethe.[1] It is nearer to our modern consciousness which has lost the belief in harmony and unity, which was a living faith in Goethe and the best minds of German idealism. To us whose experience of life is one of conflicting forces, who no longer dare to assume a unifying principle in the world as we see it, the image of evil as it was moulded by Hawthorne and Melville has the meaning of actuality. From what we know of the origin and growth of the American mind and its situation in the world of today it will seem appropriate to find a modern poem expressing the experience of evil in a language which makes use of the conceptions of Calvinist theology. The poem I speak of is by Richard Eberhart, it bears the title "The Assassin" and the date of November 22nd, 1963, the day of John F. Kennedy's death. In form it is characterized by a simplicity which is not usual with this author and may well be attributed to the conscious intention of giving utterance to a shock shared by the American nation as a whole:

> I am that vile worm of Satan
> Sent to kill the beautiful.
> I have destroyed everything that is good.
> I have drawn over my head death's hood.
>
> In the dark of my brain
> Was a primeval stain.
> I destroyed what is sacred
> Out of primitive hatred.
>
> Grace fell from my face.
> Of love I had not a trace.
> I was able to kill
> By my malevolent will.
>
> Thoughtless, abstract, evil,
> I was agent of the devil

---

[1] The following remark seems appropriate here: There is in American intellectual history one philosophy of life which stresses the unity of the mind not unlike Goethe, actually owing something of its conception to him: Emerson's transcendentalism. But Emerson in resolving the dualism of good and bad eliminates evil, which Goethe, who works it into an organic concept of life, does not. For Emerson's evasive and inadequate conception of evil and his contemporaries' reaction to this side of his philosophy of life cf. F. O. Matthiessen, *American Renaissance*, New York, 1941, Chapter V.

Who overwhelmed my humanity
And totally blinded me.

Now whatever gods there are
See in history from afar,
The repetition of the stroke of Cain
Come to the world again.[1]

The dignity of American literature and much of its meaningfulness to us do largely rise from its dedication to the truth of the human dilemma, from its readiness to record without evasion man's search for Good and his unavoidable confrontation with Evil.

---

[1] The text of the poem is taken from *The Hollins Critic*, vol. I, no. 4, October 1964, p. 11.

A. N. J. DEN HOLLANDER

CULTURAL DIVERSITY AND THE MIND OF THE SCHOLAR

Some Thoughts on American and European Thinking

No European who devotes professional attention to things American can, I believe, escape the realisation that what is true of American living is true also of American thought: both have characteristic patterns that mark them off from the patterns of other cultures. In certain respects European scholars do not think the same way their American counterparts do. To Europeans, American thought has a distinct bent of its own born from reshaping British, French and German influences to an American mold.

In the 19th century realisation of men like Marx, Poincaré and Freud that the human mind is itself an object for social study we find the beginning of the sociology of knowledge. It was the further reaching achievement of Durkheim, Scheler, Mannheim, Mead to connect the individual and his thinking with the social context, to demonstrate that thinking is continually linked with the forms of social existence. We now know that thought is always bound up with social processes and structures: the autonomy of a theoretic sphere is delusory. Our surrounding culture teaches us logical relations, it sets the goals of human problems and teaches the inferences which people in a particular culture regard as justifiable. Therefore, in order to truly understand the world of thought of any country one has to study the existential conditions of its intellectual activity.

Reflection in the humanities and in the social sciences is embedded in the social life of the society from which it comes forth. The thought of the social scientist especially, to some extent forms part of the object to which he directs his thought. Thus the object studied is one of the constituent elements of the structure of the researcher's thought: Hegel's "identity of the subject and object of thought".[1] There also is the historical dimension: people do not think the same way in dif-

---

[1] Lucien Goldmann, "The Sociology of Literature", *Intern. Soc. Science Journal*, Vol. XIX, no. 4, 1967, pp. 493-494.

ferent times. Exploring the social as well as the historical setting within which American cultural phenomena have been conceived and born carry this insight home to students with considerable force. Once they are encouraged to uncover the roots of mental structures or artistic achievements and thereby gain a better understanding of its making and meaning, its essence and existence, they realize that they reach further and deeper than they could have otherwise.[1]

Exploring this particular field means that the American students of things European, and that the European students of things American, if they accept the general view just offered, will concentrate not so much on the content of a thought or theory as on its relationship to the wider society within which it has been conceived and born. An idea ceases, then, to be only considered as such, in and for itself, it also becomes the possible manifestation of wider tendencies, forces or facts, as an expression of realities which lie behind it.

Reading American authors conveys the conviction that not only popular, unscientific thinking is conditioned by its cultural milieu; neither is the mind of the scholar freefloating, independent of any situational context. It is evident that we have to account for the bias of the man of learning also. Truth does not spring from his brain pure and pristine, free of any distortion or slanting.[2] The structure of his mind too accommodates itself to the structure of the society in which it has to function. It is not possible for any man, after his mind has been formed and conditioned by passing through that socially determined matrix of thinking which constitutes his culture and society, to cut himself adrift from it and resume the complete freedom which his mind has lost in the process of its social determination. It will be subject to the values of the nation of which he is a member; these values constitute the prism through which the worldview of the society concerned is made what it is. This, notwithstanding a large allowance for individual deviations from the norm. The scholar's perception, his apprehension of meaning will be an act of the whole personality including the specifically social sector of the mind; indeed, it is not absurd to claim that the specifically social sector of the mind will have a larger say in the matter than either the sensual apparatus or the formal intellect. Philosophically speaking,

---

[1] W. Stark, *The Sociology of Knowledge*, 1958, p. 12; Stanley Taylor, *Conceptions of Institutions and the Theory of Knowledge*, 1956, pp. 13, 14, 23.
[2] I. L. Horowitz, *Philosophy, Science and the Sociology of Knowledge*, 1961, p. 8.

it is not a transcendental consciousness which takes in the meaning, the essence, of any social fact, but an immanent consciousness, the socially determined consciousness of a man who lives within a certain order and apprehends all social events in terms of it. The social and organizational structure, too, of the learned community inside Western society, has always tended to fit itself harmoniously into the framework of the contemporary social values. Such as the wider society was, such the narrower society of learning tended to be.[1]

Let us now leave general principles and attempt to demonstrate their validity in the special field of endeavour the EAAS is engaged in. First then, it seems to me that the preoccupations of American and European scholarship illustrate the point made rather neatly.

Theories originate in the culture-bound beliefs and personal values of the theorists. Scholarly theory in the behavioral sciences in particular always has an underlying pattern of latent sentiment and assumption, rests on a particular image of man, resonates certain connotations. In the Berlin Conference of the EAAS (1961), Dahrendorf pointed out, when discussing the influence of European sociology on American sociology, that in this traffic a number of concepts and ideas have been more or less systematically neglected in America, although they played and continue to play a prominent role in the thinking of European sociologists: the concepts of class, violence, élites, the ideas of revolution, of history and of the intellectual as a "rebel". American sociologists for a long time failed to absorb those ideas of European sociologists which threatened their undisputed acceptance of the dominant values of their society. They have thereby rendered their society the dubious service of apparently protecting it from some of the more unsettling ideas of modern times.[2] In directing their attention to European sociologists and their works, Americans have, till quite recently, greatly preferred such theories and concepts that fitted in with their prevailing orientation of dynamic conservatism and have neglected those aspects of European social thinking which might be interpreted to have more radical implications. In this way, as Dahrendorf pointed out, Tocqueville has been received rather than Marx, Spencer rather than Pareto, Max Weber rather than Sorel, Tönnies and Durkheim

---

[1] Stark, *op. cit.* pp. 15, 30-31.
[2] Ralph Dahrendorf, *European Sociology and the American Self-Image* (mimeogr.), 1961, pp. 46-47.

rather than Mosca and Michels, Malinowski rather than Levy Brühl. Within the work of the chosen few, the same selective principles have been at work, so that certain very general ideas, central to European thinking, such as class conflict and élites, never played a considerable part either in American sociology or in American thought more generally. Instead the ideas of democracy, of individualism, of ethical capitalism, of rationality, community and stability were chosen, because they served well as ideological foundations of the American reality. Clearly, the selection of problems to which answers are given is a function of the values of the society in which such knowledge arises and becomes significant. In this sense, every social theory is relative to the society in which it belongs.

Every society is held together by values which glorify the existing state or trend of affairs.[1] European ideas that do not fit well into the American conception of self, that collide with the dominant, official ethos of America, have long been soft-pedalled in American scholarly thought, while they prevail in European thinking. It is clear that the structure of knowledge is dependent on a principle of selection and a principle of order, and both are to be seen as consequences of the "grid" before the eye of the student of society or history, the a priori in his mind, in short, his basic system of values. Societies are unlike each other precisely in this, that they have different preoccupations concerning what is good and bad, right or wrong, what is worthy to be pursued or better eschewed. Extra-theoretical factors are present, unrecognized, even in a view of history and society which, on the conscious level, is altogether "pure" and wholly "theoretical". Even where individual prejudice has no place, there yet obtain certain basic social pre-valuations of which we have to take note. They explain the manifest differences between American and European variants of social history, having their sources in different intellectual and practical climates.[2]

---

[1] *Ibid.* p. 50.

[2] The problem is not absent from historiography either. The world of the male is different from the world of the female. Much of the presentation of history is male-oriented because the male scribe has evolved as the main custodian of tradition. One has occasion to wonder whether the point has received as much interest on the part of historians as one might expect. The reports of anthropologists usually make a decidedly masculine impression, even when the anthropologist happened to be a woman. The main reason of this may be that the interpreters and most of the informants are almost always men. (A. N. J. den Hollander, "Social description; the problem of reliability and validity", in D. G. Jongmans and P. C. W. Gutkind, *Anthropologists in the field*, Assen 1967, p. 14).

Let us explore some of the domains where Americans and Europeans think in different ways. First I like to ask attention for the nature of theory, both American and European. I think, then, that you will agree with me that in the European sense, America has had little "grand theory", whether political, economical, social, cultural or theological. One finds fragmentary achievements rather than imposing over-all structures. The American disinclination to structure thought into systems is striking when contrasted with the continental European tradition. Much more so than Europeans, Americans have a fear of freezing thought. Being less interested in forms than in contents, being little disposed towards projections into a far away future, they have also shyed away from predictions and programs of social change covering more than one generation. It may have been one of the reasons why neither socialism nor communism ever gained much ground in the United States. To Europeans American thought seems tentative, piece meal, concrete and direct, keeping both postulates and objectives flexible. American thought has rarely strayed far away from the concerns of social reality.

Take the case of conservative thought. Unlike European conservatives, who relied upon the authority of the State and the Church, the sanctity of the family and of order generally, American conservatives took over the liberal principles of individualism and natural rights, they were in a sense liberals from the very beginning and their later protests centered in resistance against state interference in individual economic alternatives. America has little clearly delineated conservative philosophy and the European student looks in vain for outstanding conservative thinkers. It is apparent that liberalism has furnished the dominant political and intellectual climate of the United States. American radical thought in particular has had little to fight against throughout the times, historically it did not perform a similar service to the liberal movements of the 19th and 20th centuries in the United States as it did in Europe. American radical thought could not build up pressure, because of the dynamics of social change, the general awareness of considerable social mobility, the widespread myth among all classes of the reality of the American Dream. Only in recent years, radicalism seems to be gaining some importance in the United States.

Americans always wonder about the wealth of ideologies in Europe. They themselves have always been weak in creating them. European observers of American society noted equality as a characteristic of

American life. But, as Daniel Boorstin has pointed out with his un-
failing perspicacity, it is the fact rather than the theory of equality
which has flourished in America. "If European countries have been
strong in theories of equality, as in other political theories, they have
long been feeble in developing equalitarian institutions. In the United
States on the contrary, where people have had unprecedented success
in developing widespread social equality, they have never produced
a pretty or an important theory about it. This is but an example, if
one of the more spectacular, of how their talent for improving life
has excelled their capacity for perfecting thought".[1]

An exploration of American sociology provides a case study in the
influence of a social and political milieu on the presuppositions and
implications of theory and research. Sociological concepts derived
from European social and political philosophers, frequently loaded
with anti-liberal freight, underwent a subtle transformation at the
hands of American sociologists when imported into the liberal American context. Or, with perhaps equal frequency, these concepts have
been uncritically applied to the American realities without regard for
the deficiencies of the resulting analysis. The process is one of the main
reasons why European sociologists find little use for American textbooks in teaching their students. Since the textbook as such is almost unknown in European academic writing, European professors
often do use American textbooks, for better or for worse. Next to the
distorting influence just mentioned, it stands to reason that there is
another major one: American sociology textbooks are based on an
American social reality, which is so different from the social scene
in any European country, that for this reason alone such textbooks
are largely useless for European instruction.

The most interesting thing about American sociology in its relation
to European theories, is that in many instances one or two things
have resulted. On the one hand, there has been either a transformation
of the meanings of the European concepts, or the development of new
concepts more appropriate to the American liberal tradition and the
American social and political context; on the other, there has been
an uncritical application of concepts developed in Europe to American
data without regard for the resulting distortions or for the special
condition which had to be taken into account.[2]

---

[1] Daniel J. Boorstin, *America and the Image of Europe*, 1960; 1964 ed. pp. 52-53.
[2] Leon Bramson, *The Political Context of Sociology*, 1961, p. 47.

America's unique social and political tradition, her individualism and liberalism, has somehow stamped her traditional sociology, making it different from that which Europeans practice and comprehend. Those burning issues which aroused the passions of Europeans in social and political conflict are precisely the issues which have to a large extent, ceased to be matters of controversy in the United States, if they ever had major importance. Agreement among American sociologists on the absolute validity of the middle-class norm was, till fairly recently, almost unanimous,—whilst for European sociologists, the relations among the social classes is a question that is historically and traditionally defined.[1]

The concept "class" offers a good example of the fate that may befall to a product of European thinking after the idea has travelled West and has become an American immigrant. It soon underwent a radical change in meaning.[2] In Europe the notions of class, economic position and class conflict are quite inseparable, but for the ordinary American, class is not a prime category of self-interpretation. In the U.S. Marx has never exerted the enormous influence he has had in Europe, he just was not at home there, the Americans did not know what to do with him and did not bother much to make him applicable. Class in America and class in Europe refer to phenomena sufficiently different to render invalid any effort to transfer theory based on the concept from one continent to the other. Of course the concept can be used, and is widely used by American sociologists. Unavoidably their inappropriate application of theory developed for a European institution to data from the American scene has brought about considerable confusion. There would be no objection to using the term "class" in order to speak of arbitrary divisions in the United States, on any continuum—occupation, education, status or prestige, power, or one of the other bases of significant social differentiation—provided it is recognized that class is a different phenomenon in Europe. It is very difficult, however, to keep the distinction clear. Social differentiation in the United States just does not lend itself to realistic treatment in terms of arbitrary and blanket concepts.[3] There is, indeed, an increasing awareness of this among American scholars.

---

[1] Bramson, pp. 48-49.

[2] See the lucid exposition by Arnold M. Rose, "The Concept of Class and American Sociology", *Social Research*, vol. 25, no. 1. Spring 1958. Also Dahrendorf, *loc. cit*. p. 33.

[3] Rose, *loc. cit.*

Let us turn to another concept: élites. The American ethos has no use for élite groups, they are incompatible with the American ideal of democracy. Small groups of men who monopolize power is an aspect of European thinking which (till Wright Mills) has found little resonance in American self-interpretation.[1] American students find it difficult to understand European theories about élites, as many a visiting European professor has found out in his American classes. For a similar reason, Americans do not easily grasp the educational system in European countries with its heavy anchorage in a social system that may now be largely of the past but still makes itself felt. The American idea that education is by definition a good thing, and that as many people as proves to be economically possible should receive as much of it as can be provided for them, runs counter to the European idea that secondary and higher education should be bestowed in the measure in which the recipient can benefit by it, and that not more than a small percentage of the total population is intellectually capable of being educated up to the highest level. One is inclined to think that the background of this particular élitist reasoning is more influenced by old ideas about the supposed normalcy of a strict social stratification than European educationalists would admit.

We can go on with other concepts affected by the cultural diversity of the Old World and the New. Simply because people use the same word for something is no indication that they mean the same thing. Take the word "liberal". Europeans misunderstand American usage of this word again and again. They are acquainted with a historical past in which the crown and the altar, feudal lords and mighty ecclesiastics held power. For them the word "liberal" refers to the classical doctrine of political and economical individualism, with its emphasis on rationality, equality, religious liberty, constitutionalism, majority rule. All this has been associated socially, culturally, economically, with middle-class hegemony. In comparison with Europe, the U.S.A. was born a liberal country, with limited government, social mobility and economic freedom. American liberals, having no *ancien régime* to attack, have been sober, moderate and realistic.[2] In contemporary American usage, the word "liberal" indicates sympathy with democratic socialism, trade unionism, university reform, safeguarding the rights of minori-

---

[1] Dahrendorf, *loc. cit.* p. 38.
[2] Bramson, *op. cit.* p. 16, p. 50.

ties, being against discrimination of Negroes, Jews, Asiatics. It may sometimes refer to groups with conservative, even reactionary leanings, as e.g. the "Agrarians" in Vanderbilt University in the twenties of the present century. All this can be explained, yet the use of one and the same word for two different realities makes it a problem for European students to understand American usage, as their professors have frequent occasion to note.

À propos "problem"—here we have another word that shows an interesting difference of vocabulary between Europeans and Americans. It is often the case that Americans, when they speak of a "problem", imply that it is something that can eventually be solved. American activist tradition and American optimism both seem to make for a tonic attitude in such matters. When Europeans speak of "problems" they are often thinking of something which cannot be solved at all; and this is sometimes revealed in their subsequent discourse.[1] Americans may then be impressed by what they sometimes name "European negativism"; Europeans are equally impressed and slightly surprised by American optimism. It simply means that they think differently. In technical imagination and the art of "getting things done" the American mind is clearly better equipped than that of an average European but it becomes a different proposition when both set to work upon an abstract subject. If he has not yet lost his original respect for knowledge, the European with so much of the world's achievement stacked up all around him, all to aware of the temporary quality of all insights achieved, may have ceased to expect that knowledge alone will provide the key to every problem. Some problems may be entirely insoluble—including the major problem of human existence. But that any question should not eventually find an answer, and that any problem, however complex, should not at length be reducible and ultimately soluble seems an idea plainly repugnant to the American sense of fitness. European students notice this attitude, not only in matters of scholarship but also in practical world affairs and they sometimes wonder.

Having discussed the influence of cultural diversity on preoccupations, on theory, on concepts, we come to words and expressions. One can hardly make a distinction between concepts and the words they are expressed by, but one can make general statements on words and languages within the general context of this paper, because language is culturally determined as few other products of social life are. It

---

[1] Bramson, *op. cit.* p. 5.

is also true, that language is not only a device whereby knowledge already existing is communicated, but an activity, prior to knowledge itself, without which knowledge could never come into existence.[1] Words are a lens to focus one's mind. No proper human thinking is imaginable without the use of concepts framed in some language.

Mental communication requires more, however, than being able to speak the same language. Europeans speaking English to Americans still speak a different cultural language. Dictionaries carry definitions but people carry connotations and it is connotations which influence thinking and rule behavior. Moreover, connotations are not only personal, they are also heavily cultural. An Englishman, an Indian and an American may "understand" the words each is using when speaking English, but whether they will ever understand the nuances, the shades of delicate differences in meaning, is quite another matter. I do not claim that greater attention to semantics will in itself eliminate all problems of "meaning", but it should be incontestable that descriptions of "things elsewhere" can and must be conveyed with utmost precision and the most accurate interpretation, for abstractions immediately take place when one tries to substitute words for reality.

Languages are very different in how they abstract their pictures of the universe and this is why one has to learn to think another language. European students of the American scene experience this constantly. No matter how well they may succeed in mastering (American) English, they will always remain aware of the fact that one only has one mother tongue. One realizes that the variety and subtlety of English make it possible to say things in English which cannot be said in any other language. One will at the same time be aware that there are many things which can be said in one's own language that cannot be said in English. Well known are the difficulties of varying degrees in translating single words across languages. Teachers of undergraduates in the U.S. know about the problems of finding equivalents for *verstehen* or *sympatico*. On the whole the importance of the American language for the study of things American is so vital, and the difficulties for the student of finding equivalents in his native tongue are so real, that his constant larding of the mother language with American words seems almost inevitable. Even so, occasion for misapprehension remains because of the divergence of

---

[1] V. Gordon Childe, *Social Worlds of Knowledge*, 1949, p. 8.

meanings for one and the same word in various national cultures. The problem is enhanced because within a single language community there can be quite different meanings for the same word.

I do not think we should be over-concerned with all these problems. There is little ground for pessimism with respect to terms. If it is the fate of common words to be equivocal, it is the duty of discerning minds to make them less so. Some such minds have done so in all branches of knowledge by fashioning concepts and methaphors that clarify what the careless use of language has confounded, or what cultural diversity of those who use the word in common, has caused to diverge. Where intellectual integrity prevails there can never be obduracy in error. Seminar sessions in American Studies offer constant opportunities to point out to the students, how vital it is to be clear about our statements and to use terms on the conscious level.

Some differences are simple enough and pose no problem, once one is aware of the connotation they have in the other continent. American boisterousness, generosity and preparedness to glamourize make Americans say a billion when the European would not go further than a milliard, make American professors speak of a brilliant student when Europeans would consider the young man only above-average. It is perhaps a similar tendency of the American mind as what makes Americans speak of parking-hostesses, of business-colleges, of morticians, and of extermination-engineers when they mean delousers. Once the European is aware of this American proclivity he adjusts his sights, discounts heavily and is not longer surprised when he receives an invitation to attend a conference of experts on some topic. For Europeans, a real expert is a rare person, as rare as brilliancy, but America abounds with experts. It is laden with a vast bureaucracy of authorities in all areas,—of health, of aesthetics, of personal conduct. In America the expert flourishes as briskly in child care and interior decorating as in market analysis, marriage, gardening and the mixing of cocktails. Again, no real problems originate in this sphere.

These do arise when particular words are heavily loaded with sentiment and emotion. For Europeans a constitution is something that is either absent (as in Great Britain), or something that has experienced considerable vicissitudes in the course of time, but it is in no country of Europe a sacred cow. Europeans after the Second World War have therefore been surprised by the American cult of the constitution, their constitution, which, they think, has become a kind of esoteric religion in the United States, leading to the exclusive identification of a political concept like "liberty" with the American constitutional system. European journalists have been surprised by the almost magical significance for Americans of the word "republic" and they think it part of the American credo that only citizens of a republic can be free.

In the political sphere especially, cultural differences have caused frequent mis-apprehension. The European call for national unity has always been an appeal to the sacred Fatherland, in the United States the rallying appeal is more likely to be to the principles to which Americans adhere. A European nation considers itself an ethnographical entity, among the members of which all sorts of different convictions can be tolerated. The United States is primarily held together by a common creed and those who do not subscribe to this creed put themselves outside the national pale. This difference in the fundamental basis of national coherence and loyalty is not always easy for European students to grasp and their incomprehension of American witch hunts, American loathing of communists, loyaltyoath controversies and similar phenomena is quite understandable.

American nationalism is simply not quite the same thing as European nationalism. Dutch students have difficulty in understanding the semi-religious tone of certain American political pronouncements. It is difficult for Americans to imagine how strongly Europeans dislike and resent American statements on high intentions, on devotion to humanitarian tradition and ideals or moral principles. Europeans did not like the preamble of high-toned argument which accompanied the Marshall Plan. They consider such statements preaching. Such words which come naturally and sincerely to the lips of an American, often sound hollow and false to Europeans. They feel uneasy when American leaders emphasize moral principles. My students in studying such texts find them oddly at variance with comparable European documents and they fail to comprehend the particular American flavour of such writings till their study of the United States has taught them, that this simply happens to be the way Americans do these things, a way to which their history and ethos have conditioned them. From then on, they no longer look upon such statements as either hypocritical or naive.

After having considered the language we use, and the way in which we are accustomed to say things, we can go on to some other creations and expressive modes that are culturally conditioned. Inevitably we again meet significant differences between the Old World and the New. Continued study of American as well as European authors on common themes, constantly makes students aware that different cultures show a different approach to most subjects. In such a stimulating and thoughtful book as Jacques Cabau's on the American novel (*La Prairie Perdue*, 1966) the author probably answers the needs of the French but can hardly satisfy the American reader. They must object to the French method of orderly classification, divisions and subdivisions, because this search for the so-called "clear ideas" compels French critics to fit individual novelists into prefabricated compartments, thus eliminating the plenitude and inconsistencies of reality. It is a tendency Dutch readers detect in most French commentators. In spite of whatever non-French travellers in France may experience, the French are an orderly people. Perhaps less so in what they do than in the way they think and write. Their penchant for deduction is another culture trait that runs counter to the Anglo-Saxon way of handling data. How severe a logician was Tocqueville! His chief object was to derive all factors under observation from the democratic principle as the sole common denominator. What he thus gained in logical unity he lost, on the other hand, in accuracy. One may assume, though, that as a Frenchman he willingly paid the price. One easily notices the same deductive tendency in André Siegfried's book *Les Etats Unis* that appeared almost a century later.

If the French are inclined to approach and handle a given assignment differently from both the British and the Americans, the British and Americans are also differentiated by their respective national style in various matters of the mind. Sticking to novel writing, the wry detachment with which the British can write about the vagaries of human nature, Americans find difficult to comprehend and impossible to imitate. Their authors are committed to the themes they treat to a degree the less sanguine Briton would find hard to reach. This British tradition of passionate objectivity is not always understood by Americans. Occasionally it irritates them; occasionally British critics admit to be baffled by the passionate involvement of American authors.

In fact, not only the particular approach to one and the same matter sets national cultures apart, the cultural product itself demonstrates persistent differences that seem to be culture bound. Few Americans e.g. seem to realize, how convinced many people in Europe are, that America is a land of extremes. It appears to them that moral and intellectual extremism are firmly established in the transatlantic character. The student of the American novel who wishes to discover a parallel for the personages and general atmosphere of many of the books he is considering, will look, not to the narrative tradition founded in England and France during the past two hundred years, but to the work of the great Russians, notably to Dostojewsky. There we also find persons who carry to a violent extreme their personal tendencies. They have little in common with the hesitant, reflective, self-doubtful persons who fill the works of great European novelists. To my students, this characteristic of the hero in many American novels is all the more remarkable, since they cannot well understand it from the general context of American culture, which is so typically middle class.

This is, on the other hand, easy enough with another form of American cultural expression, the film. It seems an accepted view in both Europe and America, that the American film as well as the other popular arts of the U.S.A. convey a distorted image of life in America. One could mention quite a few European students of the mass media who have expressed such views. Their statements miss the fact that American mass media rather accurately reflect many of the attitudes of this intensely middle class nation.[1] They have glorified comforts, luxuries and achievements, suggested the advantages of conformity and adjustment, have used the happy ending as a device to indicate that all is basically right with the world. They have romanticized and glamourized sex, physical attractiveness, youth, so that these appear in agreeable pastel colors. Yet middle-class energy and vitality are also at a premium in the popular arts in America, which besides show technical perfection and editorial virtuosity that has made them known throughout the world. This devotion to middle class attitudes and ideals causes Europeans, accustomed as they are to élite conceptions of art, to receive the American messages in a spirit different from the one they originated from.

Different value systems result in different world-views, which all tally with the facts, however surprising that may be. Discussions across the borderlines of closed perceptional systems, such as the mediaeval and the modern, and to a lesser degree, the American and the European, have often been no more than talk at cross purposes. One party has as a rule missed the whole truth and even the signifi-

---

[1] Leo Gurko, *Crisis of the American Mind*, 1956, p. 111.

cance of the components of the other's mental universe. It means
that we should not pronounce a statement nonsensical until we have
made sure that it is so, not only from our own point of view, but
also from that of him who made it.[1] This brings us to the problem
of communication across cultural boundary lines.

We all know that here lie difficulties galore. Sometimes particular phenomena carry such different implications in different cultures,
that communication breaks down altogether. It has been said that
the American moving picture *The Grapes of Wrath* was viewed by
Hitler, who thereupon decided that a country where farmers moved
about so much could not be taken serious as a potential adversary.
A fatal conclusion indeed. Another instance: when after the war this
same picture was shown in Yugo Slavia as part of an anti-American
propaganda *The Promise of American Life*, the picture had to be
withdrawn from circulation, as the Yugo Slav audiences were too
impressed by the fact that even the most destitute of American peasants could travel about in automobiles of a sort, and also, that Steinbeck was free to speak his mind about his own country. We may say
without exaggeration that as regards our observations of a strange
country, even when one is certain of the facts, one cannot profess
to be certain of the deductions. "The fact without the truth is futile;
indeed the fact without the truth is false", to quote Chesterton.

In conveying "matters known in common", persons convey them
while entertaining as a legitimate expectation that the other person
will understand. The speaker expects that the other will assign to his
remarks the sense intended by the speaker, and that thereby the other
will permit the speaker the assumption that both know what he is
talking about without any requirement of a check-out.[2] However,
across cultural boundaries the assumption that verbal similarity means
semantic equivalence is dangerous indeed. The European investigator
working in the United States is soon enough faced with the necessity
of a probing into valid meanings which has not characterized prior
research. He cannot take it for granted that the questions he is asking
are, for his informants, identical and conceptually equivalent as compared with those he used to pose at home when soliciting information
of a similar nature.

---

[1] Stark, *op. cit.* p. 128.

[2] Talcott Parsons, "An Approach to the Sociology of Knowledge". *Actes 4me
Congrès Mondial de Sociologie*, vol. VI, p. 61.

The different meanings of simple words may already cause a break-down of communication. In the third volume of Winston Churchill's book on the Second World War he mentions how at an important top conference a long and acrimonious discussion between the Americans and the British present arose, because of the verb "to table". For Americans this is synonymous with "to postpone", for Englishmen it means "to tackle", "to take up". The discussion partners did really quite agree, yet they thought they were in opposition. One could easily present other instances of tension arising out of this sort of misunderstandings.

Translation adds further dangers. Americans will translate the French word "syndicat" by "trade union"—yet these two concepts are not at all equivalent. In a Dutch translation of an American book I have seen "corduroy road" translated as "fluwelen weg" (= "a velvety road"). It is rather the opposite, but one can well imagine how the use of the dictionary contributed to the result. Continental Europeans never know on what grounds British and American authors translate our "Bauer" or "paysan" sometimes as "peasant", sometimes as "farm-er". We are aware of certain shadings of meaning, but what exactly these connote, escapes us. It is small solace to notice, when inquiring, that our British and American colleagues do not quite know it them-selves.

Naturally, we cannot find apt words for institutions our culture lacks.[1] Yet there seems to be a constant tendency to force the insti-tutional framework of our own culture on to the other culture. For many years now, American colleagues visiting me in Amsterdam on repeated visits spoke with regrettable tenacity of "the department of sociology" they suppose me to be the head of—yet Dutch univer-sities do not know the organization in departments. My visitors inquire about the number of undergraduate and graduate students I have—again, we do not know the college system, so the American thought pattern is inapplicable. American forms ask me to state whether a student applying for an American fellowship belongs to the top 5% or, rather, to the top 25% of "his class". Our students do not belong to any particular academic "class".

---

[1] It has been said that if a word is not in a language, then the culture never has the referent. I do not believe this is true. A verbalizing species will have a word for every concept and will create new ones whenever a new concept evolves, but if the concept as such is lacking, there will be no word for it. Some of the things a culture is most familiar with may never have been conceptualized and may there-fore remain unnamed.

Institutional discordance between American and European universities has been one of the reasons why the Fulbright program could not be carried out with complete success, outside the United States. The program was conceived and blue-printed by Americans—such is part of the explanation.

Returning now to processes of thought, we have to admit that cultural diversity creates particular problems. The mental intercourse between societies has always been marred by a good deal of mutual incomprehension. The most vital concern of the scholar, the problem of truth, springs from the fact that every society sees, possesses and holds only one aspect of objective reality, in other words, one part of the truth, but is inclined to regard it as the whole truth, besides which all other world-views must needs appear erroneous. All human perception is limited; but all human beings are loath to acknowledge their limitation. Still, it stands to reason that approching any alien reality with a preconceived idea means that we shall perceive in it only what we want to perceive.

This preconceived idea is frequently something we have learned to take for granted. Things one takes for granted quite often have their particular validity only within one culture. Serious mistakes are made when we naively project these "understandings" on other cultures. The history of European thinking about the United States shows striking instances of uncritical application to American realities of European concepts and "understandings" without regard for the deficiencies of the resulting analysis. An excellent example is offered by a book written by an Irish professor, Cairnes, about the Old South, in 1862, *The Slave Power*. With impeccable argumentation and excellent data he arrived at a bizarre picture of the Southern States; one main reason why he failed so oddly was his exaggerated faith in the validity of the "laws" in his field, economics. He did not realise that such "laws" have validity only as *principia media* within a particular cultural context. He constantly extrapolated from the Old World to the New, where Ricardo's theory of rent just did not hold water, because of the abundance of free land, for one thing.[1]

The opposite happened to the thinking of another European economist, Friedrich List. His stay in the United States contributed to his refutation of the universality which the classical liberal theory

[1] A. N. J. den Hollander, "Countries Far Away", *Comparative Studies in Society and History*, vol. IX, no. 4, July 1967.

of economics demanded for itself. For him America was an eye-opener for the geographical and historical limitations of economic maxims.

The tendency to perceive distant things so that they will best fit into one's own scheme of thought can even in scholarly thought result in the incorrect assumption that something exists that does not exist and has never existed at all. An interesting illustration of this is the myth of a "Black Belt" as an extensive region of black soil containing most of the negro population of the South, extending through all the Gulf States. It is a myth that haunted European geography books for a long time.[1]

European literature on the United States as well as American books on Europe frequently show us the odd results produced by applying rules discovered in one's own culture to the "facts" of an alien culture, in any attempt to confer meaning on such facts. It is only one aspect of our tendency of projection, to relate one's own world to the alien world and vice versa. Many Europeans who wrote about the United States did little else. Tocqueville's famous book is the classic example. His real concern was not America but France and the United States crept into its pages as a source of illustration rather than as the central theme.[2] As one of the consequences of this approach, his description of the United States left much to be desired as a piece of contemporary observation. Many observers from Europe approached the New World similarly. Among those of importance Bryce was perhaps the first who directly studied America not only with sympathy but for its own sake.

Experience with European writings about the United States makes one subscribe to the tentative conclusions a student of Chinese civilisation arrived at concerning the perception of one culture by those belonging to a different one. One is that a great living civilisation may impose its self-image on those who study it and affect the ways in which studies are conducted. Another conclusion is that characterization may be affected by a wide range of factors many of which are almost irrelevant to the object being studied: greater or

---

[1] For an attempt to track down the origin and growth of this particular myth: A. N. J. den Hollander, "Het begrip 'Black Belt' in de geografische literatuur over Noord Amerika". *Tijdschrift van het Koninklijk Nederlands Aardrijkskundig Genootschap* LIII, 4, Juli 1936.

[2] As Harold Laski remarked with some exaggeration. *The American Democracy*, 1948, p. 16. See Jack Lively, *The Social and Political Thought of Alexis de Tocqueville*, 1962; Georg Wilson, *Tocqueville in America*, 1938; Seymour Drescher, *Tocqueville and England*, 1964.

lesser aesthetic appeal of the culture, products of the civilisation, the vagaries of international politics and ideologies; the changes, intellectual and social, in the society in which the student of a civilisation lives; the fortuitous organisation of learning which may place the study of a particular civilisation in an intellectual backwater.[1]

All this suggests that characterizations of civilisations are conditioned by time, culture, and circumstances, and that they have at best only a very provisional validity. Yet, any survey indicates that men who are a part of a given civilisation seek always to simplify it into a myth by which they can live and act. And those who study the same civilisation from a distance are forever driven towards some simplified general view of the object they study. Sometimes this is a purely intellectual demand for some broad conception which will give importance and meaning to the study of some particular problem. At other times the demand for some holistic view may spring from considerations of international politics, from the need suddenly to "understand" a whole people so that we can "deal with them". And the tendency in such cases is not to attempt the formidable task of the synthesis of available knowledge, but to fall back on some earlier simplification or upon a passing intellectual fad. The holistic characterization of such a civilisation as the American is a necessity for those within and those without its orbit. But experience suggests that simplification is always at war with analysis, that only rarely is a simplified image of this civilisation held as a hypothesis; rather, it usually tends, for a variety of reasons, to devolve into an article of faith.[2]

Now assuming that all thinking is situationally bound—and this seems undeniable—we are posed with a problem of a general philosophical nature. The problem is similar to the one Boulding pointed out[3] when discussing the influence of images on our thinking: there is no reason to deny that the author's thinking is also situationally bound. When one is arguing along the lines we have been following, one has to recognize oneself, unfortunately, as an exception to the rule. In Boulding's words: if one is too successful in explaining why people think what they do in terms of factors and forces lying outside the

---

[1] A. F. Wright, "The Study of Chinese Civilization", *Journal of the History of Ideas*, vol. 21, no. 2, pp. 233-255; reprinted in Ph. P. Wiener and A. Noland, *Ideas in Cultural Perspective*, 1962, p. 376.

[2] *Ibid.* p. 376.

[3] K. E. Boulding, *The Image*, 1956, p. 150.

ideational structure, this is apt to destroy the validity of the theory itself. One is always in the position of having to assert that nobody is queer except himself.

The answer is, that one may agree to the anthropological view that every man's idea of truth is a function of his group's culture, but that culture is not the sole determinant in the life of the individual. Complete cultural determinism is complete and self-refuting skepticism. No anthropologist or sociologist intends to go to such extremes. Cultural differences cannot destroy all truth or the possibility of truth seeking and truth finding. If it were true that they do, then no one can ever know that truth. Some truth is knowable in all cultures. If no truth were absolutely knowable, regardless of cultural conditions, then no communication among cultures would be possible. Anthropologists have yet to discover a human society the members of which find everything and everyone from another culture completely unintelligible. When there is any common ground at all there is some common truth.[1]

Nonetheless, the insight that the influence of social determination on human thought is omnipresent and all-pervasive, that it establishes all-inclusive frames of reference, total mental universes, remains quite valid. Thought is, not exclusively, but also social and cultural, in origin, development, function and pre-supposition. It reveals the thinker and his situation. Keeping this constantly in mind may make a positive contribution in overcoming professional insularity and insolence in matters of communication by taking knowledge itself as a problem. It will then offer a guide in measuring the extent to which extra-logical considerations enter into the formation of logically grounded methods of social and cultural explanation.

In conclusion, let me say that I believe the thought that forms the background, the main theme and the general stimulus of the EAAS conferences in Rome and Brussels to be a valid one. The theory from which the conferences issued, does not even necessarily have to be true, whatever this means, as long as it will have an effect. The point this present paper is trying to make can easily be overworked. Yet it has proved to be a fruitful one in the practice of teaching students in the behavioural sciences. Perhaps, its main value is to stimulate thought

---

[1] E. S. Brightman, "Culture and Truth", in L. Bryson et al. *Conflicts of Power in Modern Culture*, 1947, pp. 509-515.

and to confer insight into the relativity of truth. Thus the working hypothesis of a European way of thinking and an American one, is one of the ways in which American studies are proving useful. While acknowledging that the approach has only a limited relevance, restricted perhaps to particular areas of thought, it may still be an instrument for attaining a better understanding of the work of American scholars by their European counterparts, and vice versa. One could envisage it to become an additional vindication of American Studies by European students, in fact, of special study of any alien civilisation in any academic program in the fields of the social sciences and the humanities.